GENTLEMAN
JURIST
THE LIFE OF RALPH G. THOMPSON

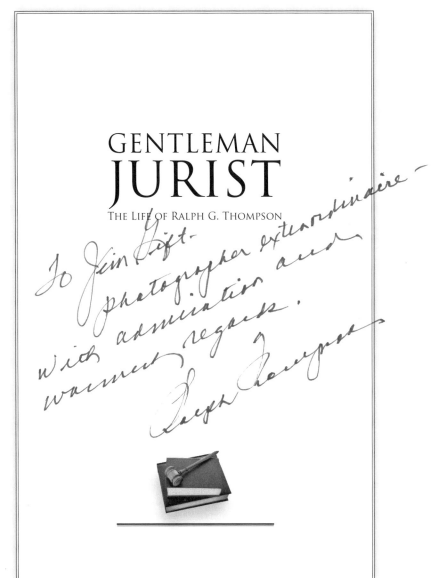

OKLAHOMA TRACKMAKER SERIES

GENTLEMAN JURIST

THE LIFE OF RALPH G. THOMPSON

BY BOB BURKE AND ERIC DABNEY
FOREWORD BY ED KELLEY

SERIES EDITOR:
GINI MOORE CAMPBELL

OHA

ISBN 9781885596901
Library of Congress Catalog Number 2011927816

Design by Skip McKinstry
Printed by Baker Group, LLC - 405.503.3207

CONTENTS

Foreword

In many ways Ralph Thompson's life has been a quintessential American—and Oklahoma—story. One grandfather, a renowned university president, the other a gun wielding, crime-fighting lawman. A lawyer for a father who answered his nation's call, distinguishing himself in war. A wife he fell for the first time he laid eyes on her. Three beautiful daughters. And a son in law who succeeded him in the work that rightfully earned him the title of "Gentleman Jurist."

But, like the stories of most successful people, his life has an unmistakable strain to it that family, friends, acquaintances, and others will recognize. It flows from more than good fortune or a supportive family. Instead it is the standards by which a man in public life in America in our times is held— in this case, to judge the judge. Is he smart and hardworking, honest and above reproach? Is he both firm and polite, tough and sympathetic? Above all, does he reflect the best of what this country, this "indispensible nation," offers to itself and the rest of the world?

In the case of Ralph Thompson, the questions answer themselves.

Fortunately, this portrait painted by our friends, Bob Burke and Eric Dabney, lovingly describes how Judge Thompson—it's still hard to call him "Ralph" even after knowing him for more than two decades—came of age, and how his experiences as a military officer, a counter-intelligence agent, and a successful politician led him to the pinnacle of his profession, as a federal jurist.

A fair amount of "Gentleman Jurist" is rightly centered on those 32 years on the bench, and readers will be taken behind the scenes of court cases both big and small. One of my favorites is the issue, hotly contested at the time, whether a high school girl had the right to play basketball on the entire court, rather than half court as the girls' game was played at the time. (She didn't). Another was a classic interpretation of the separation of church and state, on whether a school district could hold prayer services during the school day. (It couldn't). In neither case did the judge side with what would have been popular sentiment in Oklahoma at the time.

Judge Thompson is a key player in the county commissioner scandal of Oklahoma, then the largest of its type in American history. He found the commissioners' corruption unlawful and distasteful, just as he did a corrupt college president and a police chemist whose shoddy work led to at least one wrongful conviction.

But life on the federal bench, however important and long-lasting, is just one slice of the Ralph Thompson story. His adolescent years in a nurturing neighborhood on the north side of Oklahoma City will seem familiar to many of the same generation. And was there ever doubt that a grandson of University of Oklahoma President William Bennett Bizzell was going to matriculate at any other school other than OU? Probably not. Those OU years spawned lifelong relationships that continue to this day.

From there virtually all roads in his young adult life led to public service. He spent a career in the Air Force, on both active and reserve duty, much of the latter while juggling responsibilities of his day job as a federal judge. Active duty in his 20s dovetailed quickly into an interesting stint with the Office of Special Investigations. From there the young Oklahoman ended up in the Far East, heading up a small counter-espionage team. It was an exotic time for a young Ralph Thompson.

His political life began in earnest as a member of the Oklahoma House of Representatives, as one of the few Republicans at the state Capitol in the mid-1960s. So quickly was his rise through the party that he became the Republicans' nominee for lieutenant governor in 1970. He ran a spirited race, on the same ticket as incumbent Governor Dewey Bartlett, but lost to a more familiar name in Oklahoma politics: George Nigh. Those who know both men in the lieutenant governor's race that year aren't the least bit surprised they are on warm terms, some four decades later.

My relationship with him started in Washington, D.C., where I was the bureau chief for *The Oklahoman* in the late 1980s. Our interaction came from two events that couldn't have been more different.

The first was one of those stealthy rumors that took on a life of its own. In mid-1987 the Reagan administration was searching for a new FBI director, and one of the names that kept floating to the top of the list was that of U.S. District Judge Ralph Thompson of Oklahoma City. His background as a judge, free of controversy, as well as his military and political experience seemed well suited for a conservative White House. My sources convinced me the job could have been his had he wanted to pursue it with the president. Ever gracious, the judge told me his family and satisfaction with his work persuaded him to ask that his name be taken from consideration. To this day I'm certain he would have been a terrific FBI chief, bringing Oklahoma's twin sensibilities of toughness and fairness to the nation's No. 1 crime-fighting agency.

The second story occurred the following spring, in 1988, under far less stressful circumstances. His and Barbara's eldest daughter, Lisa, had been named the Cherry Blossom princess from Oklahoma. Obviously the event didn't carry the same gravity of that of an opening for an FBI director. But the Thompsons accompanied Lisa to Washington, and their time spent with the Cherry Blossom activities was a reminder to us wayward Okies in D.C. of the classy nature of one of Oklahoma's great families.

To me, nothing in Ralph Thompson's long career in public life was more impressive than the way he left it. As you'll read in these pages, the Thompsons' son in law, Tim DeGiusti, was set to join the federal bench in Oklahoma City, as a district judge. What a time it would have been! But a little known piece of the law suddenly posed a big dilemma: Members of the same immediate family couldn't serve in the same judicial court. When son-in-law Tim pointed it out to father-in-law Ralph, the elder jurist made a quick, irrevocable decision: He would retire. There were no protestations, no efforts to contact influential leaders in Washington to try to circumvent the rule, no attempts to fan sympathetic flames of public opinion. Judge Thompson simply stepped down, burnishing his usual good cheer as he sang the praises of a family member about to make the same leap to the federal judiciary as he had made more than three decades earlier.

"Gentleman Jurist" proves just that. Ralph Gordon Thompson is right out of central casting, whose experiences early in life shaped his career as a judge, admired and respected by all.

Ed Kelley
2011

Raised in Perry, Oklahoma, Kelley earned a bachelor's degree in journalism from the University of Oklahoma where he graduated Phi Beta Kappa in 1975. He has been Editor at The Oklahoman *since 2003 when he succeeded the late Edward L. Gaylord. Since 1974, Kelley has filled a number of roles at the newspaper, including Washington Bureau Chief, city editor, and managing editor. In 1996, he was named National Editor of the Year by the National Press Foundation for directing* The Oklahoman's *coverage of the Oklahoma City bombing. Kelley has served as a juror to the Pulitzer Prizes and is a member of the Oklahoma Journalism Hall of Fame. He and his wife, Carole, live in Oklahoma City.*

ACKNOWLEDGMENTS

It was a rewarding experience to chronicle the life of Judge Ralph G. Thompson. We were able to spend many hours with his lovely wife, Barbara, and their incredible three daughters to glean the many stories and perceptions of the man who has been such a major part of their lives. For more than a year, the Judge allowed us to interview him in detail about his life in which he has contributed so much to his native Oklahoma. Throughout the nation, others did as well.

We are grateful to many people for their help in this project. Michelle Douglas transcribed dozens of interviews. Ed Kelley honored Judge Thompson and us with a superb foreword. Michael Dean and Rodger Harris at the Oklahoma Historical Society provided research information. Linda Lynn, Melissa Hayer, Mary Phillips, Robin Davison, and Billie Harry at the Oklahoma Publishing Company helped select photographs from the newspaper's vast archive.

We are indebted to our editor, Gini Moore Campbell, for keeping us on the straight and narrow as we converted mountains of information into a readable and correct record of Judge Thompson's life. We also thank Skip McKinstry for an incredible design of the cover and contents of the book.

The Authors, 2011

GENTLEMAN
JURIST

THE LIFE OF RALPH G. THOMPSON

CHAPTER 1

A STRONG
FAMILY HERITAGE

*My great grandmother lived in the time of Lincoln, a
reminder of how young our nation is. Always attired in a
long, black dress with a lace collar and cameo pin, she was
a figure of unchanging, quiet wisdom and character.*

Ralph G. Thompson

From his earliest memory, Ralph Gordon Thompson associated his own family's legacy with the history of the nation and the State of Oklahoma. His great grandmother, Sarah Elizabeth Wade Bizzell, shared stories with him of watching Yankee soldiers during the Civil War remove the upright piano from her family home in Alabama and make it into a feeding trough for their horses.

Born in 1856, Sarah married George McDuffie Bizzell. She remained alive for the first 14 years of young Ralph Thompson's life. Their relationship was warm and affectionate.[1] Sarah was widowed for the last half of her life and lived with the Bizzell and Thompson families until her death in 1948. Just how close her relationship was with her great grandson is reflected by a family story that occurred when he was two years old, had a head full of straw blonde curls, and looked strikingly similar to the son of aviator Charles Lindbergh. The child had been kidnapped and his photograph appeared prominently in the nation's newspapers.

On a family trip to New Orleans, Ralph was in an elevator with his parents at the Roosevelt Hotel when a passenger saw him and gasped, "He looks exactly like the Lindbergh baby." Ralph immediately corrected the lady and emphatically said, "No! I am Grandma's baby!"[2]

George and Sarah Bizzell settled on a farm near Independence, in Washington County, Texas, where a son, William Bennett Bizzell, was born October 14, 1876. Young Bizzell, Ralph Thompson's grandfather, was baptized in the Independence Baptist Church. The congregation was organized in 1839 and is the oldest continuously active Baptist church in the State of Texas. It is the church where Republic of Texas President Sam Houston was baptized and where Houston's wife, Margaret, is buried.[3]

Independence was the original location of Baylor University. A decade before Bizzell was born there, Independence was one of the wealthiest communities in Texas, and as a result, the Union Baptist Association established a religious university there. Independence was home to Baylor University until 1885 when university officials moved the school to Waco.[4]

Bizzell was an only child and was encouraged by his parents to appreciate and collect fine books. His parents were determined he would have the finest possible education. Because of the local preference for Baylor University, Bizzell earned a Bachelor of Science degree in 1898 and a Bachelor of Philosophy degree in 1900 from Baylor. Continuing his education, he earned a Master of Laws degree from the Illinois College of Law in Chicago in 1911 and a Doctor of Civil Law degree from the same institution in 1912. Bizzell was awarded a Master of Arts degree from the University of Chicago in 1913 and a Doctor of Laws from Baylor University in 1919. He completed his incredible education with a Doctor of Philosophy Degree from Columbia University in New York in 1921. In 1944, he received the Columbia University Medal for Excellence, one of its highest honors.[5]

From the beginning of his adult life, Bizzell pursued excellence in a career in education. While he was completing his own studies, he was public school superintendent in Navasota, Texas, for ten years, and president of the College of Industrial Arts, later Texas Women's University, in Denton. In 1914, at the age of 37, Bizzell was named president of the Agricultural and Mechanical College of Texas, now Texas A&M University.

While living in Navasota, Bizzell married Carrie Wray Sangster. The couple had two children, William Sangster Bizzell and Elaine Bizzell. After assuming the presidency of Texas A&M, Bizzell moved his family into the president's home on the A&M campus in College Station. He became well known as a leader in higher education. He promoted minority higher education, especially through his support of the all-black Prairie View College of Texas.

Bizzell's daughter, Elaine, was one of only five female students at Texas A&M. Except for the five faculty members' daughters, the student body was an all-male, uniformed, officer training military institution coexisting with its agricultural and engineering studies. The high boots and swords, military marching and formations, bonfires, and legendary spirit made a lasting impression on Elaine. Ralph Thompson said of his mother, "She remained loyal to Texas A&M for the rest of her life."[6]

Bizzell's reputation spread northward to the infant state of Oklahoma. In 1925, the Oklahoma Board of Regents hired Bizzell as the fifth president of the University of Oklahoma (OU). When word came that Bizzell would be leaving Texas A&M, a local newspaper quoted an A&M regent as saying, "He has made a greater contribution to the college than any other man ever connected with the institution."[7]

Bizzell arrived in Norman to fulfill his dream of building a great research university from a frontier college through the development of human and intellectual resources. Even though he faced political op-

Dr. William Bennett Bizzell, Judge Thompson's maternal grandfather, served as president of the University of Oklahoma from 1925 to 1941.

position from recalcitrant Oklahoma Governor William H. "Alfalfa Bill" Murray in the 1930s, Bizzell's tenure was filled with notable accomplishments. Among the buildings constructed during his administration were the Oklahoma Memorial Union, Buchanan Hall, a new football stadium, and a magnificent library.

Bizzell, awarded Oklahoma's highest honor with induction in the Oklahoma Hall of Fame in 1936, was responsible for developing an OU Medical Center in Oklahoma City, established a student loan program with the help of Ponca City oilman Lew Wentz, and established the University of Oklahoma Press. However, Bizzell's greatest accomplishment at OU perhaps is his development of the university library later named for him. Bizzell was involved in almost every aspect of the construction of the Cherokee Gothic library in 1929. Its beauty and contents have been compared to the libraries at Dartmouth College, Yale University, and Harvard College, and named one of the "great libraries of the world."

In 2010, Bizzell Memorial Library was recognized as one of the nation's most beautiful university libraries. OU President David L. Boren credited Bizzell for the "beautiful design of the building and for obtaining the funds to build it." The vast holdings of the Bizzell Library include a broad range of research and rare acquisitions, including Bizzell's own Bible collection, Galileo's handwritten notes, and first edition works of Charles Dickens. With more than five-million volumes, the library is the largest research library in Oklahoma.[8]

When the William Bennett Bizzell Memorial Library was dedicated

Dr. William Bennett Bizzell, second from left, while president of Texas A & M University, hosted President Woodrow Wilson, left, during World War I at College Station, Texas.

During Dr. William Bennett Bizzell's presidency at OU, the Thompson family met many interesting and famous visitors. Dr. Eduard Beneš, president of Czechoslovakia, left, visited President Bizzell in Norman in 1939 while in exile from his country that had been occupied by Nazi forces.

in 1949, Professor of English Dr. Jewel Wurzbaugh wrote in the program:
>A book was to him "the precious lifeblood of a master spirit." He preferred one bound with artistic skill, and he liked first editions and autographs, but he did not scorn a pamphlet ample in thought. Books were near him always, piled on his desk, lining the walls of his study and home, under his arm when he crossed a barren or flowering campus.[9]

Dr. Wurzbaugh, who appreciated the intellectual and academic excellence demonstrated and promoted by President Bizzell, talked of the president's many journeys in search of rare and majestic books. Wurzbaugh said:
>He dreamed of a legacy to outstrip time, a magnificent treasure-house of books. And he made his dream a reality. There it stands. Look at it—beautiful and stately—a symbol of the man's greatness.[10]

Bizzell's wife, Carrie, known as "Mother Carrie," was "a fine president's wife." Born in 1880 in Texas, she was a refined and dignified hostess and a loving grandmother to Ralph and her other grandchildren. She called her husband "Will" and accompanied him in a happy and fulfilling life of world travel.

President Bizzell was known for his kindness. Once while attending a National Education Association meeting in Atlantic City, New Jersey, he heard the plight of a ten-year-old Oklahoma boy who had been stricken with appendicitis while at the convention with his parents. Young Denzil Garrison, later a leader in the Oklahoma State Senate and successful attorney in Bartlesville, was ordered to bed for 14 days following surgery. His parents were without a reasonable solution. They had to return to their jobs in Norman and could not afford lodging for 14 days in Atlantic City.

Dr. Bizzell had traveled to the convention by train and gave up his return stateroom ticket so that young Garrison could remain bedfast all the way back to Norman. Bizzell returned home by car and refused any reimbursement for his generosity. Garrison said, "What a kind and generous person he was. He always was a hero to my family and me."[11]

Ralph Thompson's paternal grandparents were uniquely different from his mother's side of the family. His grandfather, Plez C. Thompson, born in 1868, was a fiddle-playing, tall-in-the-saddle frontiersman, crack shot, and fearless deputy United States marshal in both the Eastern and Northern districts of Indian Territory prior to and after Oklahoma statehood. He was sworn in as a marshal on October 16, 1897, and served with three legendary deputies—Bass Reeves, the first African American deputy marshal in the nation, Heck Thomas and Bill Tilghman. Thompson only earned $1,010 in 1897 and $808 in 1898 for his dangerous service to keep crime to a minimum in Indian Territory.[12]

A frontier newspaper, *The Daily Chieftain* in Vinita, Indian Territory, reported an incident in the summer of 1901 when Deputy Marshal Thompson gunned down three armed smugglers in a gun fight at Island Ford on Grand Lake. When the smugglers reached for the guns, Thompson opened fire. The newspaper said:

> But before Nelson, who was armed with a shotgun, could raise the piece, the deputy had shattered his arm with a shot from his Winchester. The companion of the man, had opened up at short range, with a revolver, but went down, as a ball from the officer's rifle plowed through the upper portion of his body.[13]

More than 80 years later, Ralph Thompson, as Chief Judge of the

Judge Thompson's paternal great grandparents, Henry Clay Jackson and Sue Chadwick Jackson, of Louisiana, Missouri. Great Grandfather Jackson was reportedly a descendant of President Andrew Jackson and General Stonewall Jackson.

United States District Court for the Western District of Oklahoma, helped dedicate a new hangar facility for the United States Marshal Service jet air fleet at Will Rogers World Airport. Thompson noted that his grandfather, as a deputy marshal in the early part of the century, transported federal prisoners by foot, horse, and wagon. By contrast, Judge Thompson said, "I was dedicating a hangar facility for a fleet of jet aircraft used for the same purpose. Just imagine how far things have come!"[14] Judge Thompson's grandson, Tony DeGiusti, followed his ancestor's career path when he became a deputy United States marshal in 2010.

After turbulent and dangerous years as a federal marshal, Plez Thompson managed the Frick-Reed Supply Company and served as city clerk and finance commissioner of Nowata, Oklahoma. He died in 1920 in the influenza epidemic following World War I. His wife, Margerie Jackson Thompson, was left with three sons, identical twins, Lee Bennett and Ralph Gordon Thompson, and Wayman Jackson Thompson, all in high school at the time.

Margerie's father, Henry Clay Jackson, was reportedly a descendant of President Andrew Jackson and General Stonewall Jackson according to genealogical and family historical records.[15] Margerie graduated from War-

Plez C. Thompson was a deputy United States marshal in Indian Territory and in the early years of statehood. He was Judge Thompson's paternal grandfather.

Judge Thompson's paternal grandmother, Margerie Jackson Thompson.

rensburg Normal School in Missouri and taught school in Missouri and Indian Territory. After her husband's death in 1920, she took in boarders to make ends meet. She was described as "kind, strong, and dedicated to the welfare of her three sons." Margerie was determined that her boys receive a college education. While the boys attended OU's law school, Margerie developed uterine cancer. She lived with her sons in their Norman boarding house until her death in 1926. The primitive treatment of using a soldering iron in treatment of his mother's condition inspired Wayman to become a physician, specializing in obstetrics and gynecology.[16]

Judge Thompson's mother, Elaine Bizzell Thompson, was born September 27, 1904, in Navasota, Texas. She later charmed her grandchildren with stories of her distinguished father milking the family cow, outdoor plumbing, kerosene lamps, and horse and buggy transportation. Elaine was eight years old when her father became president of Texas A&M. As she became a teenager, her life was a dream on the College Station campus. She gleefully anticipated Cadet balls and dancing the night away with handsome cadets. She was voted the most popular girl in Bryan High School. After two years of being one of only five female students at A&M, Elaine transferred to the University of Texas at Austin where she graduated with a degree in anthropology and a minor in history. She was an excellent student and made lifetime friends in the Pi Beta Phi sorority house.[17]

In 1925, when Dr. Bizzell announced he was moving to Oklahoma to become president of OU, Elaine asked her father to commit to never let OU play A&M in football. Dr. Bizzell could not make the commitment, so later games between the two institutions "proved to be a loyalty tug of war for her." Elaine became a devoted supporter of OU, except anytime the Sooners played the Aggies on the gridiron.[18]

After Elaine graduated from the University of Texas, she moved into her parent's home, now Boyd House, on the OU campus. As the president's daughter, she met the president of the student council, an outstanding young man named Lee B. Thompson. Lee sensed he should "do what's right" and ask the president's daughter for a date. Their first date was to an OU baseball game. Lee was impressed that Elaine knew about baseball and, as a loyal fan with her Texas A&M background, never left the game until it was over. His previous dates were more interested in the shoes or purses of other girls at the game.

Lee knew quality women when he saw them. With his federal

Above, Lee and Ralph Thompson, identical twins, were born in Miami, Oklahoma, on March 2, 1902.

Below, left to right, Ralph, Lee, and Wayman Thompson, were a source of great pride for their parents.

marshal father gone much of the time, he had grown to revere his mother who knew how to handle three boys of keen intelligence but "with plenty of mischievous and rambunctious ways." After his father's death, Margerie had taught her sons to work hard. Lee grew radishes, lettuce, and mint in a small garden and peddled produce in a tiny red wagon to the grocery store. He also sold cold bottled soft drinks to factory workers in Nowata. He learned to barter at an early age, trading mint to a soda jerk for ice cream for him and his brothers.[19]

Lee was a baseball fan, especially of the Philadelphia Athletics managed by Cornelius McGillicuddy, better known as Connie Mack. In 1913, Lee wrote Mack a fan letter informing the legendary major league manager that he had named his local Nowata team the "Athletics." By return mail, Mack wrote Lee a generous and gracious handwritten letter thanking him for his long-distance friendship and wished the Nowata Athletics success. Mack also sent Lee a baseball autographed by stars such as Jimmy Foxx.

It was big news in Nowata County. The baseball was placed in the storefront of the Palace Clothing Store on Main Street on a purple velvet cloth. Years later when Lee visited a city when the Athletics were playing, Mack invited Lee to his hotel room and gave him tickets to the game. Their relationship continued for the remainder of Mack's life.[20]

A friend of the Thompson boys in Nowata was Welcome D. Pierson. He, too, became a lawyer after graduating from the OU College of Law. His son, W. DeVier Pierson, Jr., has been a lifetime friend of the Thompson family. DeVier was an honor graduate of the OU law school, was special counsel to President Lyndon B. Johnson, an inductee into the Oklahoma Hall of Fame, and managed a successful law practice in Washington, D.C., for decades.

At OU, the three Thompson boys were gifted students and held a variety of jobs to pay for their college education. Lee and Ralph ran a dry cleaning and pressing establishment on what is now Campus Corner. Lee sold flying lessons to other students in exchange for his own lessons.

Lee, Ralph, and Wayman all became devoted members of their college fraternity, Beta Theta Pi. Lee, in later years, was to become a national officer and a recipient of the Oxford Cup, one of Beta's highest honors. Other recipients include United States Senators Richard Lugar and John Warner, UCLA coaching legend John Wooden, and Walmart founder Sam Walton. The library at the Beta national headquarters is named

Lee B. Thompson in 1927 as a senior law student at the University of Oklahoma.

in his honor. All of his sons, grandsons, great grandsons, and nephews became Betas. Lee, Jr., also became a national officer and Ralph was an OU chapter president.

Lee and Elaine dated throughout Lee's senior and law school years. Lee was named the outstanding senior man, was given the Gold Letzeiser Award, and elected to Phi Beta Kappa and to the Pe-et men's honor society. Lee was devoted to President Bizzell, his sweetheart's father, and enjoyed many meals in the president's home during their courtship. [21]

Having an identical twin presented problems for Lee. By mistake, Ralph received much of his brother's attention after he was elected president of the student council. The student newspaper, the *Oklahoma Daily*, published an article titled, "What Good Does it do to be Elected President if Your Identical Twin Brother gets Most of the Accolades?"

Ralph benefited from his twin brother getting a free pass on trains taking the OU football team to away games. They devised a scheme. Lee boarded the train and made himself conspicuous to the conductor and ticket taker. A few minutes later, Ralph showed up and said hello to the conductor who thought he already had taken his ticket. The only down side was that one of the twins had to stay hidden during the train trip. Lee frequently had to hide under duffle bags full of football helmets and shoulder pads.[22]

Lee and Ralph graduated from law school in 1927. Ralph became an assistant attorney general serving under Oklahoma Attorney General Edwin Dabney. Lee joined the prestigious Oklahoma City law firm of Everest, Dudley, and Brewer. He and Elaine had definite plans for marriage, but he first had to earn enough money to support them.

With a solid savings account in hand, Lee proposed to Elaine. They were married at McFarlin Memorial Methodist Church in Norman on November 27, 1928. Elaine's bridesmaids were Pi Phi friends from her time at the University of Texas. Lee's groomsmen included his brother, Wayman, and Beta fraternity brother Hal Muldrow, later a highly decorated combat officer in World War II and Korea, and commanding general of the Oklahoma 45th Infantry Division. Lee's best man was his twin, Ralph. Because Lee's law firm represented a railroad, he was able to obtain passes for his new bride and him to travel by train to Kansas City for their honeymoon. His new in-laws, the Bizzells, bought Lee and Elaine a Ford coupe. Its color was "Arabian sand," and came with red-

The 1928 bridal portrait of Elaine Bizzell taken in Boyd House, the presidential home at the University of Oklahoma. The portrait is on display at Boyd House. The Oscar Jacobson painting in the bridal portrait also is displayed in the Boyd House dining room, a gift of the Thompson family.

wire wheels and a rumble seat.

Lee and Ralph built a small duplex on Northeast 16th Street in Oklahoma City. Ralph lived on one side, and Lee and Elaine occupied the other. In the fall of 1929, Ralph's boss, Attorney General Dabney, resigned and offered Ralph the opportunity to join him in private practice. As junior partner in the firm of Dabney & Thompson, Ralph learned oil and gas law. His expertise was recognized by being offered a position in the firm headed by former Judge Frank Burford, the leading authority on proration and conservation laws in the state. After Burford died, Ralph established his own practice until he was appointed assistant proration attorney for the state.[23]

Both Ralph and Lee were established young lawyers in Oklahoma City and planned to form their own partnership. Then, tragedy struck. On March 3, 1934, the day after the twins' birthday, Ralph died of pneumonia—the condition took his life in just three days. He was buried next to his father and mother at the cemetery in Nowata.

Lee continued in private practice and his brother, Wayman, established a successful medical practice. Wayman married Ruth Vaught, daughter of Edgar S. Vaught, the second federal judge appointed for the Western District of Oklahoma. Vaught, appointed to the bench by President Calvin Coolidge, became nationally famous for presiding over the trials of George "Machine Gun" Kelly and his gang in the celebrated kidnapping case of wealthy Oklahoma City oil man, Charles Urschel, in 1933.

CHAPTER 2

WARTIME BOYHOOD

*By far, World War II, with its family moves, separations,
anxious moments, and childhood adventures, had more
influence on our early years than anything else. It was good
against evil and, as little boys, we were in it to the end.*

Ralph G. Thompson

F ollowing the birth of Lee, Jr., in 1931, Lee and Elaine were
expecting a second child in 1934. To have more space for Lee, Jr.,
and the new baby, the Thompsons moved to 245 Northwest 34th
Street in the Edgemere Park addition of Oklahoma City.
Ralph Gordon Thompson was delivered by his Uncle Wayman at
Oklahoma City General Hospital on December 15, 1934. Ralph was
named for his father's twin brother who had died a few months before.

The year 1934 was the hottest year in the United States since records
were kept. The heat added to the oppressive effects of the Great Depression that gripped the nation as the worst economic downturn in modern
history, caused banks to fail and swelled unemployment rolls to unprecedented levels. Oklahoma was especially hit hard by the depression.

In other news of the year of Ralph's birth, Adolf Hitler became
Fuhrer of Germany, the American Midwest suffered some of the worst
storms of the Dust Bowl era, the FBI ended the criminal careers of the
notorious John Dillinger, Pretty Boy Floyd, Baby Face Nelson, and Bonnie Parker and Clyde Barrow, Alcatraz became a prison, and gasoline was
ten cents a gallon. Just eleven days before Ralph was born, Oklahoma
aviator Wiley Post discovered the jet stream while flying to an altitude of
more than 50,000 feet over the airport in Bartlesville, Oklahoma.

Elaine gave birth to a third child, Carolyn, on Valentine's Day,
1937. The comfortable bungalow on 34th Street was an ideal home for
the family of five. As the children became toddlers, they were wheeled
around Edgemere Park by their mother. Even before they were aware of
being neighbors, Ralph, Dave Hansen, and James "Jimmy" Fentriss, and
their mothers, met in the park. The three boys became lifelong friends.[1]

Ralph's earliest memories include his father reading the newspaper
comic strips to the three children while sitting on their father's lap and
singing his children to sleep at night with songs from his fraternity days
while rocking them back and forth in a breakfast room chair. While still
very young, Ralph received his first driving lesson sitting on his father's
lap behind the wheel of their Robin egg-blue Ford coupe.

Another early recollection is of taking naps during hot summer
afternoons next to an open window. With no air conditioning, an oscil-
lating electric fan stirred the warm Oklahoma air about the room as the
sound of buzzing cicadas and the smell of hot, freshly-cut grass drifted
through the window.[2]

"It is amazing how your senses bring back memories of so long ago,"

Ralph Thompson at age two. Note the curls.

The three Thompson children with their mother in 1937. Left to right, Lee B. Thompson, Jr., Carolyn Elaine Thompson, Elaine Bizzell Thompson, and Ralph G. Thompson.

Ralph remembered. As the Thompson children started school, they were allowed to join other children in the neighborhood to "sleep out" on canvas Army cots in the backyard. Ralph can still smell the Citronella oil used to keep mosquitoes away and remembers scary mystery radio shows such as "I Love a Mystery" and "Inner Sanctum Mysteries," listened to in the dark with the aid of a long extension cord from the house. "Every little sound seemed threatening," he said. "It all added to the backyard adventure. In the middle of the night we were always mystified at how the stars had moved."[3]

Ralph began kindergarten at Edgemere Grade School in Mrs. Snell's spacious classroom on the first floor of the stately building. The teacher reminded him of Kate Smith, a popular vocalist of the day. Ralph's playmates, Dave and Jimmy, and Danny McNatt, were at his side as they expanded their circle of friends.

Another kindergarten classmate, Suzanne Riley, later, Lawson, was Ralph's first sweetheart. Even from the first grade, class photographs show them always standing next to each other. She remembered, "Ralph was so

Ralph was a dedicated Cub Scout.

The first grade class at Edgemere School in 1941. Ralph and his first sweetheart, Suzanne Riley, stand together, front row, second and third from left. The two were pictured together in each of the Edgemere class photographs to follow.

cute. He was the last kid in the class to get his permanent front teeth."[4]

America's entry into World War II had a profound effect upon the Thompson family. Ralph's father, Lee, had taken four years of Reserve Officers Training Corps (ROTC) at OU and was commissioned a second lieutenant in the United States Army upon his graduation in 1925. While practicing law, he was a member of the Oklahoma Army National Guard and served as Aide de Camp to Major General William S. Key, commanding general of the 45th Infantry Division. The 45th traced its history back to 1890 and the formation of the Oklahoma Territory militia. By 1940, it was the Oklahoma Army National Guard.

As war clouds loomed in 1940, the 45th was called into federal service and moved to Fort Sill, Oklahoma. In February and March, 1941, the 45th relocated to Camp Barkeley at Abilene, Texas. The camp, near present Dyess Air Force Base, was huge, covering more than 70,000 acres. It was named for David Barkley, a Medal of Honor recipient during World War I. A clerical error caused the Army camp to be spelled different than its namesake.

The 1941 Thompson family Christmas card photograph was taken at Abilene, Texas, where Lee B. Thompson was on active duty with Oklahoma's 45th Division. Front row, left to right, Ralph and Lee, Jr. Back row, Lee B. Thompson, with Carolyn Thompson in his lap, and Elaine Thompson.

More than 27,000 troops from the 45th made the transition to Texas, the largest peacetime motorized movement of personnel ever made in the country. The Thompson family moved with the division to Abilene where Lee, then a major, continued to serve as General Key's aide. *The Daily Oklahoman* described the arrival of the 45th:

> You would have thought infantrymen of the 45th Division were conquering heroes as crowds lined the streets of town through which they passed and thousands jammed the business district here to welcome the men to their new home at Camp Barkeley.[5]

Lee, Jr., and Ralph attended Alta Vista Grade School. While their father prepared for possible assignment in the war that was blazing in many countries, America entered the conflict when the Japanese attacked Pearl Harbor, Hawaii, on December 7, 1941. The boys had been to a movie in Abilene and walked out to hear newsboys on the street selling "Extras" with the announcement.

Lee, Jr., and Ralph were the only small children at the Army camp and were treated kindly by soldiers who went on full alert and stepped up their efforts to get ready for war. The soldiers equipped the boys with Army packs, leggings, uniform caps, and insignia. They had the run of the base. General Key even allowed the boys to accompany officers on long hikes. Ralph remembered, "We were excited about the close order drills, the parades, the uniforms, bugle calls, meals at the officers' mess, and other Army ways."[6]

At the Camp Barkeley publications office, Lee, Jr., and Ralph became acquainted with a 19-year-old, baby-faced corporal, Bill Mauldin, a cartoonist for *The 45th Division News*. Mauldin drew funny faces, airplanes, and tanks for the boys. Later, he became the most famous wartime cartoonist. His ordinary infantry men "Willie and Joe" characters were the hit of the military's *Stars and Stripes* newspaper. Mauldin later became a Pulitzer Prize-winning cartoonist with the *Chicago Sun Times*.[7]

Forty years later, Ralph again met Mauldin who remembered drawing cartoons for his brother and him. The cartoons had been lost during the family's travels during the war and Mauldin agreed to draw a cartoon of him drawing cartoons for the Thompson boys. However, Mauldin became ill shortly thereafter and did not have the opportunity to make good on his promise.[8]

Housing in wartime was a problem for most service families. As the 45th Division prepared for assignment in the European Theater, the division moved to Fort Devens, near Ayer, Massachusetts, in April, 1942. On the night the family arrived at the train station at Ayer, they had no car and no place to live. While waiting to borrow a car from the Red Cross, a soldier gave Lee, Jr., Ralph, and Carolyn a puppy, "the last thing" they needed at the moment.[9]

Most of the lodging in the town had been taken by other officers of the 45th who arrived earlier. However, Ralph's father found the upstairs of an old farm house halfway between the tiny towns of Westford and Ayer. The house was equipped with "blackout curtains," required to be drawn at night because of German submarine activity off the Massachusetts coast. Air Raid Wardens in white helmets and arm bands and with whistles strictly enforced the blackout rules each night. The Thompsons did not have a car and traveled between towns by train.[10]

Lee, Jr., and Ralph's boyhood adventures in "soldiering" continued at Fort Devens. Lee, Jr., remembered, "We had our own room in the officers' quarters, our own dog tags, canteens, ammunition belts, and caps." The boys opened a shoe shine parlor in the enlisted barracks and charged enlisted men a nickel and officers a dime. Cartoonist Mauldin had accompanied the 45th to Fort Devens and often entertained the Thompson boys in his office above the base theater lobby.[11]

Lee, Sr.'s continuing correspondence with baseball legend Connie Mack led to an epic moment for the Thompson boys. Mack invited the family to join him for brunch before an Athletics game with the Boston Red Sox at Fenway Park. Ralph sat next to Mack at the brunch and remembered him in his customary three-piece suit, stiff collar, and straw hat. "What really impressed me," Ralph said, "were his hands. Every finger was knotted and disfigured from years of playing catcher without a good glove." At the game, Athletics star Dick Siebert broke a bat and Mack ordered the batboy to give it to Lee, Jr., and Ralph. Once they returned home to Oklahoma City, the bat became "a big item" at Edgemere Park.[12]

Ralph's father and his Army boss, General Key, were extremely disappointed in June, 1942, when Key received a letter from Army Chief of Staff General George C. Marshall. Everyone in the 45th, including Key, had assumed he would continue to command the Division when its troops went into combat. In correspondence that remained out of the eyes of the public for a generation, Marshall informed Key that a regular Army general would lead the 45th into combat. It was a profound disappointment of Key's life. Key felt betrayed—so did his Aide de Camp, Lieutenant Colonel Lee B. Thompson. The Thompson family later donated the letters between Marshall and Key to the Oklahoma 45th Division Museum.[13]

General Key was named Provost Marshal General of the European Theater of Operations and later commanded all American forces in Iceland. The 45th's new commanding general, Major General Troy H. Middleton, led the division into combat. In reorganization of the 45th, Colonel Thompson was assigned to the staff of General George C. Ken-

During World War II, Colonel Lee B. Thompson commanded air bases in the Southwest Pacific. He hosted actor John Wayne on a visit to one of the bases. The two became friends and renewed their friendship after the war. Thompson also hosted First Lady Eleanor Roosevelt on a similar occasion.

ney, commander of Allied Air Forces in the Southwest Pacific and head of air operations in the command of General Douglas MacArthur.[14]

Colonel Thompson was assigned for service in islands of the Southwest Pacific, including the Fiji Islands, where he became "the right arm" of General Kenney. He traveled under Secret Military Orders on an "emergency war mission" and was entitled to priority of space on any airline enroute home for a short leave. Unfortunately, when he left for the Fiji Islands in a B-24 Bomber from what is now Will Rogers World Airport in Oklahoma City in 1942, his family would not see him for three and a half years.[15]

Once overseas, Thompson was unable to reveal his location, but

On an unidentified island in the Southwest Pacific, Colonel Lee B. Thompson, left, greets Lieutenant General Walter Krueger who was enroute to assume command of the Sixth Army. Both officers served under General Douglas MacArthur in the war against Japan.

devised a series of codes with his wife where she could know where he was without running afoul of Army censors. For example, while in Fiji, he wrote, "I can't tell you where I am now assigned, but I can say that Bus Bass would be right at home here." Bus, a close friend, had been a member of the Phi Gamma Delta fraternity at OU which was known as the "Fijis." Through their system of hints and other prearranged codes, Elaine and her children were able to determine exactly where Colonel Thompson was as he served in such places in New Caledonia, New Guinea, and other Army bases in the South Pacific.[16]

After American forces defeated the Japanese in the Philippines, Thompson was sent to the sprawling city of Manila to find General Kenney "suitable quarters." Thompson found a luxurious, palatial home and commandeered it in the name of General Kenney. After Army engineers removed hidden booby traps left in the house by the retreating Japanese, Kenney moved in and promptly announced a cocktail party to which General MacArthur and his staff officers were invited. When MacArthur entered the house, he liked what he saw and said, "Nice quarters, George. I think I'll take them." He did—rank had its privileges. Colonel Thompson resumed his house-hunting for General Kenney.[17]

Promoted to full colonel, Thompson was the American officer who ordered the lowering of the Japanese flag and the raising of the American flag at Fort McKinley near Manila as the Japanese were forced from the facility. Thompson was present on the stage in Manila when General MacArthur ceremonially returned the liberated Philippines to the Philippine president. In the early 1970s, Thompson retraced his wartime footsteps, returned to Fort McKinley, and found the flagpole still in place.[18]

With her husband at war, Elaine was left to raise her three children alone and, like other families, dealt with rationing, and shortages without ever complaining. Lee, Jr., remembered, "She was, by her nature, a gentle and loving person who was required to discipline two young and fun loving boys whose mischievous ways were sometimes hard to handle." Elaine often used a switch that she snapped off a bush by the back door. Lee, Jr., said, "We knew trouble was brewing when we heard her fast footsteps coming down the hall and then the screen door squeaked open. We knew she was arming herself with an effective weapon." Sister Carolyn was less a challenge.[19]

At the age of eight, Ralph actually "contributed" to the war effort in a tangible way. He sent the government his "invention" that surely would help the Navy. Ralph's idea was to equip American submarines with containers of old crankcase oil. When the submarine was under enemy depth charge attack, the oil could be released to flow to the surface, giving the enemy the impression the submarine had been destroyed.

Ralph drew his invention, complete with an action scene, and mailed it to the War Department. Months later, to his great disappointment, he received a long form letter from the Department of Commerce citing various patent regulations. He remembered, "It was my first, but certainly not my last, frustrating encounter with government bureaucracy." To this day, he still believes his "invention" was a good idea.[20]

Both during the war and afterwards, the Bizzell grandparents played an important role in the bringing up of the Thompson children. While

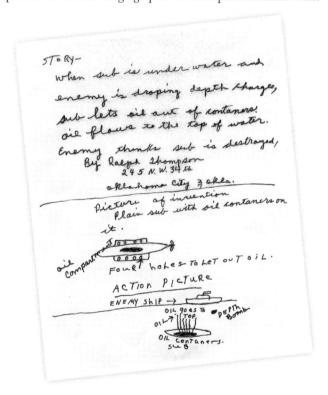

Ralph submitted this drawing to the War Department to help America win World War II. It was his idea how to trick the enemy into thinking a submarine had been sunk.

Bizzell was still president of OU, the grandchildren considered the president's home a second home. Many weekends, summers, and Ralph's first seven Thanksgivings and Christmases were spent there. Dr. Bizzell, known to the grandchildren as "Gran," was a huge influence. Ralph was proud to be his grandson. He said:

His examples of decency, scholarship, culture, refinement, and accomplishments for the public good served my family and me well...He was a saintly gentleman. He spoke of, wrote of, and lived what he called the "qualities of honesty, effort, love of truth, fidelity to high purpose, and a passion for the public good." In the closing of his inaugural address at OU, he said, "I hope to have the courage to do right, the will to be just, and the Christian virtue of being kindly, sympathetic, and open minded." What more wonderful influences could a little grandson have?[21]

Dr. Bizzell often took Ralph on walks across the beautiful campus, the start of Ralph's love for the university. He remembered, "The reflec-

The Thompson family posed for a Christmas photograph at Boyd House in 1940. First row, left to right, Barbara Bizzell, Lee B. Thompson, Jr., Sarah Wade Bizzell, Carolyn Thompson, and Elaine Bizzell Thompson. Second row, Ralph Thompson and William B.

tion pools, full of water lilies, were just hard to resist, and I have since had the odd distinction of having been fished out of each one of them by the university president." Often, both grandfather and grandson returned to the president's home soaking wet where a disapproving Grandmother Bizzell required Ralph to soak in a hot tub and gargle a cure-all of the time called ST-37.[22]

Ralph saw his first OU football game from the president's box seats. He was allowed to march with the band across campus after the game and can still feel the reverberation of the big bass drum pounding in his chest.

The grandchildren were given the opportunity to meet notable world figures who visited their grandfather at OU. Guests included Eduard Beneš, twice the president of Czechoslovakia and head of its government in exile during Nazi occupation in 1939; Bertrand Russell; Italian statesman Count Carlos Sforza; German author Emil Ludwig; and Chinese scholar and Ambassador Dr. Hu Shin.

When Dr. Bizzell retired as president of OU in 1941, *The Norman Transcript* described him as "an outstanding educator" and noted that in his 16 years he had transformed an essentially undergraduate frontier institution into a doctoral-granting research university. Even through the Great Depression, Bizzell governed the institution into a leading American university.

After Dr. Bizzell retired as university president, Lee, Jr., Ralph, and Carolyn spent a lot of time at the Bizzell's retirement home at 830 Elm Street in Norman across the street from the OU campus.

Dr. Bizzell died at age 67 on May 14, 1944, at his home. Ralph, his mother, his brother, and his sister were present. Ralph's father, serving in the South Pacific, learned of Dr. Bizzell's death over international radio. The president's body lay in state in the library he had built. The *Dallas Morning News* editorialized:

> His individual contribution to the welfare of Texas and Oklahoma and the region that we know as the Gulf Southwest was incalculable and through his part in directing the destinies of two of the Southwest's greatest educational institutions, his influence will continue indefinitely.[23]

Oklahoma Governor Robert S. Kerr said, "He was one of the great men that I have known and one of the strong men that helped build Oklahoma."[24]

Bizzell, II. Back row, Carrie Bizzell, Dr. William B. Bizzell, Edith Bizzell, William Sangster Bizzell, and Lee B. Thompson. This was one of Ralph Thompson's seven Christmases and Thanksgivings celebrated in the OU presidential home.

Above, Lee and Elaine Thompson enjoyed judicial conferences during Judge Thompson's service as a United States District Judge. Here they are at Jackson Hole, Wyoming.

Facing page, The Thompson family surprised Lee and Elaine with a Thanksgiving Day luncheon at Boyd House where they dated from 1925 to 1927.

Meanwhile, far on the other side of the planet, the war was nearing an end. Later, the Thompson children would learn about their father's dangerous yet exciting service in the war. He oversaw the construction of the military airfield which exists today as Fiji's principal airport at Nadi. Actor John Wayne visited American troops and shared Thompson's hut. After the war, while in Oklahoma City, Wayne looked up Thompson, and relived their time in the Pacific.

Colonel Thompson distinguished himself as aide to General Kenney. Thompson was awarded the Legion of Merit. Kenney personally wrote the citation for the honor, an unusual tribute to his admired and trusted top officer. Kenney recommended that Thompson be included in the first plane load of American military officers to set foot on Japanese soil after the Japanese Emperor surrendered to General MacArthur. In preparation for the flight to Tokyo, Thompson was required to be vaccinated against the Bubonic Plague. He received his injection from a bad batch of vaccine. The reaction nearly killed him and forced his return home on an American hospital ship with a 105-degree fever. The reaction denied Thompson such an historic opportunity to his bitter disappointment.[25]

Thompson returned to the United States on the hospital ship and then traveled by train to Wichita, Kansas. There, Elaine picked him up and drove directly to the Thompson home adjacent to Edgemere Park. It was the first time in three-and-a-half years the children had seen their father. He had lost weight, his skin was yellow from an anti-malarial medicine called Atabrin, and his skin in places was affected with a tropical fungus condition called "jungle rot." After a short time at home, Thompson left for the Army hospital at Fort Sam Houston, Texas, for treatment.

CHAPTER 3

THE EDGEMERE EXPERIENCE

Edgemere Park was our playground. It became the imaginary battlefields of Europe and the Pacific. It was our Owen Field, Yankee Stadium, the lawless Wild West, and whatever else our imaginations called for at the moment.

Ralph G. Thompson

Although his grade school year at Alta Vista School in Abilene had been pleasant for Ralph, he greatly enjoyed being back home. He said, "Edgemere Grade School was the quintessential neighborhood school and it was home. We walked across Edgemere Park to and from school each day, with adventures as only our imaginations could make them."[1]

Juliet Gilmer was the no-nonsense principal at Edgemere Grade School. Among the teachers was Violette Smizer, who taught music. More than 40 years later, at an Edgemere school reunion, from memory, Ralph reminded Mrs. Smizer, the last surviving of his teachers, that she had written in his fifth grade autograph book, "Music washes away from the soul the dust of everyday life." Tears came to Mrs. Smizer's eyes as she gave Ralph a big hug. Ralph assured his teacher that she had made a difference in his life—she taught him to love music. Several weeks later, the story was told at Mrs. Smizer's funeral.[2]

During his school days, Ralph was both a devoted fan and participant in all kinds of sports. His passion was OU football and basketball. During basketball season, he rode the Interurban trolley to Norman where his Bizzell grandparents would pick him up and take him to the OU field house where the ticket taker and team helper, Morris Tannenbaum, would seat him behind the OU bench.[3]

One of the young men his age that Ralph saw at OU basketball games was Ronald Howland, a "skinny, red-headed, freckle-faced kid" who took care of basketballs and towels for the Sooner players and sat under the scorekeeper's table to watch the game. Ralph envied his proximity to Coach Bruce Drake and the players. In high school, Ralph played against Howland in basketball when the Classen B squad played the Norman High School B squad. Even later, Howland became Ralph's federal court judicial law clerk and eventually a United States Magistrate Judge. Howland presided over the initial stages of the Timothy McVeigh Oklahoma City Murrah Building bombing case. The two old friends agree—it's a small world.[4]

Ralph and his friends organized a football team at Edgemere Park. The team was named the "Redshirts," for his beloved OU Sooners. The Redshirts played other neighborhood teams, although wartime shortages, especially rubber, limited their equipment. Some of the boys wore Army surplus tank helmets. Football pants were knee-length Cub Scout knickers narrowed in the legs by their mothers who also were called upon to

Fifth grade at Edgemere School. Ralph and Suzanne Riley together again, front row, first and second from the right.

sew numbers and stripes on the jerseys. During a 1986 Edgemere School reunion, film clips of one of the team's games were broadcast by a local Oklahoma City television station.[5]

"Ralph was a bit of a showman," remembered Jimmy Fentriss. Ralph's helmet was adorned with long streamers of ribbon.[6] The Redshirts even had a football queen. Ralph crowned Suzanne Riley at halftime using a shiny cardboard crown fashioned with silver model airplane paint. The queen was presented an armload of fresh flowers, cut from the Edgemere Park flower garden en route to the playing field. In 1986, on her way to the Edgemere School reunion, Suzanne was asked by a fellow traveler why she was going to a grade school reunion. She replied, "Mister, in the unlikely event you had ever been the football queen, you'd go, too!"[7]

Ralph and most of his friends were loyal to OU, but they admired Bob Fenimore, an All American halfback from Woodward, Oklahoma, who played at Oklahoma A & M in Stillwater. Ralph's teammates argued over who would wear number 55, Fenimore's number. Ralph wrote Fenimore a fan letter, not expecting a reply from the player he considered to be bigger than life. However, he received "a completely gracious

Left to right, Ralph, football queen Suzanne Riley, and William Patton at Edgemere Park, c. 1944.

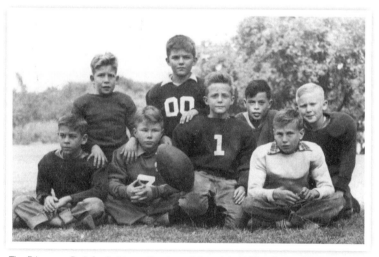

The Edgemere Park football team. Front row, left to right, William Patton, Phillip Kahler, Ralph Thompson, and Eddie Cook. Back row, Danny McNatt, Jimmy Fentriss, Ralph Thornton, and Guy James, Jr.

handwritten letter" from Fenimore who gave credit for his success to the fellow players who blocked for him. Later when Fenimore was inducted into the College Football Hall of Fame, Ralph sent him a congratulatory letter, along with a copy of Fenimore's response to Ralph as a child. As expected, Fenimore again sent a gracious reply.[8]

Edgemere Park was not just a football field, it was Ralph's playground. The rolling meadow could be an imaginary battlefield; the creek running through the park a perfect spot for amphibious attacks into enemy terri-

Ralph and two of his Edgemere Park friends annually celebrate their birthdays, only days apart, in the park with their wives. Front row, left to right, Pat Hansen, Suzie Fentriss, and Barbara Thompson. Back row, Dave Hansen, Jim Fentriss, and Ralph Thompson.

tory. It was also Owen Field, Yankee Stadium, or a fishing spot. The boys sat on the rocks by the side of the creek for hours and enticed crawfish onto strings. The creek was not environmentally sound. Once when Dave Hansen threw a lighted match into the water, the creek caught on fire and the fire department had to be called to extinguish the blaze. Ralph remembered, "We were living sort of Tom Sawyer adventures."[9]

To this day, Ralph, Hansen, and Jim Fentriss celebrate their birthdays in early December each year at Edgemere Park. Fentriss said, "Our wives patiently listen to us relive and retell all the old stories."[10] The three friends donated a park bench at the exact place where so many of their boyhood adventures played out. The bronze plaque on the bench reads, "Have a seat. Courtesy of Dave, Jim, and Ralph, Edgemere Park pals since 1934."

Adventure radio programs occupied much of the boys' afternoon time. At 3:45 p.m. each school day, Ralph and his friends gathered at one of their homes and listened to such programs as "Jack Armstrong—the All American Boy," "The Lone Ranger," "Superman," and "Captain Midnight," sponsored by the various cereal companies that offered "special deals" in exchange for box tops. Some of their favorites were the Captain Midnight secret code ring and glow-in-the-dark luminous headbands from the Lone Ranger.[11]

The boys were introduced to the outlandish claims of sponsors of their favorite radio programs of the times. Ovaltine claimed a glass or two a day could make them huskier and more popular with friends. Radio served a useful purpose during the war by suggesting that children join the Write a Fighter Corps (WAFC). Ralph and his playmates joined the Corps, a nationally sponsored kids' club encouraging letters to soldiers serving overseas. Ralph said, "Our local chapter had a membership of just three, but we took our responsibility seriously." Ralph, Dave Hansen, and Jimmy Fentriss all had relatives serving in the military in some distant land.[12]

The war, with a clear definition of evil enemies, inspired many boyhood games and the manner in which Ralph and his friends developed character. Ralph said, "It gave us strongly positive views toward the military and ambitions to someday become fighter pilots and platoon leaders ourselves." The soldier-playing activities took a particularly sobering turn when the boys learned that the father of their classmate, Ann Bell, had been killed while in a Japanese prisoner-of-war camp.[13]

In 2004, journalist Charles Osgood, the longtime host of CBS's *Sunday Morning*, wrote a book about his childhood efforts to defend his hometown of Baltimore, Maryland, against enemy attack. Like Osgood, Ralph and his friends had bragged in their adult lives of never allowing an enemy to breach the security of Edgemere Park. Osgood and Ralph exchanged correspondence about their mutual "wartime" experiences. Ralph wrote:

You captured so wonderfully the many adventures we shared as little boys growing up in the remarkable time with our imaginations going full blast. It was good against evil and we were in it to the end…We never once spotted a Zero or a Messerschmitt, but we went to sleep on our Army cots, in the backyard, covered with Oil of Citronella, knowing that we had tried.[14]

Osgood replied:
    If you enjoyed the book half as much as I enjoyed your letter, it makes me very happy. Thanks to you, Jimmy, and Dave for saving Edgemere Park.[15]

Recognized as a responsible young man by his friends' parents, Ralph was allowed to take his neighborhood pals on bus and Interurban trips. "He was a born leader," said Suzanne Riley Lawson. The friends would ride a bus to downtown Oklahoma City to transfer for the trolley ride to Norman for OU basketball or football games. Jimmy Fentriss remembered:
    Ralph knew all of the ticket takers and they would admit us free to the games. We then would spend the night at his grandfather's house where we explored Dr. Bizzell's vast library of rare Bibles. Times were different then. As young children we were free to wander and explore to our hearts content without supervision. My parents would consent to these trips, especially if Ralph was in charge.[16]

Frequently, trips to downtown Oklahoma City ended at several sporting goods stores such as Andy Anderson's, John Dunlap's, and Buck's. Hardly ever buying anything, the boys entertained themselves handling the latest baseball gloves, football shoes, and fishing lures. Then the friends spent their allowance on a movie at the old Criterion, Warner, Midwest, or State theaters to see such favorites as "Tarzan," "Sands of Iwo Jima," or Bing Crosby and Bob Hope in their road movies. Sometimes, they skipped the bus and walked home, adding to various adventures along the way.[17]
    Toward the end of grade school, Ralph played baseball with the Edgemere Robins, a team formed in the first year of Oklahoma City's little league baseball program. Home games were played at Edgemere Park against rivals such as the Wilson Mudhens and the Horace Mann Hornets.

Ralph's father, Lee B. Thompson, was a well respected lawyer and president of the Oklahoma Bar Association. The two practiced law together for 15 years before Ralph became a federal judge.

Elaine Bizzell Thompson, daughter of President Bizzell, devoted wife of Lee, and mother of Lee, Jr., Ralph, and Carolyn.

It was during this time that Ralph had his first and only brush with acting. A movie was being made of the life story of the Thompsons' minister, the colorful and inspirational Reverend William H. Alexander of Oklahoma City's First Christian Church. Ralph was asked to participate in a screen test to perhaps play Alexander as a boy. Ralph was reluctant but finally agreed, only if he could take his pal, Dave Hansen, and his baseball glove to the test.

Ralph nearly "bolted out the door" after the Max Factor makeup people applied, of all things, powder and lipstick to his face. "I was humiliated," he remembered. "After all, I considered myself a military guy and promising athlete." He flunked the screen test, although there is a unique irony to the story. The boy selected for the part was Tracy Coy "Pody" Poe, later a colorful gambling figure, who was prosecuted as a co-defendant in a federal extortion case in which Ralph was court appointed counsel for one of Poe's confederates. Later, still, in that same federal court house where Ralph was a sitting United States District Judge, Poe was convicted of a different federal crime for which he served a prison term.[18]

In 1947, the Thompsons moved from their Edgemere bungalow to a two-story house several blocks north on Northwest 38th Street. Fortunately, the house was located on another park and Ralph and his brother, Lee, Jr., had separate rooms for the first time. Ralph missed his park and his friends in Edgemere. He said, "It was a very nice neighborhood, but it seemed less personal and familiar, and it also ushered in the next big step—junior high school."[19]

Harding Junior High School was only about six blocks away from Ralph's new home. The school served students in the seventh, eighth, and ninth grades and drew from Edgemere, Wilson, Horace Mann, Nichols Hills, and other grade schools in the area. Ralph had a good working knowledge of life at Harding because his older brother, Lee, Jr., had attended the school and had been a member of the Sigma Rho fraternity, which Ralph joined. The junior high school fraternity gave students their first taste of social life with formal dances and parties. Students were taught ballroom dancing at Miss Simm's Dancing School and were introduced to the dances that were a beginning form of dating.[20]

Ralph's passion for sports competition led him to the boxing ring in the summer of 1947. He signed up for the first annual Junior Golden Gloves Boxing Tournament. Matches for the tournament were held at Brock and Oliver parks in Capitol Hill in south Oklahoma City. Ralph's

The Harding Junior High School basketball team in 1949. Front row, left to right, Ralph Thompson, Don Hart, Tom Murphy and Don Garrett Second row, Jim Frazier, Dan Brown, David Hoke, and Dick McKown. Third row, Coach Wendell White, Alfred Pugh, John Harris, Heath West, Dow Shearer, and Dick Day.

Ralph shoots a lay up against rival Taft Junior High School. He said, "I was a mediocre shooter and no help at all on the boards."

mother was less than enthusiastic, but consented to take him to his first match. About 2,000 fans sat around the outdoor ring on a hot Oklahoma summer night. Tough-looking characters smoking cigars looked more at home around the ring than did Ralph's dignified mother.

Weighing just 75 pounds, Ralph competed in the "Dram" weight division. After winning his first bout, his father and Uncle Sangster attended the finals in which Ralph lost in a close decision. He still has the medal he won as a result of the near-win. His uncle said when he looked at Ralph's skinny arm in a boxing glove, it reminded him of "a toothpick stuck in a ripe olive."[21]

A bigger thrill for Ralph was to make the Harding basketball team. It was his first experience to play his favorite sport in the "big time," on a regular, organized school team with uniforms and a gymnasium, a full-time coach, and a formal schedule. Still small in stature, Ralph became a point guard on a team that excelled. Members of the team later earned 33 letters at Classen High School and produced three Oklahoma All-State players, four state champions, a state record holder, four champion major college athletes in three different sports, two college All Americans, and a professional baseball recruit.[22]

Ralph loved wearing his white Harding letter sweater and playing rivals, especially Harding's primary opponent, Taft Junior High School. Its star, Stewart Meyers, later became one of Ralph's best friends at Classen High School. One of Ralph's few disappointments at Harding was his parents' refusal to purchase him a Cushman motor scooter or Whizzer motor bike. Most of his friends had scooters or bikes, but Ralph's parents said, "No, too dangerous!"[23]

Understanding that he might be able to buy a motor bike if he earned his own money, Ralph looked for a job. His first real job was tending Shetland ponies at a riding place on Northwest 23rd Street near present Shepherd Mall. He saved his money and convinced his father to allow him to buy a Whizzer. Ralph remembered, "I was thrilled to have it." The motor bike gave him mobility and a sense of independence. He and friends, Jimmy Fentriss, Dan Leininger, Jimmy Moore, and others drove all over town, even at night. His close friend, Joe Messenbaugh, had a small, light-weight Harley Davidson motor cycle, "the class of the bunch."[24]

While at Harding, Ralph spent many afternoons and evenings with his friends watching the Oklahoma City Indians play minor league baseball at the old Texas League Park as the top farm club of the major league Cleveland Indians. The boys were in awe of future big leaguers such as Al Rosen, Ray Boone, Bob Lemon, and Mike Garcia.

Being an Indians fan, Ralph often went to the studios of KOCY Radio in the Plaza Court Building to watch young sportscaster Curt Gowdy do the play-by-play of away games in distant cities. Gowdy, later one of America's most famous sportscasters, received play-by-play accounts of the Indians games by Western Union ticker tape, then told listeners what was happening as if he were present at the game. Gowdy said:

> I selected a block of wood with a small stick. When it came across the wire that a batter had hit the ball, I struck the block with my stick. I secured a large photo of every Texas League park so I could visualize "being there."

> The telegrapher would type out the report for the visiting ball park. B1 was ball one. S2 was strike two. He would use "single to right" or "double to left." I let my imagination soar, and it was valuable training for my ad-lib ability.[25]

Years later, Ralph stood with Gowdy at a reception during the presidential inauguration of Richard Nixon. He told the legendary sportscaster that the last time he had seen him in person was in the KOCY studios. Gowdy turned to his ABC producer, Roone Arledge, told him the story, and remarked it had been a very long time ago. Arledge replied, "Yeah, and you were a lot cheaper, then, too!"[26]

At the Texas League Park, Ralph and his friends were envious of two boys who later became dear friends and extremely successful in the sports world—Bob Barry, whose great uncle owned the team, was allowed to pitch batting practice to the Indians; and Max Nichols, later Ralph's classmate at Classen and OU, was the Indians bat boy. Barry had one of the nation's most successful radio and television sportscasting careers as the voice of OU and OSU for 50 years. Nichols was for many years baseball writer for the Minnesota Twins and president of the Baseball Writers Association of America.[27]

CHAPTER 4

A QUALITY EDUCATION

Campus life at OU was all I could have hoped for, and I was very grateful for my Classen High School preparation.

Ralph G. Thompson

There was only one logical choice for high school for Ralph—Classen High School. His popular older brother, Lee, preceded him there and Ralph had become friends with his classmates such as DeVier Pierson, Claude Woody, Tom Brett, Bob Lochridge, John Drake, Paul Lindsey, George Ellison, Bill Knox, and others. Classen was socially glamorous, and in the eyes of the Thompson family, "at the top" of the Oklahoma City high schools both academically and athletically.[1]

Classen had established fraternities—Kappa Alpha Pi, Phi Lambda Epsilon, Alpha Omega, and Delta Sigma. Lee Thompson, DeVier Pierson, and others had been Kappas and Ralph believed it "was definitely the group for me." The Kappa brothers included Dr. Joseph Messenbaugh, III, orthopedic surgeon; Dr. Don Irby, neurosurgeon; Dr. David Rose, internal medicine specialist; Dr. John Barnhill, radiologist; Ralph's cousin, Dr. Wayman Thompson, Jr., a pathologist; Dr. Tom Lekas, dentist; Joe Griffin and Lee Kennedy, architects; Jimmy Fentriss, successful businessman; Dick Sparks and Dick Day, engineers; Kon Kessee of Sotheby's; Gerald LeVan, professor of law and nationally-recognized legal author; Joe Clayton, Yale scholar and Whiffenpoof and Wall Street lawyer; and Gerald Marshall, banking leader.[2]

Ralph and his fraternity brothers often socialized with girls who were members of the two sororities at Classen—the BVGs and Merry Maids. Like gentlemen, the boys gave their dates corsages for formal dances and parties. At formal occasions the boys wore white dinner jackets in the spring and summer. Frequently, Bonnie Spencer and his orchestra provided the "dreamy, big band music." Ralph remembered, "We must have danced 25 miles to Woody Herman's 'Woodchopper's Ball,' 'In the Mood,' and to Nat King Cole's 'Unforgettable.' It was a great life."[3]

Classen had its share of teenage romances. In Nat King Cole's popular song, "Too Young," the words were, "They tried to tell us we're too young, too young to really be in love." It may have been true, but it fell on deaf ears with Ralph and his friends.

Classen had a rich basketball tradition. In 1929, Classen had placed second in the high school national championship tournament, the Stagg Invitational, in Chicago, Illinois, under 25-year-old coach Henry P. Iba. Iba later became a legend at Oklahoma State University and is a member of the Naismith Basketball Hall of Fame.

Ralph's success at Harding led him to be chosen for Classen's basketball program that recently had won two state championships. The tal-

The Kappa Alpha Pi national high school fraternity chapter at Classen High School. Front row, left to right, Jerry Parker, Lee Kennedy, Ralph Thompson, Dick Sorenson, Joe Messenbaugh, and Don Ellison. Back row, Maurice Ferris, Gerald Marshall, Dick Day, Joe Griffin, Wayman Thompson, Jim Fentriss, John Barnhill, Dick Sparks, and Dan Leininger.

ent level was still very high. He was happy to play on the B squad which was considered a grooming ground for the A squad, scrimmaged the A squad, and played its own schedule, home and away. He proudly wore his Classen Comet uniform and was excited about playing, although he admits, "I was a mediocre shooter and no help at all on the boards." "Compared to many others," he said, "it wasn't much of an athletic career, but to me, it was a great experience at a school the size and athletic level of Classen."[4]

Ralph's fraternity life also gave him opportunities to play intramural sports with competition in football and basketball. Classen was a large school with many athletes to draw from for its varsity teams, leaving a "good number of quality players" for intramurals. Football doubleheaders were played at the 38th Street Park on Sunday afternoons. After the games, Ralph and his friends usually gathered at one of the girl's houses, "rolled up the rug, put on records, and danced, usually favoring a 'Charlie

Social activities were a big part of high school fraternities. Ralph and his date are fourth and fifth from the right on the back row at the 1952 Kappa Alpha Pi Spring Formal at the Oklahoma City Golf and Country Club.

horse' muscle, knots on our heads, and with Ace bandages somewhere from the day's game. Life was good."[5]

Classen was a fine college preparatory public high school. Courses included English, algebra, plane and solid geometry, chemistry, trigonometry, physics, Latin, biology, and history. By design, one senior English class was the same as the freshman English class at OU, right down to the spelling lists. Students wrote many essays and themes in preparation for college classes. In Ralph's Class of 1952, 86 percent of graduates attended 50 different colleges and earned a total of 154 degrees. He said, "Success was part of Classen's culture."[6]

In Ralph's final year of high school, the United States was involved in a police action in Korea. With his patriotic upbringing, Ralph and several of his friends tried to join the 8th Rifle Company of the United States Marine Corps Reserve at its headquarters on Northeast 23rd Street. Several of his friends were accepted, but Ralph's father, fresh from serving in the Pacific only seven years before, refused to sign a parental consent for his underage son. Shortly thereafter, the unit was called to active duty, sent to Camp Pendleton, California, for training, shipped to Korea for combat, and sustained casualties.

As Ralph's senior year came to a close, he briefly entertained thoughts of attending college at Yale University or at West Point. But, in his heart was always OU, because of lifelong ties and appreciation for the university.

In the summers, Ralph was hired by Edward C. Joullian, Sr., founder and president of a gas-gathering and transmission company, later known as Mustang Fuel Corporation. He was a roustabout in the West Edmond Field, spending most of his time digging ditches. He and his coworkers described their jobs to friends as "earth moving engineers." It was hard work, but paid well and kept him in shape.

Looking back on his high school years, Ralph believes he received a superior education. In 2009, he was named Distinguished Alumnus of Classen. He considered it a "wonderful honor," joining previous honorees such as Admiral William Crowe, Chairman of the Joint Chiefs of Staff and American Ambassador to the United Kingdom.[7]

The transition to OU was again made easier by Ralph's personal advance man, his brother, Lee. It was a university rule that freshman live in university-owned dormitories. He roomed with Dave Hansen, his childhood friend from Edgemere and Harding. Living in the dormitory gave Ralph an opportunity to get to know other freshmen from throughout the university. Many became friends for life.

Fraternity rush was fun, but a "little stressful." Having good friends living in several houses, Ralph faced a difficult choice of which fraternity

Left to right, Judge Thompson, Barbara Thompson, Dr. Joe Messenbaugh, and Margy Messenbaugh at the Classen High School 50th class reunion in 2002.

he would join. In the end, he joined his brother and father in Beta Theta Pi. Lee, Jr., still lived in the Beta house during Ralph's freshman year. The Betas were traditionally the leading fraternity in scholarship and had high standards. Ralph said, "My college fraternity was a big help to me. It gave me positive influences, good times, and friends for life. I always appreciated one of its precepts—'urbane in deportment, courteous in expression.'"[8]

Campus life was great for Ralph. During his undergraduate years, football was definitely king. The Sooners began their 47-game winning streak and won two national championships under the guidance of the legendary and greatly admired coach, Charles "Bud" Wilkinson. Ralph never imagined at the time that he and Wilkinson would eventually become friends and political associates.

Like many of his fellow freshmen, Ralph was undecided at first about selecting a major or an eventual career. The only certainty in his mind was that he was not interested in becoming a lawyer. Too often, he had seen his father, a distinguished and successful lawyer, examining abstracts or writing contracts at the dining room table late at night. Ralph thought, "If that is what lawyers do, it has no appeal to me." However, by the end of his sophomore year, he had gained a broader perspective of law and completely reversed his previous career decision. Now, becoming a lawyer was his number one goal.[9]

As a freshman, Ralph enrolled in basic Air Force ROTC. From the beginning, he pledged to himself to pursue the four-year ROTC course that led to a commission upon graduation. After two years in the basic course, Ralph was accepted into the advanced course, passed the Pilot Aptitude Test, and looked forward to eventual active duty and flight training.

In the summers of his undergraduate years, Ralph continued to work hard, manual labor jobs. He and his friends tried to work harder than other employees, lest they be seen as just college boys. They joined local chapter 612 of the AFL-CIO Common Labor and Hod Carriers Union.

Ralph learned valuable lessons while working as a ditch digger. "We dug and dug, trying to do at least as much, or more, than our fellow workers, wearing ourselves out in the process." Yet, Ralph's ditches were never quite as long and straight as those dug by a lifelong common laborer, Lonnie Marsette, who became Ralph's mentor and friend.

Ralph remembers Marsette as a towering, wise, kind, and gentle man.

One day Marsette watched Ralph furiously trying to keep up and dig a straight line. Marsette said, "Hey slow down. Take it easy. Just take the bites you can handle, one by one. Set a goal. Keep on doing it right. Then just make the day—just make the day."[10]

Ralph listened to Marsette's wisdom. "Taking things in manageable sizes, not becoming distracted or overwhelmed and keeping the ultimate goal in sight," Ralph said, "our ditches got longer and straighter." It was a good lesson in life. Ralph has never forgotten Marsette's wise counsel and has often passed on his wisdom to his daughters and grandchildren.[11]

In the summer of 1955, between Ralph's junior and senior years of college, he and fellow Air Force ROTC cadets reported for duty at Williams Air Force Base near Phoenix, Arizona, for a four-week training camp. Ralph was selected as Cadet Colonel of the corps of cadets for the second half of the camp. One of his duties was to lead the cadets on a march through the palm-lined base each evening for "retreat," the flag-lowering ceremony. Ralph was proud to be out front and in command of the corps of cadets as the flag was lowered, the "National Anthem" was played, and four T-33 jets screamed overhead at close range.

He confessed that he was not so proud on one particular occasion when he inexplicably gave the entire group of 299 other cadets the wrong facing command, turning them in exactly the wrong direction. He remembered, "That was when the counter-command 'as you were' took on a new importance to me."[12]

The highlight of spending four weeks at the pilot training base was orientation flights in the T-34, the T-28, and the T-33 jet, including loops, rolls, and other aerobatic maneuvers to determine future pilots' aptitudes and suitability for pilot training. "I could not get enough of it," Ralph said. Once training ended, Ralph, Scott Nickson, and Bob Carey headed for the University of Colorado at Boulder to enroll in summer school. To support them while they were in classes, the friends went through the university's job placement service. Ralph became a one-time flower gardener. Nickson and Carey were hired to pick up trash at a drive-in hamburger joint. Nickson later became vice president and general counsel of Dresser Industries, a worldwide company. Carey later became bureau chief of United Press International in Little Rock, Arkansas, and a distinguished professor of journalism at the University of Arkansas at Fayetteville. The experience loosely fit Ralph's later book and speech theme, "From Modest Beginnings."

One of Ralph's most treasured honors during his final undergraduate year was being elected president of the OU Beta chapter. He always has remembered what his proud father told him when he learned of it. Mr. Thompson said, "You should appreciate and savor this honor because it will probably be the only time you will be chosen leader of the people you actually lived with—those who know you best."[13]

OU permitted an undergraduate student with reasonable grades and requisite courses to combine the first year of law school with the senior undergraduate year. As a Business Administration major, Ralph entered his senior year as a first-year law student. Things were getting serious for him. The OU College of Law accepted first-year students on a "fairly relaxed" basis with an understanding that 50 percent of them would be eliminated by the end of the year.

When Ralph walked into Monnet Hall, the "Law Barn," on OU's North Oval for the first day of law school, he hoped he would not be in the half of the class that would not return for a second year. The first thing he saw in the building was the huge oil portrait of the stern-faced former dean, Julien C. Monnet, looking down at him. Ralph said, "I swear I heard him say, 'Young man, you have no business here!'"[14]

The law school had admitted its first students in 1909 after Dean Monnet, a graduate of Harvard University, was hired by the Board of Regents to found a state-sponsored law school. Monnet brought faculty members from leading schools and developed an exceptional library. The law school became a model for other law schools across the country. Graduates were listed among the state's and nation's leaders and referred to as the Dean's "boys."

One of law students' anxious moments was from the Socratic method of teaching in which a student was called upon to stand and explain the facts, the law, and ruling of the case being studied that particular day. Ralph was the first student called upon, in the first class of the first day of the first year—a distinction he certainly had not sought and did not welcome.[15] He made new friends in his freshman law class and was elected honor council representative.[16]

It certainly was not the last time Ralph was called upon. Professors almost were never satisfied with a student's answers whom they invariably peppered with challenges and questions before mercifully being allowed to sit down. As uncomfortable as it was, Ralph understood how it worked and was a necessary part of legal training. "We didn't enjoy it, but we knew it was to test our preparation and teach us to think on our feet under pressure," he said.[17]

In law school, the final grade in each course depended upon a single final examination, usually a four-hour written essay over material covered during the semester. Results of finals were often unpredictable. All professors were known to be tough graders. Ralph survived the first year and was pleased to walk across the commencement stage to receive a Bachelor of Business Administration degree and a commission as a second lieutenant in the United States Air Force Reserve. As he and his friend, Jim Fentriss, proudly compared their Air Force and Marine uniforms, respectively, their boyhood ambitions of serving their country were coming true.[18]

As part of his agreement to receive an Air Force commission at the conclusion of his four years of ROTC training, Ralph was ordered to begin pilot training shortly after graduation. However, his active duty assignment was deferred until he completed his second year of law school. Classes went well for Ralph in the Law Barn. He was now a veteran law student who had learned the law study routine, although his mind often turned toward his immediate future—active duty in the Air Force.

Ralph was president of the Beta Theta Pi chapter at OU in 1956, his senior year as an undergraduate and first year as a law student.

CHAPTER 5

SPECIAL AGENT

While on Taiwan, it was not lost on me that if we
were invaded by the mainland Chinese Communists,
I was equipped only with a snub-nosed .38 caliber
revolver, a Ford sedan, and a World War II Jeep.

Ralph G. Thompson

I n the summer of 1957, Ralph reported for active duty at Lackland Air Force Base at San Antonio, Texas, as a member of the Officers Pilot Training Pre-Flight Class 59-B. Even though he expected training at Lackland to be difficult, it was a welcome break from school which he had experienced every year since he was five years old.

He was part of a class of 300 second lieutenants fresh from college and headed to pilot or navigator training. The six-week program focused on marching and physical conditioning with extra features such as a self-confidence course adopted from the German Lutwaffe of World War II, parachute orientation, and obstacle courses.

Ralph was assigned to the bachelor's officers quarters, four men to a room. One of his roommates was Lieutenant Thomas B. Thompson of Tulsa, an Oklahoma State University graduate. Thompson stayed at night with his new wife, Betty Jane, but spent days as a member of the foursome in the bachelor's quarters. Thompson and his wife became Ralph's close friends. Thompson later became a colonel in the Air Force, flew many combat missions in Vietnam, and commanded the first squadron of A-10 jets in the Air Force. In his role as the demonstration pilot of A-10s, he was killed in England while practicing for an air show.[1]

Years later, Ralph and his family visited a memorial to Thompson at the joint American-Royal Air Force base at Chicksands, England. Ralph also nominated Thompson for posthumous induction into the Oklahoma Aviation Hall of Fame. Thompson's wife and F-16 pilot son were present when Air Force Chief of Staff General Ron Fogleman, formerly Thompson's wingman in Vietnam, made the presentation at the Hall of Fame ceremony.

At Lackland Air Force Base, Ralph was still on track to be an Air Force pilot. The anticipation of pilot training made the long days of physical training worthwhile. As an officer, his evenings were pleasant. He and newly-made friends took advantage of 25-cent drinks and $1.75 steaks at the Officers Club and at the pool at nearby historic Randolph Field.

With the initial six weeks training behind him, Ralph received orders for primary flight training at Spence Air Base at Moultrie in southern Georgia. He received his flight gear and packed his car for the trip to Georgia. Then, the Air Force changed its policy to require pilot trainees to commit indefinitely to active duty with the first opportunity to request release after five years. That new plan did not fit Ralph's plans.

Ralph and his roommates at Lackland Air Force Base in 1957. Left to right, Jim Todd, Tommy Thompson, Dale Walentine, and Ralph.

He had one year of law school remaining, and did not believe he could justify a commitment beyond the three years he had previously been promised. He opted out of his long-awaited plans for military flying. Although he later would become a civilian pilot, it was a bitter disappointment for him.[2]

With his Air Force future in limbo, Ralph waited at Lackland for reassignment. Finally, he was asked to report to an unfamiliar building on the base to be interviewed for assignment as a Special Agent of the Office of Special Investigations (OSI). With his two years of law school, Ralph was considered an excellent candidate to be an OSI Special Agent. After a background investigation for top secret clearance, Ralph was assigned to the OSI and completed agents' school in 1957 in a World War II building at the present site of the Smithsonian's National Air and Space Museum on the Mall in Washington, D.C.[3]

At the suggestion of Congress and with the cooperation of Attorney General, and later a Justice of the United States Supreme Court, Tom Clark, Secretary of the Air Force Stuart Symington formed the OSI in 1948 to coordinate investigative activities in the Air Force. Symington patterned the OSI after the Federal Bureau of Investigation (FBI) and selected Joseph Carroll, an assistant to FBI Director J. Edgar Hoover, as the new agency's first director.[4]

By statute, the OSI was given direct access to the Central Intelligence Agency (CIA), the FBI, and other federal investigative agencies. OSI agents wore civilian clothing, carried firearms, and maintained confidentially of their rank. OSI's responsibility included investigation of major crimes in which the Air Force had an interest, crimes such as murder, arson, fraud, theft of government property, sabotage, espionage, and all of the counter-intelligence missions of the Air Force.[5]

During his first months as an OSI Special Agent trainee, Ralph received firearms and counter-espionage training and was taught the usual criminal investigative techniques, including interrogation methods, finger printing, crime scene preservation, and surveillance techniques. He said, "We 'tailed' and were 'tailed' on foot, busses, and cars around Washington, D.C." Upon graduation from the initial agents' training, Ralph was issued his badge and credentials and a .38 caliber, two-inch snub-nosed revolver and sent to the field.

With less than six months' experience as an OSI agent, Ralph was selected as the OSI Detachment Commander at Ardmore Air Force Base, Oklahoma. Never before in the history of the OSI had an agent been promoted to detachment commander so early in his service.[6]

Ardmore AFB had an interesting history. First called Ardmore Army Air Field in World War II, it was home to the Fourth Air Force from 1942 to 1946. Glider pilots and bomber aircrews were trained at the base that also served as an internment sight for German prisoners of war in 1946. The base was closed after World War II but was reactivated in 1953 and used by the Tactical Air Command and the 18th Air Force as a theater troop carrier base.[7]

By the time Ralph arrived at Ardmore Air Force Base in 1958, the base was again under a closure order. "It was a race," Ralph remembered, "to see who could close the base the fastest—the Air Force or thieves who were stealing government property." The Air Force wanted an OSI presence and Ralph was assigned the task.[8]

The official badge of a Special Agent of the Air Force Office of Special Investigations.

For nearly a year, Ralph worked with FBI and Secret Service agents investigating crimes committed on the Air Force installation. Then, as surprising as the news was of his first detachment commander assignment, Ralph was notified he was to become detachment commander at the OSI field office in Tainan, Taiwan. He had to check the atlas to see where he was headed. He did, and began learning about the ancient land that would be influential on his future in several ways.[9]

It took a long time for Ralph to travel to his new assignment. He flew from Travis Air Force Base, California, on a giant, lumbering KC-

97 propeller-driven transport. He completed lengthy legs of the trip to Hickam Air Force Base, Hawaii, Wake Island, Johnston Island, Guam, the Philippines, and finally to Taipei, the capital city of Taiwan. At Wake Island, the airplane landed at 3:00 a.m. While the plane was refueled, Ralph walked on the beach of the tiny island and thought of brave Marines fighting off invading Japanese soldiers in World War II.[10]

There was not a hint of Western influence in Taiwan, also known as Formosa or Nationalist China. The mountainous island spans the Tropic of Cancer and is covered with tropical and subtropical vegetation. It is located 75 miles off the southeastern coast of mainland China. The Republic of China (ROC) acquired the island from Japan at the end of World War II. When the ROC lost the Chinese Civil War to the Communist Party of China, its leaders retreated to Taiwan. The country's political status remains disputed more than a half century later.[11]

As an American, Ralph was well received in Taiwan. The United States government had befriended Nationalist Chinese leader Chiang-Kai-Shek and helped resist invasion of the island by the Red Chinese who claimed Taiwan as a Chinese province. The OSI headquarters in Taiwan was in the capital city of Taipei. Ralph was assigned to head

Ralph's "unpretentious" office at Tainan Air Base on Taiwan in 1959. Note the Japanese bunker from World War II in the background.

the field office in Tainan and had jurisdiction over investigations in the southern half of the island.

To get to his new post, Ralph flew an aging Nationalist Chinese C-46 passenger transport from Taipei to Tainan. The airplane had been used by the American Army Air Force as a transport in the China-Burma-India theater of operations in World War II. The aircraft had logged many miles flying "the Hump," over the Himalayan Mountains from India to China. Against the faded paint on the tail of the airplane Ralph could make out the old war-time camel insignia.[12]

Ralph sat next to a broken window alongside a Chinese man holding a straw basket full of ducks. Black smoke billowed from the plane's engines. Ralph said, "Right away I knew this was going to be quite a new experience." Flights in the antique C-46 aircraft were known as the "Mao Guan chi," interpreted as "no sweat."[13]

Ralph's primary mission at Tainan Air Base involved counter-intelligence activities, including counter-espionage. He had regular contact with the Nationalist Chinese Foreign Affairs Police and, on an as-needed basis, the CIA. His "command" consisted of another Special Agent and a file clerk. The office was a small, bare, steel, "typhoon proof" building secured to the ground by steel cables salvaged from World War II. Ralph had no problem with the unsightly cables because his office was buffeted with typhoons several times during his assignment.[14]

On Ralph's first night in his officers quarters at the Marco Polo Hostel in Tainan, he was awakened by a severe shaking that turned out to be the first of several earthquakes he experienced during his service in Taiwan.

As a plain-clothed Special Agent operating independently of local military authority, Ralph was "somewhat of an oddity" in the normal military scheme of things. But, he made friends quickly with other young officers, many of whom have remained his friends for life.

Fortunately, it was not an important part of Ralph's job to remain inconspicuous at all times. For several reasons, he stood out and "could not have been more conspicuous" in the Taiwanese culture. He was 25 years old, of fair complexion, and drove an unmarked black Jeep from World War II with Chinese license plates.[15]

Ralph investigated and put together cases to be prosecuted by Judge Advocate Lieutenant Stephen M. Boyd, a Princeton and Harvard Law School graduate. A Notre Dame law graduate, Lieutenant Michael K. Hegarty, defended the cases. The three were very close friends and lived

Above, Ralph as Detachment Commander of the OSI office at Tainan Air Base in Taiwan.

POORE
ELMER J
AF 23978581

OSI Special Agents occasionally were assigned undercover roles in criminal investigations and counter-intelligence activities. Ralph's false identity card photograph used on one occasion.

together at the Marco Polo Hostel. It was a unique relationship among the investigative agent, prosecutor, and defense counsel.[16]

When Ralph made an arrest, he placed the suspect in a confinement facility that was less than modern. It consisted of four walls, floor, and ceiling of welded, perforated steel matting left over from runway construction in the Pacific in World War II. One padlock kept suspects confined until Ralph could make provision to fly them to Clark Air Force Base in the Philippines where better detention facilities existed.

Routinely, Ralph investigated thefts of government property, armed robbery, fraud, and black marketing together with counter-intelligence activities. An unusual case involved the suspected homicide of a young missile launch officer. From his investigation, Ralph concluded that the young man committed suicide rather than face the possibility of having to launch a nuclear missile against Mainland China if ordered to do so or

Judge Thompson and his friends at a reunion 40 years after their service in Taiwan. Front row, left to right, Lee Roy Willis and Ralph. Second row, Dr. Michael Grecco and Daniel Forney. Third row, Frank Hunger, John Thorndal, and Stephen Boyd. Back row, Michael Heggarty.

if Taiwan was attacked.[17]

Another tragic case involved the flaming crash of an Air Force C-47 on take off from Ralph's base bound for the Philippines. OSI Special Agents were required to be among the first on the scene of military aircraft crashes where there existed the possibility of classified information, diplomatic pouches, or sensitive equipment on board. "It was a sobering job," Ralph remembered, "All passengers and crew were killed. They had been at the table adjoining mine for lunch at the Officers Club an hour earlier."[18]

Not all investigations turned out to be serious. In an incident in which sabotage was suspected, Ralph determined that wire surrounding a missile launch site was not cut by a saboteur, but by a Taiwanese farmer who wanted the wire to build a pen for his pigs.

Another case involved a close surveillance of drug smugglers. High-tech equipment was decades away, so Ralph hid in the closet of a cooperating suspect, holding a reel-to-reel tape recorder attached to a "softball-sized" microphone barely hidden in a potted palm in an adjoining room. The purpose was to record an incriminating conversation. Ralph said, "By today's standards, it was primitive, but it worked."[19]

The threat of invasion of Taiwan was real in the late 1950s. Red Chinese leaders were threatening and aggressive. Nationalist Chinese forces on the islands of Quimoy and Matsu regularly exchanged artillery fire with Red Chinese units on the Chinese mainland. The United States Navy's 7th Fleet was close by and Tainan Air Base was constantly on alert, equipped with Matador missiles aimed at Mainland China.[20]

Once, Ralph sat alone in the bar of an American Embassy officers club in Taipei on a monthly visit to OSI headquarters. He was envying the young officers whose wives accompanied them to the island when he saw an attractive young wife of a Navy officer walk into the room. He thought, "She looks like she could have just walked off the OU campus." She had. With her was her husband, a young Naval officer, Lieutenant Junior Grade Andrew "Andy" Coats, Ralph's good friend from OU. Neither knew the other was stationed on Taiwan.[21]

Coats, later mayor of Oklahoma City, a very successful lawyer, district attorney, the Democratic nominee for the United States Senate, and dean of the OU College of Law, was in charge of the Navy's cryptographic center in Taipei. Ralph remembered, "It seemed like we were at the ends of the earth and there we were together. What a small world!"[22]

While stationed on Taiwan, Ralph was able to travel to Japan, Hong Kong, the Philippines, and other countries in Southeast Asia. On one occasion, he accompanied his OSI boss, a pilot, on a C-47 to Bangkok, Thailand, for the purpose of picking up what was ostensibly a Navy medical research team. They refueled in Hong Kong and again at a small, sleepy airfield at Tourane, Vietnam, the French name for what became Da Nang, reportedly the busiest airport in the world during the Vietnam War.[23]

"Service in Taiwan broadened my horizons," said Ralph. "Living in such a totally different place was disagreeable to some but was fascinating to me." He began to develop an interest in the Foreign Service that, together with Ralph working occasionally with the CIA, was influential in his future career plans.[24]

One of the cultural differences that did not appeal to Ralph was experienced at a small dinner party hosted by the mayor of Tainan. Ralph had a noodle dish topped with a chewy ground meat that he later learned was from a German Shepherd. Dog meat had been a traditional dish of the Chinese for centuries. The typhoons, earthquakes, and the constant aroma of "night soil," human waste used as fertilizer on fields, also topped his list of negatives.[25]

Ralph saw signs every day of huge outlays of American taxpayer money being used to strengthen Taiwan's military forces. However, even though other foreign aid to Taiwan was used by the United States government as a shining example to the rest of the world, he was concerned that he never saw a single piece of mechanized farm machinery that could help local residents. Fields were still plowed with water buffalo. Ralph asked, "Where was all that money going? Where was the good sense to bring knowledgeable people to the local level who speak the language to help teach villagers how to make and repair a simple water pump or build a sewer system or more effective methods of irrigation or more productive ways of growing crops?"[26]

In long conversations under the bamboo roof of the Marco Polo Hostel, Ralph and his friends agreed that a new, honest, and more sensible approach to foreign aid should be employed by the United States. It was during that time that Eugene Burdick's book, *The Ugly American,* told the story of an American who lived among locals in a Southeast Asian country, understood the people and their culture, spoke their language, and offered genuine assistance. The book was banned in Taiwan by Generalissimo Kai-Shek, but Ralph's mother, in "the first and only deliberate violation of the law in her life," sent him a copy of the book hidden in a box of chocolate chip cookies. Once Ralph returned to civilian life, he was excited about the establishment of the Peace Corps, the very kind of program so badly needed.[27]

Ralph and his military friends in Taiwan have held several wonderful reunions in the half century since their service. At the first reunion, Dr. V.Q. Telford, then a pathologist, was asked what his duties had been as base veterinarian in Taiwan. He said about the only important thing he had done was to take care of Chiang Kai-Shek's dog. When another veteran asked what was wrong with the dog, the doctor said, "He had moist eczema," to which one of Ralph's friends said, "Who didn't?"[28]

Ralph's year of duty in Taiwan ended and he arrived at the airfield for his flight home and separation from the Air Force. Unfortunately, as he was about to board his flight to Taipei, alarm sirens signaled a full alert. A Communist Chinese Air Force MIG fighter had violated

Two old friends' paths cross yet again. OU College of Law Dean Andy Coats and Judge Thompson stand before their oil portraits as members of the Oklahoma Hall of Fame in 2010, 51 years after their paths crossed in Taiwan.

Taiwan's air space and was heading for Taipei, possibly for an attack. Wisely, however, the pilot of the MIG lowered his landing gear, activated his landing lights, and flew a pre-arranged pattern that American forces recognized as the signal of a defecting enemy pilot. Once on the ground and the defector secured, Ralph's flight departed.

When Ralph arrived at Travis Air Force Base, he was separated from active duty and returned home to Oklahoma City unannounced. He appeared at the door of his parents who were overjoyed that their son was home. Ralph was just in time to see his sister, Carolyn, marry her high school and college sweetheart, Don Zachritz.

Ralph's career with the Air Force did not end with separation in 1960. He voluntarily remained in the Air Force Reserve for another 24 years, reached the rank of full colonel, and was privileged to command a reserve unit of Air Force, Navy, Army, and Marine officers. He was active as liaison officer representing the Air Force Academy at Colorado Springs, Colorado. In a 1984 evaluation, Lieutenant General Winfield W. Scott, Jr., Academy superintendent, said of Colonel

Thompson, "He represents all that is praiseworthy in an Air Force officer, including excellence of education, talent, leadership, character and appearance."[29]

Ralph reflected on his long Air Force career. "I liked the military," he said, "It suited me. I liked the discipline, the orderliness, the patriotism, the camaraderie, and the sense of mission." The Air Force was good to him, generously giving him meaningful assignments, responsibilities, and advancements. He said, "It will always remain one of my most respected and valued experiences in life."[30]

In 1987, he formally retired from the Air Force Reserve in a ceremony at Tinker Air Force Base in Midwest City, Oklahoma. Lieutenant General Richard Burpee, then Air Force Deputy Director of Plans and Operations for the Joint Chiefs of Staff at the Pentagon, made a special trip to Oklahoma for the retirement ceremony at the Tinker Officers Club. Burpee said, "The highlight of the event was when I pinned the Legion of Merit, one of the highest military awards for meritorious conduct in the Air Force, on him prior to reading the retirement orders."[31]

Lieutenant General Richard Burpee, Air Force Deputy Director of Plans and Operations, left, presented Colonel Thompson with the Legion of Merit at his retirement ceremony in 1987.

Colonel Ralph G. Thompson, United States Air Force Reserve. He has worn two colors in his career—Air Force blue and judicial black—and has worn them with equal pride. Courtesy Gordon-Dinsmore Photography.

CHAPTER 6

THE LAW AND ROMANCE

That's the prettiest girl I've ever seen.

Ralph G. Thompson

Little had changed at the OU College of Law in the three years Ralph had been on Air Force active duty. The faculty and courses were the same. The Law Barn was the same. What was changed was Ralph. The three years away from school had refreshed him, and his horizons had been broadened. He was a different person in that respect.

Ralph began his final year of law school with a renewed interest in becoming a lawyer and a desire for public service. One unusual thing happened at the first home football game. When he took his assigned seat in the student section of the then 65,000-seat stadium, he was next to first-year law student, Andy Coats, whom he had last seen half way around the world in Taiwan. Their paths have continued to cross for the remainder of both old friends' professional careers.[1]

The year went quickly and Ralph prepared for graduation. He still had not decided exactly what type of law he wanted to practice. He accepted an invitation to join his father's firm in Oklahoma City. He was associated with his father and John H. Cantrell, both brilliant and respected lawyers and both presidents of the Oklahoma Bar Association.

Even though he thrived in private practice, Ralph's interest in the Foreign Service continued. After graduation, he returned to law school and took, for credit, Professor R. Dale Vliet's course on International Law which quickly became his favorite course. With knowledge gained in the course, he began to study for the notoriously difficult Foreign Service Officer examination.[2]

Ralph enjoyed his role as a lawyer. His firm had a substantial practice focused on business law and litigation. His fellow young lawyers were good friends and he believed he was off to a good start. He "carried water" for senior partners in the firm of Cantrell, Douglass, Thompson and Wilson in the First National Center.

Ralph's opportunity to learn courtroom skills was in a supporting role for veteran trial lawyers. After several months of second-chairing senior lawyers, Ralph was assigned a jury trial by himself. The firm's client, Mustang Fuel Corporation, was building new pipelines through rural Oklahoma and had to settle how much crop damage resulted from digging pipeline ditches through farmers' fields. Most landowners agreed upon the amount of damages, but occasionally the last farmer in a stretch of pipeline saw an opportunity to hold up completion of a project and demanded more damages than Mustang was willing to voluntarily pay. The result was a lawsuit to determine the amount of crop damage.[3]

The local jury trials were interesting. "It meant," said Ralph, "the heartless, bloodless corporation from the big city was pitted against the local farmer before a local jury and a local elected judge." The concern was that the company and its lawyer would be "hometowned" by being denied a fair trial.[4]

Ralph filed an action in Chandler in Lincoln County to determine the amount of damages so the pipeline project could be completed. His opponent was a difficult and elderly crusty local lawyer who had known the judge and every member of the jury for years. For two-and-a-half days, Ralph and the other lawyer put on evidence. Ralph thought the trial had gone well, but was still afraid of being hometowned. In his closing argument, the opposing attorney slid his hands behind his suspenders and, in a raspy voice dripping with sarcasm, said, "This corporation has sent this fine young lawyer here from the big city to tell you what our neighbor, old Dub's, crops are worth!"[5]

Ralph was concerned for his client, until the jury deliberated two hours and returned a verdict for the exact amount Mustang had offered the farmer. "I was as thrilled as if I had won a big one before the Supreme Court," Ralph remembered. What made it even better was the jury awarding the opposing lawyer only $75 as a reasonable attorney's fee. Ralph said, "It enshrined in me forever a respect for the value of civility in the courtroom and the price that could be paid without it. I almost literally floated back down the highway where I was welcomed warmly by my seniors." He believed his senior partners also were relieved by the performance of their new lawyer representing such a major client.[6]

From that first trial, Ralph learned valuable lessons of how to conduct himself as a judge later in his career. Judge Donald Powers' handling of such a contentious pipeline-crop damage trial with an inexperienced lawyer, with strict adherence to the rules, and courtesy to all involved, made a lasting impression on Ralph. "He was the picture of judicial dignity that has remained with me always and guided my own judicial life," Ralph said. Many times during his federal court service, Ralph expressed his thanks to Judge Powers.[7]

Even after the successful first trial, Ralph still was interested in the Foreign Service. He was contacted, however, by the CIA, although he never knew how he came to be recruited. He met with a CIA representative at night in a motel in Stillwater and was invited to take the CIA examination. He took the exam alone in a sweltering third floor class-

Ralph as an OU Law graduate in 1961.

room in a building on OU's North Oval. He was inclined to accept an offer from the CIA if it came. Then, Ralph remembered, "I got hit right in the heart with one of Cupid's arrows."[8]

Romance was not a stranger to Ralph. He had been involved in a long standing, but long distance, romance that had never ripened into marriage. One night in January, 1962, while attending a concert of the Oklahoma City Symphony with friends, Bob Bowles and Dr. Paul Houk, Ralph spotted a young woman at intermission and told Bowles, "That's the prettiest girl I have ever seen!" He was introduced to the young woman in a group and practically had to use his previous investigative experience to find out exactly who she was.[9]

The woman was Barbara Irene Hencke. In 1953, her family moved to Tulsa from their home in a suburb of Cleveland, Ohio, because her father, William Smith "Bill" Hencke, was opening a new territory for his employer. The move to Oklahoma was devastating for Barbara. Born in Cleveland, she was nearly 14 years old, had been elected president of the eighth grade, and had been chosen as a cheerleader. Beginning a new life in Oklahoma looked to be difficult, but several neighborhood families showed "great Oklahoma kindness" and Barbara became "a happy Oklahoman within one week of the move I so reluctantly made." Barbara's mother, Irene Lucy Wallace Hencke, helped make the transition easier from the big family home literally on the bank of Lake Erie.[10]

While Ralph's ancestry traveled through the Confederacy, Barbara's ancestors fought for the Union in the Civil War. Her great grandfather, Corporal John W. Hall, was a 19-year-old Union soldier in Company I, 107th Regiment, Ohio Infantry, serving for more than three years. He was wounded at Gettysburg on July 1, 1863, from being hit in the hip "from a piece of Rebel shell after firing in the line of battle."[11]

Barbara's paternal grandfather, John W. Hencke, was an active supporter of President William McKinley and a prominent Ohio Republican. He served as cashier of the United States Customs House for the Port of Cleveland for 20 years and was appointed postmaster of the Cleveland suburb of Willoughby by President Calvin Coolidge. It was in his home on Lake Erie where Barbara and her family lived before moving to Oklahoma.

After graduating from Tulsa's Will Rogers High School, Barbara earned a degree in French at OU, was a beauty queen, and active member of the Chi Omega sorority. After OU, she taught French on television

Barbara lived on the bank of Lake Erie, near Cleveland, Ohio, until her family moved to Tulsa when she was nearly 14.

to students of the Oklahoma City Public Schools system. On the fateful night at the symphony, she accompanied her friend, Alice Sparks. One of the "nice fellows" she met was Ralph, although she later admitted she could not remember which one he was when he called to invite her to their first date at the Beacon Club, a private club atop the First National Bank Building in which Ralph's law office was located.[12]

"It was pretty simple," Ralph said, "she was the girl of my dreams." He began asking Barbara for dates, going to movies, dinner, and other events such as attending Sunday afternoon overseas radio broadcasts of the Oklahoma City Symphony. Most of their friends were their age—29 and 24, were married, and many already had children.[13]

In January, 1964, Ralph and his friend, Bob Bowles, visited Europe. After a stop in Munich, Germany, the two young adventurers left the group and traveled on their own to Vienna, Austria. Then, Ralph set out alone for a week in Moscow, USSR. Times were very tense in the midst of the Cold War. It took Ralph three times the normal time to obtain a visa for Russia. No doubt the Russian authorities were aware of his military counter-intelligence background.[14]

Ralph landed at midnight in Moscow on a Russian Aeroflot airliner from Vienna via Krakow, Poland. Window curtains were drawn and an armed guard boarded the plane to manage deplaning. Other passengers boarded a bus to collect their luggage from the terminal. However, Ralph was singled out to be driven by private car to the Metropole Hotel, a "drab, threadbare" facility, where he was given a room with an "attendant" posted outside his room around the clock.[15]

Russian authorities obviously wondered why Ralph, with his background, was spending a week on "vacation" in the dead of winter in Moscow by himself. Temperatures often dipped below zero. "There were practically no other tourists there at the time," he said. His room was bugged, his luggage was searched each night, and he was not allowed to tour the city on his own. Instead, he was assigned a private guide-interpreter, private car, and driver. At one point he was "invited" to an interview with an official whose obvious purpose was to determine why he was in Moscow.

The interview was conducted in a "central casting" setting. Lenin's portrait hung from the wall where a "beefy official in an ill-fitting suit" talked to Ralph at a long, green felt-covered table. Ralph felt a "bit vulnerable" but the interview ended without incident.[16]

Ralph and his Russian guide/interpreter at Red Square in Moscow in January, 1964.

Ralph's guide-interpreter was an attractive 25-year-old Russian woman who spoke five languages, including Vietnamese. After two days of "a very cold, unfriendly attitude," the interpreter became convinced that Ralph was in Moscow purely out of interest and was not a spy. Out of the presence of the driver, she softened her approach and allowed Ralph to ask questions that she dared not answer when the driver was around.

The interpreter had an outrageously distorted view of the United States. Propaganda of the state-controlled media had convinced her that Depression-era social conditions, including soup lines, still existed in America. She was curious about Ralph's life in the United States and asked many questions.

Ralph later confirmed the obvious, through former KGB Major General Oleg Kalugin, that both the driver and interpreter were most likely KGB informers who were part of the Soviet plan to keep him under constant surveillance. In conversations with Kalugin in Oklahoma City many years later, Ralph was told that he was fortunate that a contrived "incident" did not occur to serve Soviet propaganda purposes at the time. Kalugin, the youngest general in KGB history, later was spymaster and Chief of Counterintelligence of the Soviet Union before coming to the United States and becoming a naturalized American citizen.[17]

During the week in Moscow, Ralph encountered other "travelers" who could have been part of an elaborate plan to catch a young American in an embarrassing position. At the Bolshoi Ballet, a stranger approached him asking him to accept a letter and "post it" for him. Ralph knew better. A year before, Professor Frederick Barghoorn of Yale University was standing in front of the same hotel where Ralph stayed in Moscow and was arrested for espionage and possession of state secrets after accepting papers handed him moments earlier by a stranger.[18]

At the end of the week, Ralph was ready to board a Scandinavian Airways System airliner. He was happy at the sight of colors and happy people. He had not seen many happy people in Moscow during his visit, only "drab, dreary, somber, fearful, and suspicious people."[19]

His new-found happiness was short-lived. Shortly after takeoff, the airplane developed hydraulic fluid problems and a crash seemed eminent. An emergency landing was made. Ralph's thoughts were of Barbara and his loving family back home in Oklahoma. Fortunately, the airplane

Barbara's engagement photo in 1964. Ralph called her the "prettiest girl I've ever seen."

Ralph and Barbara were married on September 5, 1964, at St. Luke's United Methodist Church in Oklahoma City.

landed surrounded by emergency equipment. The faulty hydraulic system was repaired and the flight continued to Stockholm, Sweden, and Copenhagen, Denmark.

That same year, Ralph was elected chairman of the Young Lawyers Section of the Oklahoma Bar Association and, accompanied by his friend, Scott Nickson, attended the annual meeting of the American Bar Association (ABA) in New York City. The ABA arranged for Ralph's group to attend a General Assembly session of the United Nations. Ralph and Scott were fortunate to observe the historic heated debate between United States Ambassador Adlai Stevenson and Soviet Ambassador Alexi Kosygin over the disputed North Vietnamese torpedo attack on an American Navy warship in the Tonkin Gulf that accelerated United States involvement in the Vietnam War. Following the debate, Ambassador Stevenson hosted a cocktail reception for the young lawyers. Ralph and Nickson had a private conversation with Stevenson about the significant moment in history. Later Kosygin became premier of the Soviet Union.[20]

Ralph and Barbara were married at St. Luke's United Methodist Church on September 5, 1964. It was truly an ecumenical affair. Ralph, a member of Oklahoma City's First Christian Church, and Barbara, a Presbyterian, were married by their good friend, Reverend Ron Morris, a Methodist. Barbara's bridesmaids and attendants were her sisters, Patricia and Mary; Ralph's sister, Carolyn; Ralph's sister-in-law, Ann; Eva Brasel Bogart; Susan Sparks Griffith; and Monnett Brock. Ralph's best man was his brother, Lee. His groomsmen and attendants included his cousin, Dr. Wayman Thompson, Jr.; and friends, Jim Finney, Jim Fentriss, Dan Leininger, Frank Hunger, Jack Cain, Scott Nickson, and Dave Hansen. Ralph's former law school professor, R. Dale Vliet, a Julliard-trained singer, provided special music for the wedding.[21]

After their wedding, Ralph and Barbara were joined by a one-year-old English bulldog, "Rugby," one of the puppies she and Ralph could not resist on their Sunday afternoon dates looking at puppies.[22]

With visions of serving in the CIA or Foreign Service behind him, and the realization of raising a family in Oklahoma, Ralph presented himself for public service in the legal profession. He was founding chairman of the General Practice and International Law sections of the Oklahoma Bar Association, a founding director of the Oklahoma County Legal Aid Society, and was a Special Justice of the Oklahoma Supreme

The men of the wedding party. Left to right, Jim Finney, Dr. Wayman Thompson, Jr., Jim Fentriss, Dan Leininger, Ralph, Lee Thompson, Jr., the best man, Frank Hunger, Jack Cain, Scott Nickson, and Dave Hansen.

Court. In addition, he was president of the Oklahoma City Lawyers Club and was chapter chairman of the Oklahoma County Chapter of the American Red Cross.

Ralph recognized his attraction to the law—the honor and integrity of the profession had been instilled in him by his father, "who was the very epitome of just those standards and ethical qualities." Another reason for his respect of the law was his appreciation for the honor code at the OU College of Law. The code was simple—absolutely no cheating and no tolerance of anyone who did. "It set the perfect example of the honor, trust, and high expectations that are foundations of the legal profession," Ralph said.

Then, Ralph's high esteem for lawyers and the judicial system took a blow. An Internal Revenue Service investigation revealed that three justices of the Oklahoma Supreme Court had taken bribes from lawyers to influence the outcome of cases appealed to the state's highest civil court. In January, 1965, United States District Judge Stephen Chandler learned of the written admission of former Justice N.S. Corn that he had sold his vote for $150,000 and had paid Justices Earl Welch and N.B. Johnson for their approval of a decision in a 1957 tax case before the Supreme Court.[23]

Judge Chandler shared Justice Corn's statement with Oklahoma Supreme Court Justice William A. Berry, who likewise was sickened by the obvious corruption on the high court. The statement might have been forever sealed in secret court documents unless the two judges found a way to make it public. They chose State Representative G.T. Blankenship, an Oklahoma City Republican attorney, to make public the shocking disclosure in a speech before the Oklahoma House of Representatives. Gene Howard, a member of the House at the time, and later President Pro Tempore of the Oklahoma State Senate, wrote in a 2007 editorial in *The Journal Record,* "Blankenship dropped the bombshell that changed not only the personnel of the court but the entire judicial system in Oklahoma."[24]

The House of Representatives authorized an investigation of the scandal that sent shock waves across the nation. *TIME* Magazine reported:

Little in U.S. judicial history comes close to matching the scandal now swirling around the Oklahoma Supreme Court. Though the state bar association has cleared seven of the nine justices, omitting Welch and Johnson, the court has obviously suffered a crushing loss of prestige.[25]

The Supreme Court scandal hit young lawyers such as Ralph "like a blow to the heart, shaking us and our trust and sense of honor to the core."[26] As the guilty were being brought to justice, Ralph was left with the "clear sense that judicial reform had to happen and happen then."

The Oklahoma legislature was led by Democrats who opposed Republican Governor Henry Bellmon's call for sweeping changes in the way judges were selected in the state. Ralph and many of his young colleagues became active in support of judicial reform. He and Jerry Tubb, a close friend and widely respected younger member of the bar, joined other lawyers to raise money and make speeches for the cause.

The three Supreme Court justices who were part of the high court scandal were severely punished by federal authorities and Oklahoma eventually "cleaned up its act."

Ralph's interest in effecting judicial reform and making judicial reform a reality were major motivations in his decision to enter the world of politics. It was another outlet for his passion for public service.

Ralph had chosen to register as a Republican because he and many of his friends were concerned that Oklahoma had been run too long by one party, the Democrats. He was impressed with young, civic-minded Republican professional and business leaders who offered a fresh vision for the state. Ralph said, "By watching the lives of Dewey Bartlett, G. T. Blankenship, and Henry Bellmon, I believed the Republican platform offered fresh new promise for the state." He thought a competitive two-party state would bring a higher level of candidates and policies for both parties, resulting in better government for Oklahoma.[27]

He was comfortable with traditional Republican principles. While many good friends and colleagues he would have during his career were Democrats, and with his belief that neither major political party has a complete monopoly on good ideas and ethical conduct, he maintains his choice of party was right for him. He likes the term "compassionate conservative." He said, "I believe in solutions. I just want them to be made responsibly."[28]

CHAPTER 7

TWO TERMS
AND THREE BABIES

*To have been part of Oklahoma's judicial reform
remains one of the most satisfying efforts
of my 36 years of public service.*

Ralph G. Thompson

Representative G.T. Blankenship, who had revealed the Supreme Court scandal to the world, decided to vacate his District 83 seat in the House of Representatives in 1966 to run for Oklahoma attorney general, a race in which he was successful, becoming the state's first GOP attorney general.

Ralph and Barbara lived in the same House District 83 as Blankenship that covered an area of north Oklahoma City, Nichols Hills, Lakehurst, and The Village. Ralph saw the opportunity as "a perfect one," if he ever wanted to hold public office. After discussing the idea with Barbara and with colleagues, he announced his intention to run for the open seat. One of his principal advisors was Governor Bellmon, the state's first Republican governor, who had become one of Ralph's most admired public servants.[1]

Friends, Jan Nickson and Lisbeth Alexander, served as Ralph's campaign managers. They distributed handsome yard signs and brochures and planned coffees and door-to-door campaigning. In an unprecedented move in a legislative race, Ralph sent a personal letter to every voter in the district. That would not have been possible without Governor Bellmon allowing Ralph's volunteers the use of the automatic typewriter in his office, a "big technology advantage of that time."[2]

Ralph was one of six candidates vying for the District 83 seat, the most for any House race in the state. The three Republicans were Ralph, Harvard-trained importer-exporter Jonathan Burch, and engineer and oil company executive Richard O. Bertschinger. Democratic candidates were three attorneys, A. Bob Jordan, Howard Austin, and Henry James.

During the campaign, Ralph was asked to be a groomsman in the Tennessee wedding of Frank Hunger, his former Air Force roommate in Taiwan. While stationed in Taiwan, both pledged that when each was later married, the other would be in the wedding. Hunger was a groomsman in Ralph and Barbara's wedding, so Ralph now was returning the favor.[3]

Hunger was marrying Nancy Gore, the daughter of United States Senator Albert Gore, Sr. Her brother, Albert Gore, Jr., was later senator from Tennessee and vice president of the United States. Ralph traveled to the Gore ranch at Carthage, Tennessee. He found himself at an all-family dinner the night before the wedding. Around the room were Senator Gore and his wife, Pauline; Albert Gore, Jr., recently graduated from Harvard University; and other family members.

During the dinner, Mrs. Gore told her husband how happy she was that he did not have to run for reelection that year. Nancy Gore, to draw Ralph into the conversation, announced, "Oh, but we have an active candidate with us tonight. Ralph is running for the House of Representatives from Oklahoma." To the Gores, the House of Representatives meant Congress. Mrs. Gore, ever gracious, said, "Oh, Ralph, we are so excited to know this. When you come to Washington, we'll help you get the right committee assignments. Tell us, who is your Republican opponent?" Mrs. Gore assumed Ralph, the best friend of her new son-in-law, was surely a Democrat.[4]

Ralph, who had not expected the conversation to take such a turn, responded that he was running for the Oklahoma House and that his opponent was actually a Democrat. An older gentleman, one of the grandfathers, had an old-fashioned brass ear trumpet and leaned forward to make certain he was hearing the conversation correctly. After a pause, Mrs. Gore said, "My Lawd, I would have never dreamed!"

Despite the Gores' view of Ralph's misguided political affiliation, they were "lovely, generous, and gracious friends everafter." Nancy died prematurely of lung cancer at age 46, but her husband, a distinguished lawyer and one time Chief of the Civil Division of the United States Department of Justice, has remained close friends with Ralph throughout their lives.[5]

Back in Oklahoma, Ralph picked up his frenzied campaign for the House seat. Because the cry for court reform was so loudly heard among the citizens, much of Ralph's focus in the race for the legislature was to provide voters specific ideas of ways to change Oklahoma's judicial system. He supported streamlining courts and removing state judges from partisan elections and selecting them on merit and appointment.[6]

In the primary election on May 3, 1966, Ralph easily defeated his two Republican opponents without a runoff. He polled 1,201 votes to 498 for Burch and 415 for Bertschinger.[7]

In seeking support from Republicans for the primary election, Ralph discovered that many of the same people who were supporting him also were supporters of State Senator Dewey Bartlett of Tulsa who opposed John N. "Happy" Camp of Waukomis for the Republican nomination for governor. Ralph and Bartlett became instant friends and colleagues. Ralph appeared at many events with Bartlett, a man he appreciated and admired and who was destined to play a major role in his future. Bartlett,

Ralph served two terms as a member of the Oklahoma House of Representatives from 1966 to 1970.

a native of Ohio, was a graduate of Princeton University who came to Oklahoma and built a successful oil and gas business. Ralph learned that Bartlett had trained to be a Marine dive bomber pilot in World War II and had been one of the pilots who had flown training missions over the presidential-retirement home of Ralph's grandfather on the OU campus in Norman 24 years earlier during the war.[8]

Expecting their first child, Barbara's primary role early in the general election campaign was helping with mailing letters to voters. Lisa Irene was born on July 13, 1966. After Barbara and Lisa spent a few days at home, Barbara was again available to knock on doors. By fall, she was able to put Lisa in a stroller and campaign for her husband throughout their home precinct.[9]

On election day, Ralph helped Oklahoma Republicans pick up three House seats in Oklahoma County by defeating his Democratic opponent, Jordan, 5,155 to 2,423. The GOP closed the gap in House seats in the county from 14-5 to 11-8. The political landscape was changed forever that November when House Speaker J.D. McCarty was defeated in south Oklahoma City after serving 13 terms. Bartlett became the state's second GOP governor and Blankenship was elected attorney general, but the state legislature remained solidly in the hands of Democrats.[10]

Ralph was excited about becoming a member of the House of Representatives with the leadership of new Governor Bartlett whose campaign had been based upon reforms in state government. Just before being sworn in, Ralph met a young new House member from Tulsa, James Inhofe. Ralph had been told that he and Inhofe were much alike, not only in age and background, but even in appearance. Inhofe's father had told him to look up Ralph because, "His dad is one of my best friends, and he's our kind of people."[11] The embrace and meeting in the aisle of the House chamber was the beginning of a long and close friendship. Inhofe later was elected state senator, mayor of Tulsa, congressman, and United States Senator from Oklahoma.[12]

Also sworn in as a new House member was David L. Boren from Seminole, still a law student at the University of Oklahoma. He also became a lifelong friend of Ralph. Boren ultimately was elected governor of Oklahoma and United States Senator and became president of OU.

While becoming a new member of the legislature had its serious side, there was also a lighter moment on the day of the swearing-in. The Republican minority leader opened the first caucus meeting with a warning, "A member of the House is drunk and he's got a gun and he's on the House floor." Ralph believed it was "hazing" of new members and was all a joke. It was not. The representative was "roaring drunk," was stumbling around the House chamber, and declared, "No Republican, Princeton-educated, Roman Catholic, rich Tulsa oil man is going to be governor of my state." The House member, a Democrat, obviously was referring to the election of Governor Bartlett. Safety returned to the chamber when sergeants-at-arms ushered him from the chamber. Ironically, the man later became an unlikely ally of Ralph and others pushing for judicial reform.[13]

The House was led by Democrat Rex Privett of Maramec. Speaker Privett was elected to the post after the surprise upset of former speaker J.D. McCarty. Privett was a "bridge builder" and was able to push through legislation with the support of his own party and the coopera-tion of Republicans. He and Ralph had great mutual respect for each other. Ralph said, "He was a fine man with whom I developed an excel-lent working relationship and personal friendship."[14]

Privett knew of Ralph's good reputation as a lawyer and appointed him as a minority member of the House Judiciary Committee. Privett said, "Ralph always knew the subject of each bill we were considering. He

Ralph introduced former Governor Henry Bellmon at a 1968 rally in Bellmon's success-ful race for the United States Senate. Ralph considered Bellmon one of his most admired public figures.

helped other members as well as me with the legal purpose and effect of the bills we were trying to enact. His vote always was for the benefit of Oklahoma and its citizens."[15]

The Judiciary Committee was chaired by Democrat John McCune of Tulsa. Democratic leaders recognized that the "hot-button" issue of the 1967 session was judicial reform and that no meaningful reform would be accomplished without bi-partisan support. Because it was his primary reason for entering the race, Ralph valued the opportunity to work with leaders on both sides of the aisle for court reform.

With obvious respect for Ralph as a lawyer, he was allowed to become a principal co-author of the Judicial Reform Constitutional Amendment. Among other tasks, he was assigned the job of handling the provision that would eliminate the old, scandal-ridden justice of the peace system and replace it with special district courts. "I got that assignment," Ralph remembered, "because it was a hot potato among 'Old Guard' circles because justices of the peace were a significant political force. I think I was considered to be expendable"[16]

Ralph held hearings in which some justices of the peace were crude and critical of any attempts to remove them from the system. Ralph considered it a "badge of distinction" to be publicly castigated by opponents of court reform. In the end, even many of the opponents of court reform "came around." It has been said that the legislators who opposed change "not only saw the light, but felt the heat."

Eventually, voters approved constitutional amendments that created a new system of merit selection, appointment, and retention of state appellate judges and non-partisan election of state district trial judges. Ralph favored the idea that trial judges be appointed on merit also, and removed from any elective system. But to get passage, he and other judicial reformers had to compromise on that single issue. He said, "The new system, while not going far enough, still was a huge step forward for the state and the cause of justice."[17]

Prior to the special election at which voters approved the constitutional amendments on court reform, Ralph decried apathy that he believed was growing among state voters. He said:

> Citizens should be given a good shaking to wake them up to the urgent need for court reform. Lack of interest in the issue is incomprehensible…If we want excellence in our state, it must start with justice…We now have an opportunity to

correct the situation that allowed the terrible Supreme Court scandal to develop.[18]

Ralph was part of a bi-partisan group of Oklahoma House members who were appointed to travel to Washington, D.C., in April, 1967, to oppose Congress' new highway beautification legislation which would have punished states with the potential devastating loss of ten percent of federal highway money unless strict federal beautification rules were followed.

Ralph and Representatives Boren, Inhofe, Lee Cate of Norman, and Lou Allard of Drumright appeared before the United States House Subcommittee on Public Works and testified that increased federal

Barbara and Ralph admire the plaque naming him "Oklahoma City's Outstanding Young Man" for 1967. The honor came from the Oklahoma City chapter of the Junior Chamber of Commerce (Jaycees).

guidelines imposed on the states were too punitive and were making state legislative functions "mere formalities."[19]

The Oklahoma delegation, with Representative Boren as spokesman, told Congress:

> Our people are fast becoming alienated from government and the governmental process. There is a growing feeling that they no longer have a real and effective voice in government… Often there are no alternatives for state legislative policy because the sanctions attached to the guidelines leave no room for choice by state legislatures…We feel that federal grants are sometimes the technical means by which decision to initiate, expand or alter public services and polices are carried out. While the states are not being outright abolished, their functions are being increasingly preempted.[20]

In January, 1968, Ralph was named by Governor Bartlett to a special commission to study the effects of crime on Oklahoma. The commission, chaired by Attorney General Blankenship, included lawmakers, law enforcement officials, private citizens, and prosecutors from around the state. Prominent members joining Ralph were Hugh Collum, Represen-

Ralph was one of "Three Outstanding Oklahomans" honored by the Oklahoma State Junior Chamber of Commerce in 1967. Left to right, Ronald Gilbert, State Senator Al Terrill, and Ralph.

tative Jerry Sokolosky, Preston Trimble, Thomas R. Brett, Dr. Hayden Donahue, Burke Mordy, Senator Roy Grantham, and Representative Lou Allard.[21]

Ralph was a respected member of the Republican leadership in the state. At the GOP state convention in early February, 1968, Ralph nominated former OU football coach Bud Wilkinson as the interim Republican national committeeman from Oklahoma, a position vacated by the death of John W. Tyler of Bartlesville. When the votes were counted, Wilkinson scored a landslide victory over C. Hubert Gragg of Oklahoma City.[22]

Others recognized Ralph's growing prominence in state government. At the conclusion of his first term in office, he, State Senator Al Terrill of Lawton, and Dr. Ronald W. Gilbert of Miami were named the "Three Outstanding Young Oklahomans" by the Oklahoma State Junior Chamber of Commerce (Jaycees) and, the same year, the Oklahoma City Jaycees selected Ralph as "Oklahoma City's Outstanding Young Man."[23]

In June, 1968, Ralph announced his intention to run for reelection in House District 83. He cited his accomplishments in leading the passage of court reform, being the author of a new drug control law, and sponsoring legislation on riot control, tax reform, and other advances.[24]

Ralph had long-range plans. He anticipated that John Jarman would

House Speaker Rex Privett, right, welcomes the Thompson family to the Speaker's office. Left to right, Ralph, holding Elaine, Lisa, and Barbara, holding Maria. Ralph and Privett had a warm and productive bi-partisan relationship.

soon retire as the congressman in the fifth congressional district that covered the Oklahoma City metropolitan area. He believed that he could win the support of many longtime Jarman friends, among them E.K. Gaylord, publisher of *The Daily Oklahoman* and the *Oklahoma City Times*. He was Gaylord's representative in the legislature and believed the two had a favorable relationship.[25]

The summer of 1968 was exciting in the Thompson household. Barbara was expecting a baby in mid-October. Ralph had drawn no primary opponent in his reelection bid, and prepared to face Democratic challenger Andrew L. Hamilton, an Oklahoma City attorney, in the general election. Three days before Barbara was due to deliver, she and Ralph were "flabbergasted, but delighted" to learn that she was going to have twins.

On October 18, 1968, Elaine Bizzell Thompson and Maria Louise Thompson were born. They were identical, "absolutely indistinguishable." Ralph remembered, "As with the birth of Lisa, our lives were again changed forever." Ralph's father, who was an identical twin, was exuberant with the news.

On November 5, Ralph easily defeated Hamilton 7,390 to 2,912 in an all-time high voter turnout in Oklahoma County. He received more

Proud grandparents, Elaine and Lee Thompson, with, left to right, Lisa, Elaine, and Maria.

than 71 percent of the vote, only slightly behind the percentage of the total vote received by Congressman Jarman. Much of the interest in the election surrounded the presidential race which brought the election of Richard M. Nixon. More than 189,000 voters cast ballots in the county, surpassing the previous turnout record in the 1952 presidential election.[26]

Three weeks after Ralph and Barbara experienced the joy of the birth of twins, and a few days after the satisfying victory in the general election, they were shocked to learn of a plane crash that killed three of Ralph's close friends. The single-engine aircraft carrying attorney Tom Lynn, neurosurgeon Dr. Dick Earnest, and oilman Jim Harrell, crashed in Kansas on a pheasant hunting trip. A fourth empty seat in the airplane had been reserved for Ralph, who, at the last minute, had cancelled in order to take Barbara to an Ella Fitzgerald concert. Ralph said, "It was a close call for me and a horrible tragedy for my friends and their families left behind."[27]

CHAPTER 8

THE RACE FOR LIEUTENANT GOVERNOR

The trouble with a politician's life is that somebody is always interrupting it with an election.

Will Rogers

Along with his service in the legislature, Ralph's law practice continued to grow. Frankly, he liked the adversarial role in litigation and his service in the legislature. "Courtroom work was a natural for me and the legislative duties naturally put me on opposite sides of issues with others on a daily basis," he said. He particularly enjoyed and valued his ability to "do battle" professionally and remain good friends with colleagues when the battle ended.[1]

Ralph was elected Assistant Minority Floor Leader for the 1969 session of the legislature. His strong working relationship with members of his own party and his Democratic friends served him particularly well in that role. In the back of his mind, Ralph still considered himself as a reasonable choice to replace Congressman Jarman when he retired, the only future office he considered. He obviously was familiar with the problems of Oklahoma City and was interested in national and international issues. Then, a telephone call in the summer of 1969 changed his political plans.[2]

Shortly after Ralph and his family returned from vacation, the telephone rang. On the other end of the line was Governor Bartlett, who stunned him with a request that he run for lieutenant governor and campaign with him as a team. Bartlett was the first Oklahoma governor eligible to be reelected, due to a change in the state constitution, and had privately decided to run for another four years.

Ralph never had considered the office of lieutenant governor that was occupied by George Nigh, who Ralph considered to be a friend. There was no doubt Nigh was the most popular Democrat in the state, although rumors suggested Nigh might be considering running for governor against the incumbent, Bartlett.[3]

Bartlett asked Ralph to think about the offer overnight and meet with him the following afternoon at the governor's mansion. After a sleepless night, Ralph appeared at the mansion at the prescribed time. Bartlett reiterated his invitation to Ralph to effectively become his running mate. Bartlett outlined his reasoning that the governor and lieutenant governor work together, similar to the way the president and vice president of the United States run and serve together.[4]

Ralph was intrigued with the prospect of running with Bartlett, his admired friend. He knew he needed the team approach in order to have a reasonable chance of winning. He had never run for statewide office and lacked name recognition outside Oklahoma City. "Unless we could combine our effort to offer a sensible and appealing concept of running the state as a team, my chances would be pretty slim," Ralph said.[5]

Ralph talked with friends and supporters privately until word leaked out at the State Capitol. On August 26, 1969, *The Daily Oklahoman* ran a story about the possibility of several top Republicans running as part of the "Bartlett team." The newspaper reported that "informed capitol sources" confirmed that chief contributors of Bartlett's 1966 campaign were supportive of the team concept in which Ralph would run for lieutenant governor and Attorney General G.T. Blankenship and State Superintendent of Public Instruction Dr. D.D. Creech would run for reelection.[6]

By December, 1969, Ralph still had not publicly announced his decision on whether or not to be a candidate for lieutenant governor. The incumbent, Nigh, also had not announced his intentions of running for

Ralph campaigning for lieutenant governor in 1970. He considered meeting Oklahomans from all walks of life to be invaluable, one that helped him in his judicial career to follow.

The entire family at a campaign event in the summer of 1970. Left to right, Lisa, Ralph, Elaine, Maria, and Barbara.

reelection or trying to unseat Governor Bartlett. However, Nigh had told his friends that he would stick by his principle of never running against an incumbent governor. That principle had served him well.[7] Ralph noted that he and Nigh were friends but that Nigh's decision to run for reelection or for governor had no bearing on his own decision.[8]

Ralph visited every corner of Oklahoma, talking to Bartlett supporters who needed to champion his cause in the lieutenant governor's race if that effort was to be successful. He was strongly encouraged in talks with Republican legislators and other GOP leaders from both Oklahoma City and Tulsa and throughout the state.[9]

Many of those contacted by Ralph believed that the governor and the lieutenant governor should work more closely together. Ralph said, "It doesn't make sense to a lot of people that the highest Republican office holder in the state has a lieutenant governor who is the highest office holder in the Democratic Party." Ralph told supporters, "A friendly lieutenant governor could almost double the outreach of the governor's office."[10]

Both political parties had talked about candidates for the state's two top elective posts running as a team. An interim constitutional revision study group recommended a plan in which the gubernatorial nominee for each party would choose a running mate who would become lieutenant governor. Newspapers suggested that the Bartlett-Thompson team would demonstrate that such a system would work.[11]

By January, the races for governor and lieutenant governor were clear. Former Tulsa County prosecutor David Hall and Oklahoma City attorney Bryce Baggett became the front runners for the Democratic gubernatorial nomination. Additional Democratic candidates included former Commissioner of Public Safety Joe Cannon and Wilburn Cartwright. Lieutenant Governor Nigh announced he wanted voters to return him to office. He was opposed by an unknown candidate, Jack K. Gillespie of Oklahoma City. Ralph was unopposed for the GOP nomination for lieutenant governor.

True to his promise, Bartlett included Ralph in campaign planning meetings and the actual campaign. The Bartlett-Thompson combined campaign theme was that the top two elected officials in the state should be "working partners." Ralph's motto was, "Give our governor a working partner."

Barbara and the three Thompson daughters were active in the campaign. Ralph said:

> Having a wife and three little girls who were all so sweet and pretty and friendly was a big asset. They were so appealing and well received that I used to say I should just stay in the shadows and not undo the good they were doing.[12]

Barbara especially enjoyed traveling around the state with wives of other Republican candidates for state office. It was her honor and delight to spend time with First Lady Ann Bartlett and Libby Blankenship, the wife of Attorney General Blankenship.

Even though Barbara had campaigned for Ralph in his local House district races, it was a new world and "a big state." At a fundraising event, Barbara sat next to United States Senator and former Governor Henry Bellmon who impressed Barbara with his vast knowledge of almost every GOP supporter in attendance. Barbara said, "I loved being on the campaign trail with Ralph. He was always so well received." Barbara especially enjoyed meeting "so many genuinely wonderful people dedicated to making our country a better place to live." For Barbara, it was an education, "inspiring and a real learning experience," meeting so many patriotic, genuine, and diverse people who made up Oklahoma in 1970.[13]

Ralph took his message to all 77 counties in parades, stump speeches, and campaigning up and down main streets with Barbara and the girls. Radio, television, billboard, and newspaper advertisements carried his call for good government. A brochure for OU football games was developed in which the Bartlett-Thompson team was endorsed by former Sooner greats Clendon Thomas, Billy Pricer, Ron Shotts, and Heisman Trophy winner Billy Vessels.

An invigorating part of the campaign for Ralph was meeting Oklahomans from all walks of life. He remembered, "Meeting all kinds of people with all kinds of hopes and needs gave me a new perspective and helped me be a better judge later on in my judicial career." As a "city boy," rural Oklahomans left an especially "warm spot" in Ralph's heart for their "goodness, natural decency, and intelligence and common sense."[14]

When Ralph and Bartlett campaigned together, they hired the legendary Leon McAuliffe and his country swing band to draw crowds. McAuliffe had been a member of the famous Bob Wills band. Many people enjoyed his music and packed outdoor venues and conven-

The 1970 campaign helped cement the lifelong friendship of Ralph and Governor, and later United States Senator, Dewey Bartlett, left.

tion halls where Ralph and Bartlett had captive audiences in which to convince voters their team approach was best for Oklahoma. McAuliffe knew that one of Ralph's favorite songs was "San Antonio Rose." When the entertainer saw Ralph approach the stage, he gave Ralph a friendly wink and the band struck up the familiar strains of the classic Bob Wills song. Hearing the song today takes Ralph back to those moments.[15]

In the closing weeks of the general election campaign, Ralph won the approval of three major Oklahoma metropolitan newspapers. On October 25, the *Tulsa World* wrote:

We have long believed that the governor and lieutenant governor should be elected as a team—or at least be members of the same party…The opportunity exists now. Governor Bartlett has an attractive, articulate teammate in State Rep. Ralph G. Thompson of Oklahoma City…Thompson is young (35) but experienced as an attorney and as a legislator. In this third year in the House he was elected Assistant Minority Floor Leader, the only member of Oklahoma County's delegation to have a leadership post…He is frankly running uphill against Lt. Gov. George Nigh, an accomplished democratic vote-getter in Oklahoma. But even Nigh has agreed that the governor and lieutenant governor should run together…

We would not be in favor of replacing Nigh with just anybody, simply to satisfy a "system." But Thompson is a candidate worthy of the office—which after all holds the potential of substituting for the governor. We do not hesitate to recommend the Bartlett-Thompson Team.[16]

On October 27, the *Tulsa Tribune* editorialized:

Thompson has worked to strengthen drug laws and for tax reform. He is a close associate of Dewey Bartlett and well qualified to serve as the governor's strong right-hand man. The *Tribune* endorses Ralph G. Thompson, G.T. Blankenship, and J. Michael Donahoe to aid Governor Bartlett in providing better state government for all Oklahomans.[17]

The state's largest newspaper, *The Daily Oklahoman*, published a front-page endorsement of Ralph on the morning of the November 3 election. It was the second official endorsement of Ralph by *The Oklahoman*

Wives of GOP candidates on a statewide bus campaign tour. Left to right, First Lady Ann Bartlett, Libby Blankenship, wife of Attorney General G.T. Blankenship, and Barbara.

Ralph, right, with legendary OU football coach Bud Wilkinson at a 1970 campaign event.

The Thompson and Nigh families were close friends before, during, and after the 1970 lieutenant governor race. At an OU Evening of Excellence banquet in 1988 are Ralph and Barbara and Governor George Nigh and First Lady Donna Nigh.

in three days. The newspaper said:

> For lieutenant governor, Ralph Thompson is a man of integrity and a respected public official with experience in the legislature. The offices of governor and lieutenant governor should not be separated on the ballot, and in time will be linked by law. Ralph Thompson has worked well with Gov. Bartlett in the past, and should be elected to cooperate with him during the next four years.[18]

Even though Ralph had the support of the three largest newspapers in Oklahoma, Nigh put together a group of more than 200 rural newspaper editors in his camp. Larry Hammer, editor and publisher of the *Fairview Republican*, was the chairman of the group.[19]

In a major upset that shattered all predictions, David Hall defeated Governor Bartlett by slightly more than 2,000 votes out of more than 670,000 cast. Bartlett lost by less than one vote per precinct. Observers believed that Hall, the 40-year-old silver-haired underdog, had ridden a tide of rural support to the surprise victory. Hall's victory led a Democratic "clean sweep" that ousted Republicans from every state office.[20]

Bartlett's loss and the huge vote in rural areas were too much for Ralph's effort to become the state's first Republican lieutenant governor. When the votes were counted, Nigh won reelection 382,249 to 270,535. The American Party candidate, Jack Davidson, polled 11,588 votes. Even though Ralph fell short of his goal, it was an incredible experience of getting to know the people of Oklahoma. He said, "While realizing there is no such thing as a prize for a runner-up in an election, to me our statewide campaign and the entire Bartlett-Thompson experience was a wonderful one."[21]

History places the loss to Nigh in perspective. It was the second closest race for Nigh, who later became governor and is looked upon by many as one of Oklahoma's most popular public servants in the state's first century.

Ralph and Barbara congratulated Nigh and his wife, Donna. In the 40 years since, the couples have remained good friends. Ralph recognizes Nigh's superb contributions to Oklahoma. Nigh said Ralph is "a bastion of integrity" and "a truly great Oklahoman." Both truly value their unique relationship.[22]

Approaching the Federal Bench

*My four-year involvement in elective office was over.
It had been interesting and engaging, but it did not compare
to the 32-year, life-defining career that awaited me.*

Ralph G. Thompson

When the dust settled from the race for lieutenant governor, Ralph returned to his law practice. The firm represented many successful and distinguished businesses, especially in the oil and gas business.

Ralph's father had been instrumental in the formation of one of the firm's major clients, Mustang Fuel Corporation, a highly successful natural gas pipeline gathering and transmission company. Years before, Mr. Thompson had represented Edward C. Joullian, Sr., an engineer for another gas pipeline company, who wanted to form his own company. Joullian did not have resources to pay Mr. Thompson for the legal work, but offered him a percentage of the common stock of the new company. Mr. Thompson accepted, and the commercial potential of the new venture blossomed. Later when Edward C. Joullian, III, took over the company that his father founded, Mr. Thompson continued as general counsel.[1]

Ralph assisted his father in representing the interests of Mustang Fuel. Once when his father was preparing to close a major loan from financial institutions in New York City for pipeline expansion, Mr. Thompson suffered a detached retina and was hospitalized. Ralph took over the project and successfully concluded the complicated financing package at the offices of a prominent New York City law firm. Once completed, Ralph and Ed Joullian, III, celebrated at the venerable Union Club in Manhattan, complete with mahogany-paneled walls and oil portraits of famous members.[2]

Ralph was "enormously relieved" to have survived the occasion with a successful closing and with his "self respect intact." During the lunch, he turned to Joullian and said that it had never occurred to him while digging ditches and shoveling grease and bugs from Mustang's compressor stations years ago, that he would someday be the company's lawyer and be sipping a martini and enjoying lobster bisque at the elegant Union Club.[3]

Ralph especially liked trial work in federal court. In addition to handling his own firm's cases, he sometimes was hired by other Oklahoma City firms that had a conflict and needed an outside trial lawyer. Ralph's strong preference was federal court. He particularly enjoyed the orderly and dignified practice, the quality and professionalism of the judges, staffs, and superior facilities. In the back of his mind, he thought a federal judgeship certainly would fit his continued interest in public service, but it was only a thought for the time being.[4]

In 1971, Ralph served as a Special Justice of the Oklahoma Supreme Court in a case to determine whether a disbarred critic of the judicial system should have his license to practice law reinstated. Harlan Grimes, a controversial Dallas, Texas, attorney, had lost his license after publicly accusing members of the Oklahoma Supreme Court of bribery and corruption. Believing the ultimate revelation that three former justices had accepted bribes had vindicated him, Grimes sought reinstatement to the bar. The appointment of Special Justices was necessary because members of the Oklahoma Supreme Court disqualified themselves from any consideration of Grimes' reinstatement application.[5]

A proud father, Lee B. Thompson, congratulates his son on becoming a new judge on October 20, 1975. Daughter Lisa is holding the gavel.

Other members of the special court included Judge Neal Merriott of Idabel and attorney John Wallace of Miami. After hearing testimony and conducting a thorough investigation, the special court found that Grimes had been practicing law without a license for the 11 years since his disbarment. That fact alone was enough for the special court to refuse Grimes' reinstatement.[6]

Ralph's life was full, with family, his law practice, and occasional dabbling in politics. In December, 1971, he attended a three-day briefing in Washington, D.C., with a group known as Friends of Richard Nixon.[7] He and Inhofe were selected as surrogate speakers for President Nixon in Oklahoma. In the meeting, they became good friends with Kay Bailey, at that time the press secretary for Anne Armstrong, co-chair of the Republican National Committee, and one of the surrogate speakers from Texas.

Later, Bailey was the first woman elected to the Texas House of Representatives, was elected State Treasurer, and even later, then married, was elected to the United States Senate as Kay Bailey Hutchison. Ralph, Inhofe, and Bailey shared the belief that the people and policies of the Nixon administration at the time represented their personal commitments to the high standards of honesty and ethics in public affairs. With the glitter of being hosted at the White House by President Nixon, they took their responsibilities seriously.[8]

Then, Ralph and Inhofe were unsettled by events at a group meeting with top Nixon advisors John Ehrlichman and H.R. Halderman who addressed the group about how to speak on behalf of the president. When one particular policy was addressed, a member of the group stood and respectfully asked what he should do in his home state in which that policy was extremely unpopular. Ehrlichman said bluntly, "You do what we tell you to do!" Ralph remembered, "We all felt rather stunned. After all, we had been handpicked to be speakers for the President. We hadn't expected such arrogance and disrespect, especially from the President's top aides."[9]

Ralph and Inhofe did not dwell on the incident and served as Nixon surrogate speakers in the campaign. But the incident was not lost on them, later, when Ehrlichman and Haldeman were key figures in the Watergate scandal and were convicted and sentenced to prison for their part in the cover up which resulted in President Nixon's resignation.[10]

During Senator Bartlett's campaign for the United States Senate in 1972, he invited Ralph to introduce California Governor Ronald Reagan at a campaign event in Oklahoma City. Reagan was in Oklahoma speaking in support of Bartlett. Ralph was greatly honored to be asked to introduce Reagan, but on the day of the rally, Ralph came down with a genuine case of influenza with a fever of 102 degrees. "No amount of fever was going to keep me off that stage with two of my most admired people," he said. He gave a rousing introduction of Reagan, according to Barbara, because the fever clouded Ralph's memory of the event.[11]

Ralph had been a lawyer for 15 years and had become more interested in seeing that the "right thing" was done rather than just representing one side of a controversy. His senior partner said, "I think you should be a judge—a federal judge if possible." At about that time, it was rumored that United States District Judge Stephen Chandler wanted to retire, but only if a particular lawyer friend be selected to replace him. Chandler had long been highly controversial. Efforts to remove his caseload resulted in a much-publicized lawsuit against the United States Court of Appeals for the Tenth Circuit.[12]

Oklahoma's two United States senators, Henry Bellmon and Dewey Bartlett, sent word to Judge Chandler that he could retire whenever he wanted to, but they would not be told who to select as his successor. Eventually, Chandler wrote Bellmon and Bartlett of his intention to retire. The news was received "with such relief" that Senator Bartlett immediately dispatched his legislative aide, David Russell, to deliver the letter to the White House before Chandler changed his mind. The retirement became official, a vacancy in the Western District of Oklahoma was created, and opportunity for Ralph was created.[13]

It has been said that "stars have to align precisely" for a federal judgeship to be a possibility for a lawyer. Ralph remembered, "It looked as if the stars were aligning for me—the prospect of public service and federal trial practice was coming together perfectly." Ralph's name was suggested as a replacement for Judge Chandler almost immediately. Privately, when asked, Ralph confirmed he was interested.[14]

Federal judges were selected in a traditional way. The top-ranking United States senator of the party in power in the White House recommended potential judges to the President for appointment. President Nixon resigned because of the Watergate scandal on August 9, 1974, and

United States Senator Dewey Bartlett, left, welcomes Ralph to the confirmation hearing before the Senate Judiciary Committee. Bartlett later inscribed the photograph, "Congratulations on a new career which will raise the quality of justice in Oklahoma."

was succeeded by Vice President Gerald Ford. Because a Republican occupied the White House, Senators Bellmon and Bartlett, both Republicans, exercised great power in the selection of federal judges. There was a gentleman's agreement between the two senators they would take turns in taking the lead in selecting a federal judge nominee.

It was Senator Bartlett's turn. He directed his chief of staff, Don Cogman, and legislative assistant, David Russell, to begin the tedious and lengthy process of poring over lists of lawyers, soliciting ideas from multiple sources, and getting recommendations from both friends and adversaries. Cogman and Russell were thorough in their work. In his autobiography, Cogman, who later became president of the world's largest public relations company, Burson-Marsteller, wrote, "Finally we prepared a lengthy report, ending with our recommendation, backed by pages of rationale and other people's recommendations that the person be Ralph Thompson as [the obvious and best choice]."[15]

Fully agreeing with Cogman's assessment was Russell, who later served twice as United States Attorney and eventually United States District Judge in the Western District of Oklahoma. He became Ralph's close colleague on the court for many years.

Senator Bartlett knew Ralph well and wholeheartedly concurred with his aides' recommendation. He called Ralph and advised him of his decision.

Meanwhile, Ralph was appointed by United States District Judge Fred Daugherty to represent an indigent defendant, Ivan Pearce, who was a co-defendant of Pody Poe in a federal extortion trial. Poe was accused of using Pearce and another co-defendant, Keith Parton, both recently released from the federal penitentiary in Leavenworth, Kansas, to collect unpaid gambling debts. Poe had been a notorious gambling figure for years, making the case a big one for federal prosecutors.[16]

Poe was represented by James Patrick Quinn, a well-known criminal defense lawyer from Kansas City, Missouri. Ralph's only criminal trial experience was from several lesser cases in which he was appointed by federal judges. He remembered, "Never had I taken on a criminal case of this magnitude. It was to be a crash course in federal criminal trial practice."[17]

The FBI had tape-recorded telephone calls in which Pearce and Parton were threatening Poe's debtors. The evidence was substantial against them, but proof of Poe's actual and specific personal direction on how they were to collect his debts was not as strong. Neither Pearce nor Parton would consider pleading guilty and testifying against Poe. Both told prosecutors they would never go back to prison "wearing a snitch jacket."

The case was scheduled for trial before Judge Daugherty at a time when news reports were circulating that Ralph would be selected by President Ford to succeed Judge Chandler. During a recess in the trial, Senator Bartlett reached Ralph by telephone to tell him he was his choice and that the choice had been ratified by Senator Bellmon. Despite Ralph's excitement, the trial resumed. Pearce and Parton were found

Judge Thompson's first official judicial portrait at age 40 in 1975.

guilty of extortion, but the jury acquitted Poe. He was later convicted on other federal charges and served time in federal prison.[18]

It was a financial sacrifice for Ralph to defend Pearce. In those days, there was no federal public defender's office and lawyers were expected to serve their turn representing indigent defendants. They received no compensation for their time or expenses. It was considered an obligation of the profession. Ralph literally dipped into his savings account to pay office and home expenses during the protracted case.

Shortly after the trial, Senators Bartlett and Bellmon formally recommended Ralph to President Ford to fill the vacancy in the Western District of Oklahoma. The United States Department of Justice began its inquiry and the FBI started a full field background investigation. The American Bar Association also conducted an extensive investigation of Ralph's qualifications to become a federal judge and found him to be fully qualified.[19]

The Senate Judiciary Committee held a hearing on Ralph's nomination on October 6, 1975. Senators Bartlett and Bellmon spoke on his behalf. Bartlett was generous in his unequivocal support for Ralph describing him as "an exceptionally well qualified candidate for the federal judiciary." Bartlett said, "His experience intelligence, age, training, temperament, and character uniquely qualify him for the federal bench." Senator Bellmon concurred. There were no negative recommendations or comments introduced into the record.[20]

After a unanimous committee vote, the full Senate unanimously confirmed President Ford's nomination of Ralph three days later on October 9. The *Congressional Record* officially recorded the vote as "without debate or dissent."[21]

The President officially appointed Ralph on October 14. After the official commission was signed by Attorney General Edward Levi, he took the oath of office on October 20 in the ceremonial courtroom of the federal courthouse in Oklahoma City. Judge Chandler, who took senior status, administered the oath and handed the new Judge Thompson his gavel he had been given when he was sworn in as a federal judge in 1943, 32 years before. The gavel was originally owned by Oklahoma Supreme Court Justice Samuel W. Hayes, considered by some historians as one of the most dominant delegates of the Oklahoma Constitutional Convention. Present at the ceremony were Senators Bartlett and Bellmon, other judges of the court, his family, and many friends, attorneys, and other well-wishers. Ralph was presented his robe by his father.[22]

Ralph's long awaited opportunity to combine federal trial practice and public service finally officially had arrived.

After taking the oath of office, at age 40 one of the three youngest federal judges in the nation, the new judge promised to carry his full share of the load in the Western District. He said:

> And to the lawyers and litigants who come before me as a judge, I pledge that to the extent of my abilities, every day, every case, every question, every procedure, to provide a place of courtesy and dignity and order for the resolution of your differences, and to strive to administer justice without regard of any kind, ever once, to race, origin, or station in life; and to strive to administer justice and apply the powers of this office without favor to or fear of anyone.[23]

Thereafter, and here, he appropriately became "Judge Thompson."

Judge Thompson and Barbara with President Gerald Ford, right, who appointed the judge to the federal bench in 1975, at an outdoor symphony concert at Vail, Colorado.

CHAPTER 10

FEDERAL JURIST

*The complete independence of the courts of justice is peculiarly
essential to the Constitution. If the courts of justice are
to be considered as the bulwarks...against legislative
encroachments, this consideration will afford a strong
argument for the permanent tenure of judicial offices.*

Alexander Hamilton

The Founding Fathers of America believed that an independent federal system of justice was critical to the success of the Republic, to prevent encroachments by the executive and legislative branches of the federal government upon rights guaranteed by the Constitution.

At the constitutional convention in Philadelphia, it was argued that the only way politics and the winds of change could be eliminated, or at least diminished, was to appoint judges of the United States Supreme Court, the federal courts of appeal, and federal district courts for life, with removal only by impeachment. When considering the proposed federal constitution, Alexander Hamilton, in *The Federalist No. 78*, wrote:

> This independence of the judges is equally requisite to guard the Constitution and the rights of individuals from the effects of those ill humors, which the arts of designing men, or the influence of particular conjunctures, sometimes disseminate among the people themselves, and which, though they speedily give place to better information, and more deliberate reflection, have a tendency, in the meantime, to occasion dangerous innovations in government, and serious oppressions of the minor party in the community.[1]

When ratified by the states, the United States Constitution contained Article III which provided that the President, with the consent of the Senate, appoint for life, during "good behavior," judges of the Supreme Court, the federal courts of appeal, the federal district courts, and the Court of International Trade. Article III gave Congress the power to determine how many federal district courts were necessary and the power to remove federal judges by impeachment. It is not a constitutional or statutory requirement that Article III judges even be attorneys. However, since the beginning, all federal judges have been appointed only after having a legal education, usually a distinguished one.[2]

Former Oklahoma Governor and United States Senator Henry Bellmon said of the federal judiciary:

> The founders of our Constitution showed unbelievable courage and foresight when they set up the federal judiciary and made it more or less independent of the electoral process. The problem was—and is—that in our society some questions arise that are simply too tough, too hot, too politically dangerous for the political branches—the elected officials—to

deal with. And the federal judiciary, which is bound only by the Constitution and the law of the land, and not by the will of the voters at the next election, makes these tough decisions that elected officials have a difficult time making…Without this system, we would not have a country of which we would be so proud.[3]

Federal judges must follow the ethical standards set out in the *Code of Conduct for United States Judges*, guidelines to make certain a judge does not show partiality or oppression in the conduct of presiding over a case. Financial disclosure is required annually and federal judges are strictly prohibited from taking sides in elections and asking people to contribute money to civic and charitable organizations.[4]

Judge Thompson had practiced in federal courtrooms many times, but he never had been there as the judge and final arbiter of the proceedings taking place before him. He was aware that his entire previous legal career had been a preamble, a preparation, for "the perfect role for me, one by which my identity and professional life would be defined and judged."[5]

The new judge began his duties with an outstanding staff. He brought his "capable secretary," Lyn Marshala, from his private practice and hired an outstanding court reporter, Larry Marks, from Tulsa. He also hired the first of a long succession of "very able" law clerks. He said, "We were all committed to do our best to provide in every case the highest quality of justice, in the least possible time, for the least possible expense." He also promised to do all he could to never keep lawyers, litigants, or jurors waiting.[6]

The federal district courts in Oklahoma were relatively small in 1976. The Chief Judge of the Western District was Fred Daugherty. The other active judge was Luther B. Eubanks. Judge Luther Bohanon had taken senior status, but still was assigned cases. Daugherty and Bohanon had been appointed by President John F. Kennedy. President Lyndon B. Johnson appointed Judge Eubanks.

Previous district judges in the Western District included John Cotteral, appointed by President Theodore Roosevelt; Edgar S. Vaught, appointed by President Calvin Coolidge; Alfred P. Murrah, appointed by President Franklin D. Roosevelt; Stephen Chandler, appointed by President Roosevelt; W.R. Wallace, appointed by President Harry Truman;

and Ross Rizley, appointed by President Dwight D. Eisenhower.

As a new judge, he learned from watching the judicial temperament and practices of Judges Daugherty and Bohanon. Daugherty had "a great legal mind," was a former state district judge, and commander of Oklahoma's 45ᵗʰ Infantry Division. He was also one of Judge Thompson's father's best friends. Bohanon had been assigned the difficult and volatile Oklahoma City school desegregation and state prison cases. His controversial rulings brought him severe criticism and personal vilification. More than once he was hanged in effigy during the long arduous litigation involving school busing and integration. In chambers, Bohanon often spoke of his love for, and his commitment to, the Constitution and how he had been greatly influenced by his OU Law School dean, Julien C. Monnet.[7]

Judge Thompson was well aware of the uniqueness of being appointed for life and the deference paid to federal judges leading some to have "an overly inflated self regard." He knew, or had heard of, a few federal judges who took on a new persona when they donned robes. He enjoyed reciting the story of a federal judge from North Carolina who said, "I'm a rather dull man. I've always had trouble telling jokes or stories. But ever since I became a federal judge, I am one of the funniest men in North Carolina!"[8] Judge Thompson consciously tried to avoid the pitfall by being courteous and professional to others.

It was a daunting challenge to inherit Judge Chandler's cases. Many cases were stagnant and needed immediate attention. In addition, H. Dale Cook, who recently had been appointed as a federal judge in the Northern, Western, and Eastern districts of Oklahoma, transferred, by agreement, cases involving litigation generated by the collapse of the Standard Life Insurance Companies to his good friend Judge Thompson. Those cases, along with an equal draw of cases shared with Judges Daugherty, Eubanks, and Bohanon, presented him, "a full experience to be sure, but one that I was determined to do right."[9]

The United States District Court for the Western District of Oklahoma was a court in which civil cases of multi-million dollar magnitude and complexity were not uncommon as were cases of importance in public affairs, often implicating Constitutional issues.

The court's jurisdiction included the entire western half of Oklahoma which included the crossroads of I-35 and I-40 in Oklahoma City. These routes provided a uniquely ready access to drug smugglers from

Mexico, other drug source countries, and California to distribute their drugs throughout the United States. Consequently, the Western District was commonly the forum for major, often international, drug conspiracy cases of huge significance. Such cases became commonplace for the judges of the court and placed heavy demands on the court system and law enforcement agencies involved.

CHAPTER 11

COLORFUL AND INTRIGUING CASES

Judging is an enormous responsibility.
You often wished for the wisdom of Solomon.

Judge Ralph G. Thompson

Whether criminal or civil, many cases had some importance, sometimes major importance, in their social value. In Judge Thompson's 32-year career, he heard both large and small cases. Some were noted for their colorful facts, while others are still quoted because of their national significance.

His first civil trial was surprisingly an admiralty law case, the law of the sea, and involved a collision of a Kerr-McGee barge on the McClellan-Kerr Arkansas River Navigation System in eastern Oklahoma. It was a challenging first case and the only time in his many years on the federal bench in which a case involved admiralty law.

His trials involved quite a colorful variety of cases. Some were bizarre, such as a criminal case involving an Arkansas man operating a nine-state rabbit raising mail fraud scheme. Many cases required hours of study to master the facts of the case, providing a "liberal education" on a wide variety of subjects. Among them was a case to determine the cause of the disintegration of a giant electric turbine, requiring study of the laws of physics and harmonic vibrations.

There were trials of collapsed corporate empires and embezzled Indian tribal funds. Others called for knowledge of the molecular make up of cocaine, the unraveling of complex international fraudulent securities transactions, the tracing of assets of failed banks and understanding the tensile strength of limestone in the collapse of a vast underground petroleum storage cavern. Was it an earth tremor or union sabotage? In most cases he was to determine truthfulness from falseness as well as intention.

One of the most important cases of Judge Thompson's judicial career, and one whose decision impacted the nation's natural gas industry, was unique in several respects. Several gas producing states, including Oklahoma, filed suit to challenge the constitutionality of the Federal Natural Gas Policy Act under the Commerce Clause of the federal Constitution. In an exhaustive, 35-page ruling, he upheld the constitutionality of the law, holding that Congress acted within its powers. It was a complicated set of issues, calling on him to emphasize that the issue before the court was not the wisdom or practicality of Congress' chosen action, but whether it was permissible as a matter of constitutional law. He wrote:

> This decision does not find the Act to be wise or fair or best suited to meet the present and future economic and energy needs of the nation. But it is fundamental that establish-

ment of policy in these respects is the business of the elected legislative branch—the Congress. As long as the laws enacted are within its constitutional authority, the Courts are not empowered to re-write, or veto them, or to second-guess or otherwise undo its chosen policy despite errors of judgment.[12]

An intriguing issue in the case was urged by the State of Texas that claimed any regulation of natural gas produced from its public lands was contrary to the terms of Texas' admission into the Union and thus violative of the Tenth Amendment. To rule on that issue, Judge Thompson and his law clerk, Robin Cauthron, who later was appointed to serve alongside him as a federal judge in the Western District, spent a great deal of time reviewing the pre-admission history of the Republic of Texas to the Union and the conditions and guarantees provided in the Joint Resolution of Congress and even the floor debates in the United States Senate.[3]

He ruled that Texas came into the Union on equal footing with the other states, and thus was properly included in the application of the regulation passed by Congress. His rulings in the case were ultimately affirmed by the Tenth Circuit Court of Appeals, which took the unusual step in congratulating the court for his excellent ruling. After the decision became public, *The Daily Oklahoman also* complimented the court for emphasizing that it is not the role of federal courts to rewrite congressional actions. The editorial said:

> Mixed emotions attend the ruling…upholding the authority of Congress to regulate intrastate natural prices… Thompson's order, while questioning the act's wisdom, merely confirmed the reality of congressional power to cloak virtually any kind of regulatory move with the mantle of [the Commerce Clause]…
>
> But conservatives who still cherish the concept of states' rights and a judiciary of strict constructionists…can take cheer from Thompson's declaration [that federal courts should not interfere with Congress]…Would that we had more federal judges who shared that view of their role in our tripartite governmental structure.[4]

A significant 1980 oil and gas case called upon Judge Thompson to make a careful analysis of certain critical aspects of oil and gas law. He ruled that a lessor who knows from the size of royalty checks that the lease is not producing in paying quantities, who demands that a protection well be drilled, and who acquiesces in the drilling of the well, will not be allowed by law to assert that the lease was not producing in paying quantities prior to the demand, and will be held to have waived any right to assert that the lease has terminated.[5]

In addition to being reported in the federal case reporting system, the case was selected for inclusion and review in the *Oil and Gas Reporter,* authored by Eugene Kuntz, dean emeritus of the OU College of Law, and the preeminent national legal scholar in oil and gas law. In his discussion notes, Dean Kuntz wrote, "Judge Thompson's opinion deserves to be preserved in legal literature as an incisive analysis of the defenses of estoppel, waiver, and bar." When the judge wrote Kuntz a note of thanks for the comment, Kuntz replied, "Your exhaustive analysis left very little for comment and certainly justified my description…I also know that we at the College of Law are very proud of you and your work."[6]

Judge Thompson was the assigned judge in the nation's first enforcement action of the Employee's Retirement Income Security Act (ERISA) by the Secretary of Labor. The owners of a popular Oklahoma City steakhouse, Glen's Hik'ry Inn, sold assets of the company, including an employee retirement plan, to a man professing to be an expert in such plans. However, rules of the retirement plan were changed and longtime employees lost $1.5 million in retirement money. After the United States Department of Labor filed suit, the judge ordered the sham raid on the retirement fund rescinded, resulting in the reinstatement of the retirement fund. The decision was affirmed by the Tenth Circuit Court of Appeals and was reported nationally by the *Wall Street Journal, US News & World Report,* and labor and industry publications. He still hears from the employees whose retirement money was rescued.[7]

Sometimes, Judge Thompson heard cases that he ruled simply should never have been brought. In 1977, a high school girl who played six-on-six, half-court girls basketball believed her constitutional rights were violated because she was not allowed to play full court. Under state high school regulations at the time, boys played full court with five players on each team. The girl's parents sued the Oklahoma Secondary School Activities Association, the Oklahoma City Board of Education, and various school officials on the grounds that the girl was deprived of equal protection of the law and that, more particularly, she was denied the full pleasure of the game, including fast break and full-court strategy.[8]

As the case progressed, the girl's attorneys conceded that their client had no constitutional right to play interscholastic sports. She was left with one argument—she was being denied benefits derived from interscholastic competition that was available only to boys. The judge analyzed the position from a constitutional standpoint. Was the difference in the rules by which an elective game is played by some students for part of a school year equal to fundamental values such as freedom of speech? He concluded otherwise. He dismissed the suit, saying there was no constitutional basis for the action. He wrote:

> There are, or should be, sensible limits to the extent courts should go in characterizing as real and substantial deprivations of constitutional rights the myriad of asserted complaints and grievances being brought before them…The present rules of which plaintiff complains of, i.e. full or half court games, may well be out of step with other states' rules and may not be in the best interests of the high school girls who play basketball in Oklahoma. However, absent a substantial deprivation of a constitutional right, such a policy decision is best left to the judgment of those who play, coach, and administer interscholastic basketball, and not the federal court.[9]

Judge Thompson heard from a number of old friends from earlier political years who seriously disagreed with his decision. Even though he knew them in the past to be passionately committed to states' rights and non-involvement of the federal government in their lives, their daughters had become high school basketball players who wanted to play full court, and their approach to public affairs had amazingly changed. It reminded him of the old saying that it matters whose ox is being gored, at least, to them, where full court girls' basketball was concerned.[10]

His personal view was that the basketball rules should be changed—and they later were. But the case was asserted as a constitutional issue and he followed the well established rule of law. Later, his ruling in the basketball case was upheld by the Tenth Circuit Court of Appeals.[11]

Judge Thompson dismissed a bizarre $1-trillion suit against the federal government. An Oklahoma couple had filed an inch-thick lawsuit alleging their family members had been kidnapped 28 times in California, Texas, and Oklahoma. The lawsuit asked that the $1 trillion be deposited in the First National Bank of Coyle, Oklahoma. The complaint also contained allegations against the Oklahoma Bar Association, several lawyers and doctors, the FBI, the Internal Revenue Service, and the Chief Justice of the Oklahoma Supreme Court. The plaintiffs acted as their own attorneys.[12]

Being disdainful of baseless suits that burden the courts and abuse the legal system, he quickly ended the matter, ruling that the complaint and other papers filed by plaintiffs were "lengthy, confused, and do not state either a jurisdictional basis or identifiable cause of action." Privately, he recalled another old saying, "One who represents himself has a fool for a client."[13]

While waiting to take his own caseload, new United States District Judge Lee Roy West, appointed in 1979 by President Jimmy Carter, observed Judge Thompson sentencing Wilma Marler, a woman inmate in the Oklahoma prison system, who was convicted of sending a death threat to the United States Attorney. Judge Thompson was struck by the pitiful circumstances of the woman's life. She was extraordinarily short and mentally challenged. She had known rejection and mistreatment at all stages of her life. Even in prison, she had been abused by other inmates and stabbed in her stomach with sharpened pencils.[14]

After pleading guilty for writing a threatening letter to the federal prosecutor, perhaps to escape her rough life in state custody, the woman appeared before the judge for sentencing. With heartfelt compassion, Judge Thompson told the woman that he did not think she meant the threat to the prosecutor and she needed, for the first time in her life, a positive break. He told her he would not send her to federal prison and hopefully that for once in her life a positive break would be a springboard to a law abiding life.[15]

The woman sobbed in gratitude and even Judge West was choked with emotion. Judge Thompson closed the case and wished the defendant well. After the hearing, West complimented Judge Thompson on his compassion, admitting that he was pleasantly surprised in light of his reputation as being a rather tough sentencing judge in criminal cases. Judge Thompson was shocked two weeks later when the woman was arrested for shutting down the Los Angeles, California bus terminal with a bomb threat and sending him a letter threatening to kill him. He thought, "So much for compassion." To this day, Judge West has not allowed his dear friend and colleague to forget the story and has told an embellished version of the tale both privately and publicly around the country, gleefully claiming that "Judge Thompson was never compassionate again."[16]

One completely routine and unremarkable trial stands out in Judge Thompson's memory for a special reason. A former worker had sued his Ponca City, Oklahoma employer, a family-owned machine business, for racial discrimination. The evidence conclusively proved that the owners of the family business had tried for years to help the employee who suffered from acute alcoholism, through Alcoholics Anonymous and other programs. Eventually, once the company feared the employee would fall into the equipment in a drunken condition, they fired him.[17]

The judge took evidence in the case and found the plaintiff's allegations wholly without merit. He was very impressed with the testimony of a young man whose father had died and had joined his brother in running the defendant's company. Even with the burden of the costs of litigation, the young man was still compassionate for the fired worker during his testimony. The judge said to his staff, "We will hear from that young man again!" They did. The young man was Don Nickles, later elected to the United States Senate from Oklahoma, who became one of Judge Thompson's closest and most admired personal friends.[18]

The judge believed every American should have access to the federal court system, but he castigated a plaintiff in December, 1981, who, under the facts, had irresponsibly sued a police officer in the Oklahoma City suburb of Valley Brook for groundless civil rights violations, including brutality, in the aftermath of a bar disturbance which the officer had stopped. When the jury exonerated the police officer, Judge Thompson ordered the plaintiff to pay the officer's $12,000 legal fee, an action rarely taken by federal judges in civil rights cases. In making the ruling, he said, "Irresponsible civil rights litigation such as this has become a national problem. Such frivolous suits result in the trivializing, depreciating, and devaluing of this most important process which should be providing fair and prompt trials of claims brought in good faith."[19]

The following morning, *The Daily Oklahoman* cited the judge's actions in an editorial titled "Deterring Frivolous Suits." The newspaper editor said:

> Let's hear it for...Judge Ralph Thompson...whose
> blast at frivolous civil rights law suits is a welcome and long
> overdue putdown of such abuses of our judicial system...Judge

Thompson expressed the not unreasonable hope that socking it to those who bring such unwarranted suits will serve as a deterrent to others in the future. As he put it, "if the price of irresponsibility is high enough, perhaps there will be less irresponsibility."…If more of his colleagues on the federal bench will follow Judge Thompson's lead, the true purpose of civil rights protection can be more effectively preserved.[20]

The ruling later was reversed by the Tenth Circuit Court of Appeals.

In his courtroom, Judge Thompson not only dealt with cases that made headlines, his docket included less famous, yet colorful and intriguing cases.

He presided over an international art fraud case in which a Kansas lawyer, a self-described Israeli archeologist, and an Oklahoma City art dealer were accused of conspiring to defraud art collectors and investors. The men claimed they had discovered a series of caves in Guatemala that contained 960 ancient pre-Columbian Mayan stone carvings worth nearly $13 million.

Investors were told that buyers in Belgium were waiting to buy the artifacts but funds were needed to remove them from the Guatemalan mountains. A local sculptor had been hired to fabricate the artifacts in a factory. Two defendants pleaded guilty to conspiracy and Judge Thompson was left to try the Kansas lawyer's case. The Guatemalan sculptor, testifying as a government witness, related how he was commissioned to make 600 fake stone copies of Mayan art work from a book of photographs he borrowed. The Kansas lawyer was found guilty by the jury of conspiracy to defraud, wire fraud, mail fraud, and causing fraudulently taken property to move in interstate commerce. His conviction and prison sentence were affirmed on appeal.[21]

Another intriguing case of international scope, showcasing the extent to which some can go in gall, fraud, and a willingness to cheat others, was the case of *USA v. David D. Brunson*. The defendant, a lawyer, devised a scheme to pass himself off to the Russian Coal Company as an expert in the construction of an automated brick factory. Russia was just emerging from the previous Soviet state and was eager to provide subsistence level materials such as bricks to its people.[22]

Seizing the opportunity, the defendant contracted to build a brick plant for more than $4 million and received a $1 million cash advance. In fact, he had no experience whatsoever in the construction of brick factories. To enhance his credentials, he arranged to take his Russian visitors on a phony tour of someone else's brick plant, posing as a knowledgeable partner.

The defendant spent the $1 million advance on luxury items such as a home, [17] automobiles, and vacations, all totally unrelated to building a brick factory. The only item he ever sent to Russia was a box of bolts. With Russian witnesses testifying through interpreters in Judge Thompson's courtroom, the defendant was found guilty of all 51 counts of wire fraud, money laundering, and other acts of fraud. The judge sentenced him to a substantial term in federal prison. The conviction and sentence were upheld by the Tenth Circuit Court of Appeals. [23]

Another fascinating case was the trial of *USA v. Graham Kendall.* After a jury trial, the defendant was found guilty of conspiracy to possess 1,500 pounds of marijuana with intent to distribute. The evidence showed that he had conspired with drug smugglers to acquire an airplane that had been refitted with extra fuel tanks to give it additional range to fly from Oklahoma City to Mexico and Columbia for the purpose of smuggling the large cache of marijuana. [24]

The dramatic fact was that, unknown to the smugglers, the plane was secretly fitted with a transponder device by federal agents pursuant to Judge Thompson's court order authorizing such action. This enabled authorities to keep the aircraft under constant surveillance throughout its travels. One of the groups had bribed several local officials in Mexico to facilitate the smuggling operation which proceeded on to Columbia where the plane was loaded with the contraband. Returning to Mexico, and then bound for Oklahoma, severe weather necessitated landing in Louisiana. Because of the tracking surveillance, to the defendants' astonishment, they were immediately arrested by government agents. [25]

All pleaded guilty except Kendall who stood trial, was convicted, and sentenced to prison. His conviction was affirmed by the Tenth Circuit Court of Appeals which called the case "a large, complex and lucrative smuggling adventure involving a large quantity of marijuana and a large number of people in the United States, Mexico, and Columbia." After the trial, jurors said that with the evidence of smuggling, bribery, international intrigue, and secret tracking, they were reminded of an old-fashioned gangster movie. [26]

An especially colorful and compelling case involved defendant Joseph William Dougherty, who was being tried in the Thompson court-room for the 1982 robbery of the Quail Creek Bank in Oklahoma City. Dougherty and a confederate, Joseph Conner, held a vice president of the bank and his wife hostage in their home overnight and took them to the bank the following morning and robbed it of $750,000 in cash. Conner later was arrested in California, tried and convicted in Judge Thompson's court, and sentenced to federal prison.[27]

In the Dougherty trial before Judge Thompson, the prosecution presented witnesses against Dougherty, three of whom positively identified him as one of the robbers. Dougherty had Conner subpoenaed from federal prison to appear as a defense witness. While being transported with Dougherty to the federal courthouse in anticipation of resuming the trial, the bank robbers overpowered two deputy United States marshals and escaped. Conner had imbedded a handcuff key in his gums. The deputies were in the front seat of the government car which was not equipped with a protective screen separating them from the prisoners. Conner slipped the key from his gums, unlocked the handcuffs of both prisoners, and the two overpowered and disarmed the deputies, and handcuffed them to a tree. Before they escaped in the government vehicle, one of the robbers wanted to kill the deputies. The other objected, saying the deputies had treated them decently.[28]

United States Marshal Stuart Earnest informed Judge Thompson of the details of the escape of the defendant and the supposed witness. Declaring that Dougherty had voluntarily absented himself from the trial, the judge said the defendant would not be allowed to benefit from the escape. He opened the third day of the trial without explaining Dougherty's absence. Public defender David Booth rested the defense without offering any testimony and jurors heard closing arguments from Booth and Assistant United States Attorney John Green. Despite the absence of the defendant, the jury quickly convicted Dougherty of robbing the bank. He and Conner later were recaptured after a nationwide crime spree and sent to federal prison to serve their sentences. Their convictions were affirmed on appeal.[29]

CHAPTER 12

GIVING EACH CASE ITS REQUIRED DIGNITY

If there were a book, Plato on Federal Judges, *the definition of an "ideal federal judge" would be Ralph Thompson.*

Chief Judge Robert Henry

As a lawyer, Judge Thompson had known what he expected from a federal judge. Now that he was one, he set out to make his courtroom a place of respect, order, safety, fairness, courtesy, and equal treatment. He understood that in every case, no matter how large or small, the matter at hand was the most important case to the parties and deserved full respect from the system, particularly the judge. Proper decorum in the courtroom was of paramount importance, and he insisted upon it. He was fair, but kept a tight rein on lawyers and witnesses. The rule of law was very important to him. He held lawyers practicing before him to high standards of civility and integrity.[1]

After visiting Judge Thompson's courtroom as an "awestruck fledgling federal probation officer," Debra James Marshall said, "I believed he exemplified all the qualities I would expect in a U.S. District Judge. With his formal, aristocratic courtroom demeanor, he commanded respect." Marshall, who rose through the ranks to become Supervising United States Probation Officer, said, "He was congenial and appreciative of even an inexperienced probation officer's opinion, absolutely firm, yet fair, exceedingly articulate, and particularly attentive to details." To Marshall, Judge Thompson could be stern, yet encouraging when sentencing defendants, "frequently expressing his hope that they would turn their shattered lives around."[2]

"It was a pleasure, not an ordeal, to try a case before Judge Thompson," said William "Bill" Paul, Oklahoma City lawyer and former president of the American Bar Association. "He was courteous to counsel, parties, witnesses, and the jury. Although he was firm, he was also patient and understanding. Most of all, he was fair and impartial."[3]

Other lawyers echoed Bill Paul's opinion that Judge Thompson was tolerant with lawyers and allowed them to "try their case," to proceed based upon their respective theories of the litigation. Trial lawyer Reid Robison said, "Trying a case in front of him was to try a case in front of a consummate gentleman, who had a wonderful judicial temperament and who was always fair to the litigants and counsel. He let us try our cases, but did have suggestions for moving things along!"[4]

There was never any question that Judge Thompson was in control of his courtroom. "When he stepped through the courtroom doors behind the bench, between those two giant American flags," said attorney Drew Neville, "there was no question who was in charge. He had an uncanny command of the courtroom." Neville said, "As his deputy courtroom clerk announced his presence, his 'icy' eagle-like stare left no doubt that serious business was about to begin, and that the lawyers and litigants before him had best be ready, as 'nonsense' would not be tolerated." One lawyer said, "You feel his presence as a judge. He was born wearing a black robe."[5]

He was a judge who took special note of the rights of the government, victims, and defendants in criminal trials. Neville, both as an assistant United States attorney and civil practioner, tried many cases before him. Neville was aware of the judge's reputation as having respect for the role of law enforcement officials because they too had dedicated their careers to demanding public service. "But," Neville said, "he was obviously aware that the government had to prove its case beyond a reasonable doubt. He held the government to this burden, but it was always made clear that defense counsel also would be held to the same very high standards of conduct and the rules of evidence would be followed in his courtroom."[6]

Neville said "shenanigans" often seen in television courtroom dramas were not allowed in the Thompson courtroom. His "stare and glare" quickly suppressed conduct that was on the edge. Neville learned when he had gone too far during a trial. He said, "If Judge Thompson's ears turned red, you better throttle it back, or risk the consequences."[7]

Judge Thompson's preparation for a trial caused lawyers to come prepared. Mack Martin, a veteran of several jury trials in his court, said, "We knew we had better come prepared, because he had and he expected nothing less from all parties. He was the consummate professional even during the heat of trial when emotions and tempers might flare."[8]

The judge paid particular attention to putting at ease members of juries who left their daily private lives to serve in his courtroom. "I have never failed to be impressed and grateful and appreciative of the good citizens," he said, "who make up our juries." Jurors often were not willing participants—they had been summoned to appear for what they believed was inconvenient and somewhat scary.[9]

He is a great believer in the integrity of the jury system. In the multitude of jury trials over which he presided in 32 years on the federal bench, he agreed with their decisions 95 percent of the time. After a trial, he and other judges of the Western District met with jurors, not to discuss their deliberations, but to give them the opportunity to talk about jury service. "Almost without exception," he said, "our jurors expressed their respect for the manner in which the trials were conducted and told me of their renewed confidence in our system of justice from their experience." Many jurors said they gladly would serve again.[10]

CHAPTER 13

IMPACT ON SOCIETY

It was a volatile dispute over prayer meetings in the tiny community of Little Axe that resulted in a widely publicized trial complete with assaults and suspected arson against the plaintiffs.

Judge Ralph G. Thompson

Little Axe, Oklahoma, was an unlikely place for a major constitutional battle over the Establishment Clause of the First Amendment. In the 1980s, cases involving religious issues, especially prayer in public schools, evoked emotions and caused public sentiment to be sharply divided. America was founded on freedom of religion. The Founding Fathers, fresh from having the Church of England mandate the official beliefs of the English people, took special effort to ensure that the new American federal government would not establish religion. Their goal was to strictly maintain a separation of church and state to allow absolute freedom of religion, tolerance, and mutual respect between citizens of different faiths and beliefs.

In 1981, Judge Thompson was drawn into the center of one of the most publicized national battles over separation of church and state. During the 1980-1981 school year, several teachers supervised and participated in religious sessions or "prayer meetings" for students each Thursday morning at the Little Axe school. Little Axe was actually not a town, but an independent school district in a rural area of Cleveland County a few miles east of Norman.

Two women, Lucille McCord and Joann Bell, had children who attended the Little Axe school. Both were religious—McCord was Nazarene and Bell attended the local Church of Christ—but they objected to the childrens' essentially required attendance at the weekly prayer meetings, called the Son Shine Club, at the school. McCord and Bell disliked the fact that in the winter, the only way students riding buses could get out of the elements and into the school building was to attend the religious meetings. The mothers regularly took their children to church, but did not want them to be forced to attend what they considered a school-sponsored religious exercise.[1]

McCord and Bell complained to the Little Axe school board about the religious meetings. The board voted 4-1 to continue the meetings. The board president said, "Bring on the ACLU (American Civil Liberties Union)." McCord and Bell were met by more than 300 people at the school board meeting, some chanting, "Atheists go home." One school board member handed out homemade placards to the crowd that read "Up with Jesus" and "Commies go home."[2]

The women contacted the ACLU who referred the matter to Norman attorney Michael Salem, who often participated in cases supported by the ACLU. Salem filed a civil rights lawsuit in the Western District, claiming that the school policies violated the Establishment Clause of the First Amendment.[3]

From the beginning, Salem hoped that the case would educate people about the law. He wanted the public to know that his clients were not atheists, they were active church members. He said, "My clients are coming from the most conservative position possible, this is not some hot-shot liberal cause. The McCords and Bells have a right not to have their children exposed to religious beliefs that they don't hold."[4]

The community reaction to the McCord-Bell lawsuit was immediate and bitter. The plaintiffs received hundreds of threatening telephone calls and letters. Their children were called "devil-worshippers." An upside-down cross was hung on Robert McCord's school locker. At a school sports banquet, the plaintiffs' sons were the only children not recognized as being Little Axe athletes. Joann Bell was the victim of hair pulling by a school employee and the Bell's trailer home was burned by a fire considered to be arson.[5]

Judge Thompson decided the merits of the case without a jury. Federal law in such cases required a district court judge to hear the evidence and render a decision. The plaintiffs' attorney Salem said, "Judge Thompson allowed us to introduce a wide range of evidence not ordinarily admitted if the case was heard by a jury. The judge was incredibly accommodating to the parties, recognizing there had been no trial of this sort in the state before."[6]

The evidence was largely undisputed. On March 11, 1983, Judge Thompson issued a formal ruling that the actions of the school district were unconstitutional, that by sponsoring religious services on school grounds, in the school building, during the school day when it had mandatory legal custody of the children, requiring non-participating students to remain outside, with teachers or school officials attending, the school was providing "the type of governmental support and entanglement prohibited by the Establishment Clause."[7]

"The ruling should not have been a surprising one," the judge remembered, "the facts being what they were. It was solidly supported by the evidence and controlling law." The school district appealed the decision to the Tenth Circuit Court of Appeals. The emotional nature of the case prompted a humorous editorial cartoon in the *Oklahoma City Times,* drawn by editorial cartoonist Channing Lowe, son of actress Carol Channing. Assuming the judge was spending sleepless nights trying to decide the case, torn between siding with the angels or the devil, the cartoon depicted him with bulging, bloodshot eyes in a four-poster bed with an angel on one post and the devil on another, sharing time monitoring him while he deliberated. "It was a good cartoon," Judge Thompson said, but the decision was not quite that difficult under the facts and law.[8]

Ultimately, the Tenth Circuit Court of Appeals in June, 1985, affirmed the unconstitutional actions of the Little Axe school district. The appellate court agreed with the judge's opinion that holding the prayer meetings during the school day under the circumstances was tantamount to state-supported religion. The Tenth Circuit opinion, written by Circuit Judge Stephanie Seymour, said:

> The policy promulgated by the District is unconstitutional insofar as the District…construes it to permit concerned religious activity on the school grounds during the school day. Those sections which specifically protect such religious activity cannot withstand scrutiny under the Establishment Clause. By holding this, we do not express hostility toward religion as the District fears…To hold otherwise would inhibit the development in our schoolchildren of tolerance and mutual respect for a diverse range of beliefs—essential values in the pluralistic society we have cultivated.[9]

In the nearly 30 years since the case, Judge Thompson has continued to wonder why the school district did not simply change the sessions to after school. He said, "It was a simple solution so that the required neutrality of the government could be satisfied." He even suggested such a solution in his original order. No such agreement was reached by the parties.[10]

The plaintiffs' attorney, Salem, was awarded the Courageous Advocacy Award by the Oklahoma Bar Association in 1984 for his work in the Little Axe case.

Also in the early 1980s, a county government scheme of equipment suppliers paying kickbacks to county commissioners in Oklahoma became the largest scandal of its kind in the nation's history. A three-year federal investigation found that graft was routine among many county commissioners. Thirteen counties saw all three of its commissioners indicted. Eventually, more than 200 county commissioners, from 60 of the state's 77 counties, and equipment suppliers were indicted in federal court and found guilty. Most were convicted of taking kickbacks paid by suppliers on orders, or phony orders, for county road-building supplies.

The FBI called the investigation of corruption in county government "OKSCAM."

Judge Thompson and fellow federal district judges in Oklahoma's three federal districts were kept busy from 1981 to 1984 accepting guilty pleas from former commissioners and suppliers. Very few cases went to trial. There was only one acquittal in the Western District.

On November 4, 1981, the judge accepted guilty pleas from three commissioners who agreed to cooperate with the FBI and the United States Attorney's office by naming 22 suppliers who had paid kickbacks for a number of years. Normally, a county commissioner was paid 10 percent of the purchase price for giving the supplier the order or 50 percent of the price of supplies or equipment that never were delivered.[11]

The significance of the appearance of the three commissioners before Judge Thompson was the vast amount of information federal prosecutors obtained as to suppliers involved in the scandal. As a federal grand jury continued its investigation and releasing of indictments, many defendants began negotiating plea agreements. When all three commissioners from Tillman County were implicated and resigned, Governor George Nigh had to appoint two commissioners to conduct county business.[12]

The judge was amazed by the level of corruption uncovered by OKSCAM. Most of the commissioners had been in office and engaged in corrupt practices for years. He said, "To some, it had become virtually a way of life and the way of doing business. To them, despite its blatant criminality, the routine had blunted somewhat its effect on their consciences." For some commissioners appearing before the judge, "they professed the preposterous view that it was just part of their pay."[13]

Many commissioners were defiant when first confronted with FBI wiretap evidence of their activities. Judge Thompson said, "They had become little giants in their home counties, wielding power and influence over other local officials and public affairs and considered themselves beyond the reach of the law." Commissioners were angered by the "feds" coming into their kingdoms and "stirring things up."[14]

While some commissioners expressed outrage at their plight, others promptly admitted their guilt and acknowledged the seriousness of their corrupt dealings. Most of those convicted in the County Commissioner Scandal had no previous criminal record. Once a defendant was convicted or pleaded guilty, the United States Probation Office prepared a comprehensive Pre-Sentence Report for the judge's use in sentencing. As in all federal criminal cases, virtually every aspect of the defendant's life was reported in great detail. All judges had to consider that information along with the magnitude of the crime as well as its impact upon the public.[15]

Most of the convicted county commissioners were sentenced to federal prison, but the length of punishment varied greatly. Some commissioners were old and in ill health. Some were contrite, regretted their crimes, and arranged to make some form of restitution. Judge Thompson said, "Others remained less contrite, retaining some of the arrogance that had led to their troubles."[16]

As in many criminal cases, the County Commissioner Scandal tested the metal of "judging" for all federal judges in Oklahoma. "It is a very human endeavor," Judge Thompson said. "It can be a challenge to keep one's revulsion at the evidence of despicable behavior in the course of a trial from influencing the judge's critical responsibility of ensuring a fair trial to the very ones who have committed the crimes." The judges heard wiretapped conversations of the corruption day after day, but still had the "overriding responsibility" to conduct a fair trial for both sides.[17]

The county commissioner cases were front page news for several years. Judge Thompson was concerned that defendants could not get a fair trial because of the extensive publicity. However, he became convinced that jurors in cases tried in the Western District were conscientious about their responsibility to fairly weigh the evidence presented in the particular case.[18]

As a result of cleaning up the corrupt system, prices of road-building materials and equipment purchased by county commissioners dropped, in some counties, by 40 percent—a huge savings to the taxpayers of the state.

United States Attorney William "Bill" Price said, "To me, the most important part of the scandal was not in convicting so many defendants, but in ending the corruption's tremendous cost to Oklahoma. With inflated invoices and phony sales, both forms of corruption robbed Oklahoma counties of much of their wealth probably since statehood."

Price spent a great deal of time observing Judge Thompson during the County Commissioner Scandal. He said, "At every step of every trial and sentencing, he was thoughtful and wise. He discerned different levels of guilt and gave sentences based upon those differences. There was no automatic for him. He carefully considered each defendant in a balanced and fair manner."[19]

Judge Thompson was particularly repulsed by cases of public corruption—betrayals of the public trust, especially defendants corrupting the justice system. He said, "Even in a state whose people are decent, hard working, and law abiding, there are always the 'bad apples' who damage our society and prey on innocent victims." He believes it is important that such cases be remembered.[20]

He presided over several politically-charged trials in the 1980s involving public servants. In 1983, former Oklahoma County Assistant District Attorney and Special District Judge William C. Page was convicted of racketeering and extortion based upon government evidence that he regularly "fixed" cases and shared sensitive investigative information with criminal associates. Page was accused of interfering with ongoing criminal investigations as both a prosecutor and judge.[21]

The Page trial was well attended, with spectators standing in the aisle as attorneys made arguments to the jury. In sentencing Page to four concurrent seven-year terms in the federal penitentiary, Judge Thompson called Page's "disgraceful" betrayal of the public trust "so profoundly repugnant that it speaks for itself."[22] The conviction and sentence were affirmed by the Tenth Circuit Court of Appeals. Sixteen years later, Page's petition for a pardon was denied by the United States Department of Justice and the president of the United States. In 2004, Page's request for reinstatement to practice law was denied by the Oklahoma Supreme Court, that found:

> …the case against him was based on multiple episodes of his accepting bribes from more than one person or attempting to do so, in exchange for fixing or interfering impending criminal investigations and litigation, in his role as Assistant District Attorney or Special Judge….At present we can think of no worse white collar criminal transgression of the law than a prosecutor and a judge could commit in such roles.[23]

Another public corruption case of interest, importance, and intrigue was the criminal trial of former Southeastern Oklahoma State University President Leon Hibbs. In 1989, Hibbs was convicted by a federal jury on 38 counts of mail fraud and one additional account involving misappropriation of state funds while he was president of the university, causing aggregate losses of more than $3.5 million to the State of Oklahoma and other victims. Testimony and 3,000 exhibits supported the convictions.

The Hibbs case was a milestone for law enforcement in Oklahoma. For the first time, state and federal prosecutors worked together on a major case of public corruption. Oklahoma's young attorney general, Robert Henry, faced major criticism from Hibbs' political friends. Henry said, "Dr. Hibbs had some pretty powerful allies in the legislature and they tried to shut down the investigation."[24]

The Hibbs case had the direct involvement of United States Attorney Bill Price and Assistant United States Attorney Arlene Joplin, now a judge of the Oklahoma Court of Criminal Appeals. Price said, "From the beginning, we saw Hibbs' conduct as blatant and arrogant. He sincerely believed that he was so powerful he was above the law."[25]

Attorney General Henry made a conscious effort not to attend the trial. He said, "I couldn't appear because, behind the scenes, our critics were saying that I was seeking a higher political office by taking part in the trial. They tried to make it look like a political witchhunt."[26]

Judge Thompson had never met Henry before the Hibbs trial. After the sentencing, he called Henry into his chambers and told him how much he admired his political courage and his commitment to the cause of justice and the rule of law. He said, "The world needs more Robert Henrys." Later, they became close friends. Henry left the attorney general's post to become dean of the Oklahoma City University School of Law. He later was Chief Judge of the Tenth Circuit Court of Appeals and president of Oklahoma City University.[27]

Judge Thompson sentenced Hibbs on September 19, 1989, to 10 years in federal prison and ordered him to repay $3.5 million in restitution, one of the largest white collar crime punishments in state history. The punishment was editorially supported by *The Daily Oklahoman:*

> The 10-year rap is tough. It is in contrast to the perception that white-collar crime generally calls for slap-on-the-wrist punishment. It should deter white-collar crime by sending a powerful message to those in coat and tie who would try to use state funds for their own gain…
>
> The case also should serve as a reminder to citizens to demand vigilance and prosecution by their local district attorneys of prominent persons involved in wrongdoing.[28]

The newspaper criticized the local district attorney in Bryan County for not participating in the prosecution and making a "shameless written appeal to the federal judge not to send Hibbs to prison." The editorial concluded, "That should be intolerable to the people."[29]

The state's other major metropolitan newspaper, the *Tulsa World*, also supported Judge Thompson's handling of the case:

> Hibbs attempted to compare himself with "an old roping horse" who just needed to be slapped in the face a couple of times to get his attention. As if all that he needed was to be reminded that diverting public money into his own pockets was illegal.
>
> Obviously the problem went beyond mere inattention. The judge said he found Hibbs' remarks during the sentencing hearing "superficial and disingenuous." Hibbs' sentence is harsh. The judge's reasons for levying it, and his statements to Hibbs, are compelling.[30]

In 1999, Judge Thompson sharply criticized the forensic work of Joyce Gilchrist, a laboratory chemist for the Oklahoma City Police Department. He was assigned the *habeas corpus* petition of Alfred Brian Mitchell, who was on death row in the Oklahoma state penitentiary, and had exhausted state appeals of his rape and murder convictions. Mitchell claimed he had been denied access to evidence that would have proved him innocent of the forcible rape. Due to the seriousness of the allegation, the judge granted Mitchell an evidentiary hearing at which an FBI chemist totally refuted the opinion of Gilchrist that had resulted in Mitchell's rape conviction. In addition, the FBI chemist said he had told Gilchrist that Mitchell's DNA was not found in the FBI testing of the victim's body fluids. In the *habeas* hearing, Gilchrist admitted that the DNA evidence did exclude Mitchell, evidence that had been denied to his lawyers at the original trial.[31]

By 2001, the FBI began a formal investigation to determine if Gilchrist's tainted testimony had resulted in the wrongful conviction of defendants.[32] Before Judge Thompson's suspicions of Gilchrist's work were made known, Oklahoma City police had never questioned her work. She testified in cases for more than 20 years. The FBI reviewed the evidence in eight cases in which Gilchrist had conducted tests between 1982 and 1991 and found that in at least five of the cases, "she had made obvious errors or had improperly stretched her interpretation of the evidence."[33]

Gilchrist was suspended with pay while state investigators urgently reviewed 12 pending death penalty convictions. They also studied 11 other cases in which defendants already had been executed. In April, 2001, a DNA analysis showed that defendant Jeff Pierce had been wrongfully convicted of rape, "thanks largely to the forceful testimony of Gilchrist," and served 15 years.[34]

Few things compare in gravity to an innocent person being convicted of a crime through the judicial process which is painstakingly committed to justice. The evidence confirmed the judge's worst fears. A widening investigation found that Gilchrist appeared to push the limits shockingly beyond her expertise. David Autry, an Oklahoma public defender who helped free Pierce, said, "She's an incompetent, malicious pseudoscientist who's done everything she could in every trial to help the prosecution get a conviction."[35]

In September, 2001, Gilchrist was fired and state and federal investigators began poring over the evidence in 1,200 felony cases. The Oklahoma legislature appropriated $650,000 to perform DNA analysis in questionable cases in which Gilchrist's testimony may have been the difference between acquittal and conviction of a defendant.

The Washington Post gave credit to Judge Thompson for beginning the unraveling of Gilchrist's actions:

> It was not until August, 1999, when a respected federal judge in Oklahoma City harshly rebuked Gilchrist, that things began to unravel for her. U.S. District Judge Ralph Thompson bluntly labeled as "untrue" her testimony that semen samples in a rape and murder cases were "inconclusive," when he said Gilchrist knew for a fact that the sperm could not be from the defendant. Thompson overturned the rape conviction of Alfred Brian Mitchell. Stung by Thompson's remarks and mounting criticism, police removed Gilchrist from the lab… In 2000, she was expelled from the Association of Crime Scene Reconstruction for giving testimony that misrepresented the evidence.[36]

Reporters wondered how Gilchrist had escaped detection for so long. Questions had been raised about her work for a decade. Judge Thompson was deeply disturbed that the system of justice which he so revered had failed. But he was pleased that his decisions could have particular social value and contributed affirmatively to advancing the cause of justice.

A decade after he first "blew the whistle" on Gilchrist's often exaggerated and incorrect conclusions of her testing, Internet legal expert Edmond Geary wrote:

It took the heroic act of U.S. District Judge Ralph Thompson to bring Gilchrist down. Only someone so respected as Judge Thompson, when he ruled so unequivocally and extensively about her mistakes, could call attention to her wrongdoing and stop her. What about others who could have called attention to her wrongdoings. No state judges had the courage or the understanding to do it.[37]

CHAPTER 14

HARVARD AND JUDICIAL PHILOSOPHY

*Judge Thompson's rapid and thorough analysis of our
students' renditions and his incisive and courteous
critiques have made him one of our most prized and beloved
of his 27 years as a visiting faculty judge...one of a small
group of our core "superstars."*

Harvard Law School Professor Peter L. Murray

In 1982, Judge Thompson attended a special event for judges at the Harvard Law School in Cambridge, Massachusetts. It was a concentrated review of several areas of law taught by professors at Harvard and arranged by the Federal Judicial Center. He particularly enjoyed the session on evidence, taught by Professor Charles Nesson, who invited a group of judges to his Cambridge home for cocktails one evening. It was there that the judge was invited to become a member of the visiting faculty of Harvard's Trial Advocacy Workshop. The faculty consisted of selected judges and lawyers throughout the nation.

Judge Thompson was honored and flattered to be asked to teach at the three-week elective intersession law course teaching trial advocacy to second and third-year law students. Harvard Law School , established in 1817 and the oldest continuously-operating law school in the nation, has produced many luminaries in law and politics. Its graduates include presidents of the United States, several world leaders, including the presidents of the Republic of China and Ireland, and numerous American congressmen and senators. In 2011, six of the nine justices of the United States Supreme Court were graduates of Harvard Law School.[1] Judge Thompson said, "The antiquity and tradition were never lost on me."[2]

In the winter of 1983, he participated in the Harvard teaching experience for the first time. As he arrived in Cambridge, snow was falling and people were cross country skiing along the Charles River. He looked out the windows of the venerable paneled classrooms, with their oil portraits and fire places, and watched the snow blanket the campus. To him, it looked like a scene from a Currier & Ives painting.

Teaching days began in the morning hours with individual preparation in the judge's hotel room adjacent to the campus. A teaching luncheon followed at which the day's exercises and assignments were made. Classes were held from 2:00 p.m. to 6:00 p.m. After dinner with students, a 7:00 p.m. session highlighted demonstrations by experienced lawyers of the exact exercises that students had struggled with earlier in the day. Each teaching day ended at 9:00 p.m.[3]

Trial skills taught included opening statements, direct examinations, cross examinations, the use of evidence, and closing arguments. Ethics of trial practice were an important component as well and were consistently emphasized. The exercises were based on actual cases with the use of witnesses and actual items of evidence. By the end of the third week, each student had actually tried a mock jury trial in courtrooms in the Boston

Judge Thompson and Barbara on the snow-covered Harvard campus, a scene repeated for 27 years that the judge taught as a member of the visiting faculty of the Harvard Law School Trial Advocacy Workshop.

area. The method of teaching students skills in the afternoon classroom session, followed by the masterful performance of experienced trial lawyers in the evening demonstrations, was an "exceptionally effective way of teaching." It was intense because each student had to perform each day the skill being taught.[4]

Professor Peter L. Murray, the course director, chose Judge Thompson as his teaching partner—a partnership that lasted 27 years until Murray's retirement in 2010. The judge presided over the classroom sessions, with Professor Murray in overall charge and other faculty members participating. Professor Murray said, "Judge Thompson's rapid and thorough analysis of our students' renditions and his incisive, but always sensitive and courteous critiques, have made him one of our most highly prized and beloved of his 27 years as a visiting faculty judge."

Professor Murray continued, "Judge Thompson models for our students the kind of public service representing the best aspirations of our profession. He is one of a small group of our core "superstars."[5]

Faculty critiques were exacting, but constructive, with the goal of ensuring a high level of skills being taught while not being discouraging in the process. The students' skill levels rose astonishingly quickly, never ceasing to amaze Judge Thompson how students could progress from no experience to commendable performances by the end of the first intense week. "It was gratifying," he said, "and that alone would have kept me coming back."[6]

He remembered presiding as the judge in his first evening demonstration, always held in the Ames Courtroom of old Austin Hall, with the scrutinizing eyes of the oil portraits of Harvard's Supreme Court Justices Felix Frankfurter and William J. Brennan looking over his shoulders.

The routine virtually was unchanged for each week for the next 26 years. Whenever he could, the judge took Barbara and their teenage daughters with him. "I was always amazed," he said, "at how much more valuable my advice to the young male law students seemed to become when I was accompanied by my beautiful daughters, but I figured it out!" He was impressed with the students, "so bright, able, anxious to learn and appreciative of our efforts to help them learn." He said, "I truly believe it to be the premier trial advocacy course in the country. Once our students completed the course, they had the basic trial skills to try a case anywhere."[7]

The judge emphasized to the Harvard students that once they

Two of Judge Thompson's longtime and favorite colleagues at Harvard were Harvard Law professor Peter Murray, left, and preeminent New York City trial lawyer, Maurice Nessen.

learned basic trial skills, the key to success was preparation along with experience. Each student was accomplished, but none had experience in the courtroom. Some were intimidated by performing something entirely new and doing it in front of their classmates. The judge encouraged them by repeating former South African President Nelson Mandela's saying, "Courage is not the absence of fear, but the triumph over it," and UCLA Coach John Wooden's admonition, "Failing to prepare is preparing to fail."[8]

The overriding theme of Judge Thompson's teaching was that the trial process, with its seemingly difficult rules of evidence and procedure, was to best make it a search for the truth. This meant excluding unreliable information, requiring direct and responsive questions and answers of witnesses, and testing the accuracy of testimony through cross examination. He also stressed that, contrary to theatrical portrayals, and the occasional, highly-published horrible examples of actual trials, the trial process is not "gamesmanship" or one that allows trickery, show boating, or disrespect. The judge said, "it is to provide for the resolution of even the bitterest conflicts in an orderly, safe, and respectful forum, under the control of a neutral judge, as the old saying goes, 'Where neither the strongest arm nor the loudest voice prevail.'"[9]

It was a pleasure for Judge Thompson to teach with Professor Murray, a native of Maine and first in his Harvard Law class of 1967. He was a sailor, having built his own sea-going sailboat, a pilot, author of at least three books, and regularly taught in German in a law school in Freiburg, Germany. He was a masterful teacher, one of Harvard's most popular, a grand person and true friend. In addition, the judge made lasting friendships with other judges and lawyers who served with him on the Harvard workshop faculty.

Upon Professor Murray's retirement, Judge Thompson decided it was perhaps a good time for him "to say goodbye." He realized he was teaching students who were not yet born when he first began teaching there. At a retirement party, his Harvard colleagues gave him an engraved silver bowl which commemorated his contributions of more than a quarter century to the law students at the esteemed school.

In Oklahoma, Judge Thompson accepted numerous invitations to speak, especially to groups of attorneys and judges. In a 1976 speech in Tulsa at a luncheon honoring the judiciary, he commented on the partnership between lawyers and judges in the administration of justice.

He was concerned that the increase in caseloads in both federal and state courts might slow down justice with clogged dockets. He said, "In such circumstances courts cannot take a laissez-faire approach to the movement of a case toward disposition or more generally to the production of justice—that is, courts must be managers in the production of justice, not mere referees presiding over a fair fight."[10]

He also called for "order in the courts," a return to integrity and civility during courtroom practice. He said, "The adversary system is inherently contentious and, by its very nature, necessarily full of abrasive conflicts. Advocacy must be vigorous, but always within fixed rules of personal conduct and civility between the contending lawyers and the court…Good manners, disciplined behavior, and civility are the ingredients that keep lawsuits from turning into alley fights."[11]

Addressing the convocation ceremony at the OU College of Law in May, 1978, he urged graduates to reject the road of mediocrity and be committed to excellence. He told the future lawyers:

Whether you enter a courtroom or a conference room it will be clear that class has arrived. You will enjoy the respect of your clients, adversaries, and professional colleagues, and by your example you will contribute to the public's respect of lawyers and the rule of law. Leadership in your communities will naturally follow, and I assure you that self-respect, self-confidence, and the joy of true accomplishment will be yours.[12]

Even though he was known as a "law and order" judge, he always did his best to follow the law and protect the rights of individuals guaranteed by the Constitution, and encouraged others to do the same. As an example, he accepted a 1979 invitation to speak to a meeting in Oklahoma City of members of the American Civil Liberties Union (ACLU). He said:

While is its entirely understandable that people are anxious, frustrated, and afraid of crime, civil disobedience, and racial conflict, it is disturbing to hear criticism expressed about many of the protections of the Bill of Rights and to see them characterized as mere technicalities or loopholes for criminals. These "procedures" are essential to an orderly society and we must not permit their importance to be demeaned by expediency.[13]

He stressed that from his own experience as a Special Agent, he never had forgotten or failed to appreciate the realities facing officers in the field. However, dealing with those realities need not be at the expense of constitutional protections.

Later, he expressed the same convictions in addressing the Oklahoma Association of Chiefs of Police and as the guest speaker at the graduation ceremony for new FBI Special Agents at Quantico, Virginia.

In May, 2004, Judge Thompson was the principal speaker at commencement of the Oklahoma City University School of Law.

Two old friends say goodbye. Judge Thompson, left, presents Harvard Law professor Peter Murray a retirement gift in 2009 on behalf of the visiting faculty of the Harvard Law School Trial Advocacy Workshop.

He challenged graduating law students:

> You are different now. As one has said, "As people of law, you are uniquely educated and trained to make intelligent distinctions between fact and fantasy; to better confront life's problems—yours and your clients'—because you have learned the essential distinctions and relationships between individual rights and societal needs; to distinguish between knowledge and feeling; to understand, on a new plane, the demands and rewards of effort; and to gain a new appreciation of the pursuit of quality and the imperatives of equity, equality, human dignity, and justice."[14]

When he retired from the federal bench, Judge Thompson reflected on his 32 years of "ruling on difficult issues that so often profoundly impacted peoples' lives, sometimes, inevitably, deciding publicly unpopular cases in order to be faithful the law, trying to ensure fair trials for all, including those of disgusting people who have done disgusting things, and deciding what sentences are fair and appropriate in very different and compelling circumstances."[15]

The judge said, "When I took my oath of office, I swore that I would, as it provided…administer justice without respect to persons; and do equal right to the poor and to the rich, and that I will faithfully and impartially discharge and perform all the duties incumbent upon me… according to the best of my abilities and understanding; agreeably to the constitution and laws of the United States."

Judge Thompson continued, "Although I surely fell short of those lofty responsibilities from time to time, the responsibility itself was never lost on me."[16]

The judge respects the critically important role of the institution of trials. He said, "Vigorous advocacy is necessary and proper as a way to search for the truth." He believes that the role of the judge, lawyers, and jury is to, functioning under the constitution and laws, to produce fairness and justice in even the bitterest controversies. "But," he said, "it must always be within the rules in a forum of dignity, civility, orderliness, safety, and mutual respect." The judge had a reputation of being intolerant of anyone dishonoring that high calling and he conducted his trials and hearings accordingly.[17]

CHAPTER 15

REFORMING THE JUVENILE JUSTICE SYSTEM

As a result of the Terry D. *case, Oklahoma was the first state in the nation to have achieved accreditation of its entire juvenile justice system.*

Attorney Steven A. Novick

In 1978, Oklahoma City Legal Aid attorney Steven A. Novick filed a class action lawsuit challenging Oklahoma's handling of delinquent and deprived juveniles. The protracted litigation, called the "Terry D. case" for the unnamed juvenile chosen as the representative plaintiff, became a massive class action case that attracted the attention of social services and civil rights groups across the nation. It eventually was featured on ABC's *20/20* news program and was the subject of congressional hearings.

The case accused the Oklahoma Department of Human Services (DHS) of operating juvenile institutions in a manner that denied juveniles basic rights such as clean facilities, adequate food, and lack of showers, and allowed the use of solitary confinement as punishment. Attorney Novick alleged that juveniles housed at the L.E. Rader Center were subject to excessive use of force, sexual assault by kids on kids, and inappropriate relationships between staff and children.[1]

The *Terry D.* case threatened to be another incident of federal court intervention into state government business. In the previous two decades, the Oklahoma City school district was basically under control of the federal court during battles over school desegregation and forced busing. Also, the Oklahoma prison system was under federal court supervision for many years as a result of a civil rights case brought by inmate Bobby Battles.

Attorney Novick was lead counsel for three civil rights groups that supported prosecution of the case—Legal Aid of Western Oklahoma, the National Center for Youth and Law, and the National Prison Project of the ACLU.

Judge Thompson, to whom the *Terry D.* case was assigned, did not set out to take over another state institution. Instead, he sought cooperation of lawyers and parties. He appointed an expert to help avert federal court takeover of the Rader Center and the state's juvenile justice system. In January, 1982, nearly four years after the *Terry D.* case was filed, a proposed settlement to revamp the system was presented to the court.

Legal Aid attorneys, DHS Director Lloyd Rader, and attorneys for the parties entered into an agreement that would result in half the institutionalized juveniles in the state being placed in foster homes. The plan called for the state to provide psychiatric care for juveniles held in the state system, which meant either turning older buildings into psychiatric hospitals or building new facilities. Children who were not found to be delinquent would not be placed in institutions unless a court found them to be mentally ill and in need of treatment. Only court-adjudicated delinquents would be incarcerated.[2]

On its face, the agreement appeared to satisfy concerns of child welfare advocates. However, legislative leaders thought the agreement fell short and directed Attorney General Jan Eric Cartwright to intervene in the case. *The Daily Oklahoman* agreed with the legislature:

> The way to get at the truth of the conflicting stories and allegations, and to put the facts in proper perspective as a foundation for appropriate reform of the system, is not by a cover-up. Yet, that would be one result of the settlement agreement—forged in secret session by lawyers for the DHS and civil rights groups that brought the lawsuit four years ago. If the court approves that agreement, the public in all probability will never get a factual, balanced picture of what's been going on in the state's juvenile institutions.[3]

On March 1, 1982, Judge Thompson rejected the proposed settlement of the *Terry D.* case for many of the same reasons and ordered all parties, including Attorney General Cartwright, legislative leaders, lawyers representing DHS, and lawyers and representatives of the three civil rights groups bringing the case, to spend 60 days working toward a new agreement.[4] While rejecting the agreement, he still declined to take over the juvenile system. He stressed it was not the business of the court to order a restructuring of social policy that wasn't acceptable to all involved state agencies and the state legislature. The judge's opinion said:

> This case has the potential of becoming an example of what is widely recognized as one of the most important disputes in the history of the American judiciary—What role should the federal judiciary play in overseeing, correcting, setting standards for, and directly administering the social services of the states? Protection of constitutional rights is clearly and indisputably the role of the Court. The Court is, and always shall be, available and unhesitating in that role. Beyond that, the administration of social policy is properly for the state itself. A state's decisions affecting social policy, with the attendant philosophical considerations and consequences, should be as free from federal judicial intervention as protection of constitutional entitlements will permit.[5]

The Daily Oklahoman suggested Judge Thompson's ruling was "a model of judicial restraint."[6]

When a new agreement was not reached, attorney Novick called on the judge to set the case for trial. Novick said in June, 1982, "Kids are still being abused, kids are still being placed in solitary confinement cells, and non-offenders are still being incarcerated."[7] In an effort to prevent an elongated trial, the parties were ordered to continue to look for a solution.

With closely-monitored court control and the cooperation of the counsel for the parties, a landmark settlement and reform of Oklahoma's juvenile justice system was accomplished. Novick, who was awarded the Oklahoma Bar Association's Courageous Advocacy Award for his work as lead attorney for the plaintiffs, said:

> After many years of litigation and monitoring, the case brought about sweeping reform in the state's system of childcare. Longstanding practices of physical abuse, solitary confinement, and shackling were eliminated.[8]

As a direct result of the *Terry D.* case, Oklahoma was the first state to have its juvenile justice system accredited by the American Correctional Association.

Judge Thompson approved the "final chapter" of the lawsuit on April 30, 1991. Under the final plan, the state was required to develop a wide range of community-based services for children. The plan also called for constructing a secure, 32-bed training school designed to serve central Oklahoma, in addition to regional diagnostic services for juveniles. On April 5, 1996, 18 years after *Terry D.* was filed, the judge dismissed the class action lawsuit. In his final ruling in the case, he said:

> Oklahoma has passed from darkness to light during these 18 years and the state no longer needs federal oversight. Oklahoma has actually seized on a poor and dangerous circumstance and transformed it into something that is perhaps a model for the country.[9]

CHAPTER 16

CHIEF JUDGE

Judge Thompson is directly responsible for the collegiality of the Court in the Western District. He took extra pains to create and maintain harmony.

Court Clerk Robert Dennis

Never has a more talented man devoted so much energy and commitment to a career dedicated to public service.

Judge Robin J. Cauthron

By 1986, the caseload for the federal judges of Oklahoma's Western District was the heaviest in the nation. For several years, the courthouse was the busiest place in Oklahoma as political figures, especially county commissioners, were indicted by the hundreds. As a result of the failure of Penn Square Bank in Oklahoma City, a flood of lawsuits and more than $1.5 billion in claims against the Federal Deposit Insurance Corporation clogged the already overburdened system. Judges Thompson, West, Phillips, and Russell heard the bulk of cases. Senior judges could occasionally be assigned cases, but only Judge Bohanon had a regular docket. To relieve the docket overcrowding, Judge Thomas Brett of Tulsa spent a week out of each month in Oklahoma City.[1]

"These cases were not only burdensome from their sheer numbers," Judge Thompson remembered, "but they were complex and often involved legal issues that were of 'first impression,' having never been litigated previously." It put the onus on local federal judges to make initial rulings on federal and state issues as well as to establish innovative methods of case management for the unprecedented caseload.

Even with the burden, the Western District surprised the nation's judiciary by often ranking first in the prompt disposition of those cases, a seemingly impossible accomplishment. From 1982 to 1986, the Western District had either the heaviest or among the heaviest weighted case loads per federal judge in the nation. As a result of its record, the court was named one of only ten Civil Justice Reform Act pilot courts to write proposed new rules to improve the efficiency of the handling of federal civil cases throughout the nation.[2]

After succeeding Luther B. Eubanks as Chief Judge, Judge Thompson contacted Oklahoma's congressional delegation to seek the creation of additional judgeships in the Western District. Robert Dennis, who became Court Clerk in the Western District only a few months prior to Judge Thompson becoming Chief Judge, said:

> He insisted that matters be handled in an expeditious and competent manner. It was his way of thinking that if something was worth doing at all, it was worth doing right. He demanded perfection of himself, as well as others. He is a wordsmith who values the precise usage of the English language…Many times while preparing a document which required his signature, I labored long and hard with sweat on my

Judge Thompson became Chief Judge of the United States District Court for the Western District of Oklahoma in 1989.

brow trying to come up with just the right word that Judge
Thompson would use in the context of a document.[3]

During his years as Chief Judge, Judge Thompson made "many far
reaching changes and innovations to the court." Court Clerk Dennis
cited the judge's greatest administrative accomplishments as the realign-
ment of the federal courthouse with the General Services Administration
adding eight new courtrooms and eight additional judicial chambers
during the judge's tenure. [4]

The Court, under the judge's leadership, also converted from paper
docket sheets to an automated system called the Integrated Case Management System (ICMS). Because of the successful modernization of systems
and courtrooms, the Administrative Office of the U.S. Courts (AO) recognized the Western District as a court of innovation and change.[5]

During the construction of new courtrooms, Dennis was looking
at new judicial chambers on the fourth floor of the courthouse. He was
accompanied by Judge Thompson and new judge, Wayne Alley. The three
were looking at a beautiful new corner office complex. Judge Thompson
recited the World War II story of his father's commander being booted
out of his quarters in The Philippines by General Douglas MacArthur.
Alley, a retired Army general, said to Judge Thompson, a retired colonel
in the Air Force Reserve, "Wait a minute. Since I outrank you, I claim
the corner office." Judge Thompson quickly responded, "This is not a
military matter, General. You may outrank me militarily, but judicial se-
niority counts here. These are my new chambers and I believe I will keep
them." Of course, it was all a joke, although Judge Thompson did retain
the chambers. The general-colonel bantering went on for years between
the old friends. Judge Lee West claimed that having been a Marine
captain, he outranked them both.[6]

Dennis believes that Judge Thompson's greatest contribution to the
Western District was his ability to bring collegiality to the courthouse. In
the not too distant past, "very independent" federal judges worked their
own caseloads without a lot of interaction. "Judge Thompson was different,"
Dennis said, "He was friendly, served as a mentor to several judges who followed him, and worked overtime to make certain there was air of complete
harmony and cooperation among all judges, staffs, and the clerk's office."[7]

The judge's genuine sense of humor helped establish collegiality
at the court. Dennis remembered one occasion when a tense situation

In his judicial career, Judge Thompson has been presented numerous opportunities to meet interesting public figures of the world. In 1992, he was hosted in London by Sir Peter Imbert, head of Scotland Yard, London's famous law enforcement agency.

Judge Thompson, right, and Judge David Russell, left, meet with Andrew Bossard of Paris, France, who was Secretary General of Interpol, The International Police Organization, in 1983.

threatened the longstanding friendship between Judge Thompson and another judge. In an attempt to defuse the situation, he donned riot control gear, including a bullet proof vest, assault helmet, and shield borrowed from the United States Marshal's office, and went to the other judge's home for dinner. Dennis said, "All trepidation vanished and things returned to normal."[8]

As Chief Judge, he took a great deal of time to speak with every employee of the Western District who received a promotion. He not only talked to his own staff, but members of the Court Clerk's office and the United States Probation office. He also presided over ceremonial occasions and informal "court family" gatherings to honor employees and acknowledge their achievements. Robin Cauthron, who served as the judge's law clerk, United States Magistrate Judge, and United States District Judge, said, "These recognition ceremonies were done completely out of his own thoughtfulness and generosity for others…He was unfailing in his ability

Attendance at judicial conferences gave Judge Thompson opportunities to become friends with justices of the United States Supreme Court. Playing tennis, left to right, are Judge Earl O'Connor, Justice Sandra Day O'Connor, Judge Thompson, and Judge Joe Morris at Sedona, Arizona.

to recognize the achievement of others and reward them for it."[9]

On another occasion, Judges Thompson and Russell learned that a courthouse janitor had been diagnosed with cancer and was facing serious financial problems. The two judges sponsored a wine and cheese fundraising reception at the Thompson home, invited courthouse employees, judges, and staffs, and raised several thousand dollars for the stricken "honoree" who was able to attend. Court Clerk Dennis said, "The term 'courthouse family' is more than a name. It is a reality."[10]

Judge Thompson had to work out the details of new judges coming onto the court. Judge Alley began his term on the court in August, 1985, after serving four years as dean of the OU College of Law. He was an honor graduate of Stanford University and the Stanford law school, a retired brigadier general in the United States Army Judge Advocate General Corps, and had served as the Chief Trial Judge of the United

States Army. He was appointed to the Western District by President Ronald Reagan and assumed senior status in May, 1999.[11]

In 1987, Layn Phillips was appointed by President Reagan to the Western District seat vacated by Luther Eubanks. A graduate of the University of Tulsa and the University of Tulsa College of Law, Phillips was an Assistant United States Attorney in the Central District of California, Special Assistant Attorney in Miami, Florida, and United States Attorney for the Northern District of Oklahoma. He was known as a superstar among prosecutors, never having lost a case or even a single count of an indictment. He later left the court in 1991 to pursue an extraordinarily successful private national and international practice in California.[12]

In his position as Chief Judge, Judge Thompson became a mentor to both judges on the court and to other judges and lawyers. Steven Taylor was a young state trial judge in McAlester and shared military service ties. Taylor, named chief justice of the Oklahoma Supreme Court in 2010, said, "He was a constant source of encouragement and motivation to me. He helped instill in me the importance of the work of a trial judge and enforced my decision to permanently leave the practice of law for a lifetime on the bench."[13]

Active judges of the United States District Court for the Western District of Oklahoma in 1989 were, front row, left to right, Lee West, Ralph Thompson, and David Russell. Back row, Wayne Alley and Layn Phillips.

CHAPTER 17

DIRECTOR OF THE FBI?

It can be described as a blessing and a curse—having to decide between, literally, the two jobs in the world you would most want to have. As unlikely as it is to happen in anyone's lifetime, it was about to happen to me.

Judge Ralph G. Thompson

In 1987, toward the end of President Reagan's second term of office, Judge William Webster resigned as director of the FBI to become director of the Central Intelligence Agency. As the White House began the search for Webster's successor, Judge Thompson's name was mentioned in high circles in Washington, D.C. Newspapers quoted high-placed sources that he was on a "short list" and that he had the support of Oklahoma's two United States senators, Don Nickles and David Boren, and Senator Kay Bailey Hutchison of Texas, among other leading senators and executive level FBI officials. All were close to President Reagan, his chief of staff, former Senator Howard Baker, and Attorney General Edwin Meese.

The national media initially reported that the most likely candidates to replace Webster were United States District Judge Lowell Jenson of San Francisco, former Pennsylvania Governor Richard Thornburgh, and Associate Attorney General Steve Trott. With such nationally prominent names in the field, Judge Thompson did not believe he would be picked as FBI director, but "the unlikely prospect" was never completely out of his mind. Judge Jenson, Governor Thornburgh, and Trott withdrew from consideration. While other names became public, Senators Nickles and Boren told the judge to expect a call from Attorney General Meese and to be prepared to make a decision whether to be considered for appointment or not. [1]

While the judge was very happy with his job on the federal court, he was not sure what his decision would be. He believed he was right for his job, was doing it well, and he enjoyed his colleagues and loved his family life in Oklahoma City. "But," he remembered, "being director of the FBI was hugely appealing and I was torn between what I would say if lightning struck and I was asked to be the one candidate considered."[2]

Rumors from the White House said he was the first choice of the administration. It was assumed he could be confirmed by the United States Senate in a reasonable and timely manner. Still, he had doubts. FBI directors serve for a period of not more than ten years, but actually serve at the pleasure of the sitting President. The politics in the summer of 1987 were uncertain. Massachusetts Governor Michael Dukakis, the Democratic frontrunner, led in polls over Vice President George H.W. Bush who was expected to gain the Republican presidential nomination the following year.[3]

Judge Thompson believed that if Bush were elected, he would stay on as FBI director. However, if Dukakis became president, he would have the right to name his own FBI chief. If that happened, the judge would have given up his lifetime appointment for less than two years guaranteed as FBI director. "It was not an appealing prospect," he said.[4]

His close friend, prominent attorney Drew Neville, offered his thought on whether or not he should take the post. Neville said, "No," although he admitted it was a selfish response. Neville and many lawyers looked to the judge as the "leader" of the Western District and "the standard bearer for judicial excellence." Neville believed the federal bench at that point in time was in a "somewhat fragile state," and his leadership was desperately needed.[5]

According to Neville, those close to the Reagan-Bush administration said there was a respected body of thought that if Judge Thompson took the FBI job, it would put him into a perfect position for a seat on the United States Supreme Court should Bush be elected president. Neville said, "Judge Thompson was a perfect fit for the Reagan/Bush judicial philosophy. Observers of the Washington scene at the time believed that the FBI directorship could have springboarded him into consideration, if not the nomination, to the High Court."[6]

In the midst of his being considered for the FBI job, Judge Thompson took his family on a European vacation that had been scheduled for many months. He was preoccupied with the FBI possibility. Every time he checked into a hotel, the first thing he did was to see if the telephone message light was on.

The day after the Thompsons returned home to Oklahoma City, the judge received calls from both Senators Nickles and Boren saying that he most likely would be called by Attorney General Meese within "a day or two." Things were getting serious. Like clockwork, two days later, on July 15, 1987, Meese called and asked the judge to come to Washington, D.C. to meet with President Reagan, Chief of Staff Baker, and him. The judge said, "General Meese, I have been hoping you would call, and also hoping that you would not." Both men laughed. Meese said he certainly understood and gave the judge a couple of days to decide what to do.[7]

The following day, Judge Thompson flew to Martha's Vineyard, Massachusetts, for a Judicial Conference committee meeting. He was "absolutely torn down the middle with indecision." He was being forced to choose between the "two jobs in the world" that he most wanted to do. News that the judge perhaps was the administration's top choice leaked out. A film crew was sent by a network bureau in Chicago to take footage of him in his chambers. He received private expressions of support from FBI executive-level friends. After all, he had high regard for the FBI and the opportunity to serve his country at the national level hugely appealed to him.[8]

He had come to know Oliver "Buck" Revell, former special agent in charge in Oklahoma City and the number two man at FBI headquarters; Anthony Daniels, also the top agent in Oklahoma City and later Deputy Assistant Director of the FBI; supervisory special agent Errol Myers; and special agents Henry "Hank" Gibbons and Jon Hersley. Later, Hersley was the co-case agent in the investigation of the 1995 bombing of the Alfred P. Murrah Federal Building in Oklahoma City.[9]

An important Washington, D.C., lawyer, and former high school and college mate, DeVier Pierson, was among a group of Washington insiders urging Judge Thompson to accept the FBI post. Pierson, who served as Special Counsel to President Lyndon B. Johnson and commanded great respect on Capitol Hill and at the White House, said, "He would have been a superb choice and I urged him to do it."[10]

It was time for a decision. Although his love of the judiciary was a major factor, family considerations were paramount in Judge Thompson's mind. Barbara was entirely supportive. So were Lisa, Elaine, and Maria who were all college students. In the end, the judge decided that being a federal district judge in Oklahoma City was best for him and his family. He called Attorney General Meese from a telephone booth outside the Edgartown Drugstore on Martha's Vineyard and respectfully reported his decision. Meese was "most gracious" and told him to let him know if he changed his mind. Senators Nickles, Boren, and Hutchison and Chief of Staff Baker also understood and, although disappointed, accepted his decision.[11]

Being considered to lead the FBI was "the biggest honor" of his life. The decision was the hardest one of his life. "But," he said, "it was the right one." He told Ed Kelley, then chief of the Washington Bureau of *The Daily Oklahoman*, "It was a matter of timing, personal considerations, and my satisfaction with my work on the court here." Kelley wrote in a special story on July 25, "He was a candidate who matched what the White House wanted: A conservative judge who would bring no ideological baggage or controversy to the FBI."[12]

With the judge taking himself out of consideration, the White

House turned to other candidates. President Reagan settled on Judge William Sessions of Texas who had served as United States Attorney and federal district judge in San Antonio. Sessions was quickly confirmed by the Senate.

Planning to continue on the court, Judge Thompson was not looking for another job, but was mentioned for another position in 1988. This time, the job was closer to home. The Presidential Search Committee of the University of Oklahoma notified him in August, 1988, that he had been nominated to become a candidate to serve as president of OU. With his deep roots, loyalty, and strong family and personal ties to OU, he was "deeply touched just to be thought of." [13]

The idea of leading OU caused the judge to reflect upon how much OU meant to him. OU had given him a wonderful college experience and the "happy, friendly, beautiful" campus had become virtually a second home. He was proud of "a wonderful education," two degrees, a military commission, and close friends among students and faculty. He had been active as an OU alumnus. He said, "Anything I had ever done for the university had indeed been a labor of love." [14]

In addition to his individual admiration for OU and its excellence, Judge Thompson thought of the importance of the institution to his family. Among a long list of achievements, his family had earned 16 degrees, including six Phi Beta Kappas. [15]

But, making short work of the opportunity, Ralph gratefully and respectfully declined to become an active candidate. He said:

I knew in my heart of hearts that I was a federal trial judge for whom the courtroom had become a second home. Second, a great research university needs someone with qualifications far more appropriate than mine. [16]

These two tempting opportunities, the FBI and OU, seemed to always come with a tug at the heart.

CHAPTER 18

NATIONAL SERVICE

*As a judge of the U.S. Foreign Intelligence Surveillance Court,
I routinely read and listened to recorded secret conversations of spies
and terrorists. I can absolutely state that our country would have
been seriously harmed had it not been for the courageous and effective
work of our agents surveilling and countering their efforts.*

Judge Ralph G. Thompson

*Judge Thompson's dedicated service on the FISA Court
greatly protected our nation while maintaining the rule of law
his professional life served so well.*

Former FBI Director Louis J. Freeh

As recognition of Judge Thompson's rising importance as a federal judge, he was appointed in 1981 by United States Supreme Court Chief Justice Warren Burger to serve on a committee of the prestigious Judicial Conference of the United States (JCUS). Burger asked him to serve on the Committee on Court Administration for the JCUS which is the principal policy-making body for the nation's federal court system. It is an important committee because its members suggest national policy on jury usage, financial support, court personnel, and trial dockets in federal courts. [1]

As one of the youngest federal judges in the nation, he was, by far, the youngest member of the committee, made up of "the old bards of the federal judiciary." At the first meeting of the committee in Palm Beach, Florida, he received curious glances from participants who thought he was one of the judge's law clerks. After the matter was straightened out, the judge and the others became good friends.

In 1988, Chief Justice William Rehnquist appointed him as a member of the Committee on Federal-State Jurisdiction. When Supreme Court Justice Anthony Kennedy invited him to join him on a three-member panel to select the recipient of the Edward J. Devitt Distinguished Service to Justice Award, the highest honor a federal judge can receive, he and Barbara learned that traveling with a justice of the high court had its distinct advantages. He also served with Justice Clarence Thomas on the Devitt selection committee the following year.

In 1998, Judge Thompson was elected as the federal district judge representative of the Tenth Circuit to the Judicial Conference, in addition to serving as president of the United States District Judges Association for the Tenth Circuit. Then, Chief Justice Rehnquist selected him for membership on the executive committee of the Judicial Conference, a rare honor for a federal judge. The executive committee is the senior executive body of the policy making arm of the federal judiciary.

United States District Judge Wm. Terrell Hodges of the Middle District of Florida was chair of the JCUS Executive Committee. Hodges said:

> He listened quietly. He was thoughtful and deliberate. He was smart and wise. He was innovative and persuasive. He was compassionate, and without prejudice. He was helpful, cordial, and collegial. He was a friend and supporter of anyone interested in justice.[2]

After Judge Hodges' term as chair of the committee expired, Judge Ralph L. Winter, chief judge of the Second Circuit Court of Appeals and longtime Yale law professor, headed the prestigious committee.[3]

Another judge with whom Judge Thompson worked closely on the JCUS Executive Committee was United States District Judge Lloyd D. George of Nevada. Judge George said:

> Judge Thompson's keen sense of personal responsibility and excellence made him a hallmark, both in and out of the robe. One recognizes in this man a sharp mind and acute wit melded with the perfect balance of modesty and reserve— something that gives his ideas and demeanor a unique author- ity and authenticity...He has been a marvelous compliment to the judiciary.[4]

The meetings of the Judicial Conference are held in the stately con- ference room of the Supreme Court building in Washington, D.C. It was "awe inspiring" for Judge Thompson to sit two chairs removed from the Chief Justice in such a historic setting.

Judge Thompson's service was observed closely by United States

Judge Thompson and Chief Judge Procter Hug were asked by Supreme Court Justice Anthony Kennedy to join him to serve as the selection committee for the Edward J. Devitt Distinguished Service to Justice Award. At a meeting in New York are the judges and their wives. Left to right, Barbara Hug, Chief Judge Hug, Mary Kennedy, Justice Kennedy, Judge Thompson, and Barbara Thompson.

District Judge Fern Smith, former Director of the Federal Judicial Center. She said, "I was aware of his reputation as a credit to the federal bench in all ways. He was thoughtful, scholarly, imminently fair, and kind." After both the judge and Smith retired, they, together with Judge William Webster, served on an arbitration panel in a complex case.[5]

In June, 1990, Judge Thompson was appointed by Chief Justice Rehnquist to the United States Foreign Intelligence Surveillance Court (FISA Court), sometimes called the "Spy Court." The FISA court was created by the Foreign Intelligence Surveillance Act to provide for judicial authorization of clandestine electronic surveillance, including physical searches, of foreign powers and agents of foreign powers for foreign intelligence purposes. The court is comprised of seven federal district court judges, appointed by the Chief Justice for seven-year, non-renewable terms.[6]

Federal law requires the FBI, the National Security Agency, the Department of Defense, and other federal agencies to apply to the FISA court for permission to conduct clandestine foreign intelligence surveillance of foreign spies and suspected terrorists. A cabinet level officer had to certify that the activities were meant solely to collect foreign intel-

Judge Thompson is reunited with friend, Justice Sandra Day O'Connor, in Oklahoma City. The two had met so often, Judge Thompson asked her, "Aren't you getting a little tired of me?" Justice O'Connor replied, "Not yet!"

The Judicial Conference of the United States in 2000. Chief Justice William H. Rehnquist is at front center. Judge Thompson is on the top row, center, directly below the oil portrait

of Chief Justice William Howard Taft. Courtesy Franz Jantzen, Collection of the Supreme Court of the United States.

ligence. The FISA court reviewed the applications to determine if there was probable cause to support such representations. Only with the FISA court judge's authorization could the operations be conducted. It was a serious responsibility to make certain that FISA surveillance was used as a tool to combat espionage and terrorism by foreign powers while, at the same time, protecting the rights of Americans from unauthorized intrusion by intelligence-gathering agencies.[7]

Judge Thompson's prior experience in counter-intelligence assisted him in his decisions regarding the highly sensitive matters. The judges of the FISA court served individually, not as a panel. The judge considered applications and conducted hearings in a highly secure location in the Department of Justice Building in Washington, D.C. Testimony was taken from agents of the applying intelligence agency in a special enclosure invulnerable to all known listening devices. The information gleaned from the hearing was top secret. Reading and listening to conversations of spies and terrorists were routinely part of his service on the court for the seven years of his term.[8]

The only time that the judges of the FISA Court met together was at an annual luncheon hosted by the Chief Justice in a dining room of the United States Supreme Court. Also in attendance were the attorney general and the directors of the FBI, CIA, and the National Security Agency. During these luncheons he became acquainted with national leaders such as Attorney General Janet Reno, CIA directors George Tenet and James Woolsey, and FBI director Louis J. Freeh.

Judge Thompson drew great praise from Freeh. "He was one of the most highly-regarded federal judges within the Department of Justice, and particularly within the FBI," Freeh said. "This esteem and respect is the direct result of the many years of selfless public service wherein he always demonstrated fairness, justice, and the highest personal integrity."[9]

For the seven years of his term, the judge traveled to Washington, D.C., every few months to hear a docket of surveillance cases that lasted several days. He said, "To become intimately privy to the workings of spies and terrorists, and our agents' gallant efforts to counter them, was an intensely vital, serious, stimulating, and fascinating experience." He will never be able to discuss his work on the FISA Court except to say, "I can absolutely state that our country would have been seriously harmed had it not been for the courageous and effective work of our agents surveilling and countering their efforts."[10]

Chief Justice William H. Rehnquist presents Judge Thompson a certificate of appreciation for his service on the United States Foreign Intelligence Surveillance Court in 1997. Judge Thompson said, "I could have never imagined that it would have been the Chief Justice of the United States who so influenced my life." Courtesy Franz Jantzen, Collection of the Supreme Court of the United States.

The Chief Justice annually holds a luncheon for judges of the FISA Court and agency heads at the Supreme Court. Luncheon guests in 1994 included, front row, left to right, Admiral William O. Studeman, acting director of the CIA; Chief Justice William H. Rehnquist; Judge Joyce Hens Green; Judge James C. Cacheris; and Admiral John M. Mc-Connell, director of the National Security Agency. Back row, Robert M. Bryant, assistant director of the FBI; Jamie Gorelick, Assistant Attorney General of the United States; Judge Earl H. Carroll; Judge John F. Keenan; Judge Thompson; Judge Wendell A. Miles; Judge Royce Lamberth; and Allan N. Kornblum, Deputy Counsel for Intelligence Operations, United States Department of Justice. Courtesy Franz Jantzen, Collection of the Supreme Court of the United States.

An extraordinary circumstance arose during the judge's term on the FISA Court. His daughter, Lisa, was an Intelligence Operations Specialist in the National Security Division of the FBI headquarters across the street from the Department of Justice where her father held FISA Court hearings. Lisa was assigned to the FBI section dealing with Soviet counter-intelligence. As part of her duties, Lisa prepared applications to the FISA Court and was intimately familiar with those surveillance operations. The information, involving identities and activities of Soviet defectors and spies, was so sensitive that it was a hugely guarded secret.

Down the hallway from Lisa was Robert Hanssen, a veteran FBI agent who later pleaded guilty to selling American secrets to the Soviet Union over a 22-year period for $1.4 million in cash and diamonds.

He is serving a life sentence without the possibility of parole. Hanssen admitted selling secret information that most likely resulted in the execution of CIA operatives in the Soviet Union and KGB agents who had become secret sources for the FBI.[11]

Given the years and subject matter involved, it can be assumed that both Lisa and her father were reviewing much of the information that Hanssen had sold to the Soviet Union, although both father and daughter are sworn to never discuss it.[12]

There were other potential opportunities for national service. In June, 1991, Judge Thompson was suggested as a possible replacement for retiring United States Supreme Court Associate Justice Thurgood Marshall. In a joint letter to President George H.W. Bush, Oklahoma's two United States senators, Boren and Nickles, said:

> We are confident Judge Thompson would receive strong bipartisan support and would greatly appreciate your consideration of his qualifications. We believe his expertise and experience would be valuable assets to the U.S. Supreme Court and the nation.[13]

The release of the letter fueled speculation by the press. *The Journal Record* reported Boren and Nickles' request to the President in a story with the headline, "Oklahoma Senators Back Thompson for Court Post." It was significant that senators from both major political parties endorsed the judge for the high court.[14]

It was not the first time that Senator Nickles recommended the judge for elevation to the Supreme Court. In 1981, Nickles wrote to President Reagan, suggesting that Judge Thompson fill the vacancy by the retirement of Associate Justice Potter Stewart. The judge considered both recommendations as wonderful and much appreciated, but he termed them "long on the honor—short on the chances."[15]

In 2000, Chief Justice Rehnquist recommended him as a Judge of the International Criminal Tribunal for the Former Yugoslavia to replace former Circuit Judge Patricia Wald. Judge Wald had suggested to the State Department that a federal judge with substantial trial experience be appointed for the demanding international judicial responsibility. The post was fascinating to the judge, stirring the coals of his interest in international affairs and criminal law. However, it would have required full-time service in The Hague, Netherlands, and relinquishing his federal judgeship. He did not feel he could give up "the perfect job" and move to the Netherlands for an indefinite period of time. He respectfully declined the offer.[16]

A significant sidebar to serving on the Judicial Conference executive committee and on the FISA Court was the judge's frequent contact with Chief Justice Rehnquist. He said, "While the Chief Justice's brilliance and 'crisp' management style was intimidating to some, I knew him to be a kind man with a good sense of humor." An example of Rehnquist's nimble mind and extemporaneous wit occurred during a breakfast of federal district judge members of the Judicial Conference with the Chief Justice. He had received a special tribute from the United States Senate for the manner in which he presided over the impeachment trial of President Bill Clinton.[17]

Judge Thompson congratulated Rehnquist. As a devotee and student of opera and operettas, the Chief Justice quickly and modestly answered:

Thank you. But I am reminded of a line from "Iolanthe," sung by Lord Mountarart—"When Wellington thrashed Bonaparte, as every child can tell, the House of Peers throughout the war, did nothing in particular, and did it very well."[18]

The judge was impressed with the Chief Justice downplaying such a high honor and with his ability to quote such a passage in doing so.

In September, 2005, Judge Thompson attended the Chief Justice's funeral at St. Matthew's Cathedral in Washington, D.C. Rehnquist's friend of more than five decades, Justice Sandra Day O'Connor, and President George W. Bush eulogized the late Chief Justice, recalling his brilliant mind, the distinction of his leadership of the nation's highest court, his devotion to family, and wonderful personal qualities. He was buried at Arlington National Cemetery.[19]

As Judge Thompson listened to the beautiful eulogies, he personally reflected that no one had given him more opportunities or positively influenced his judicial career than Chief Justice Rehnquist. He said, "I could never have imagined that it would have been the Chief Justice of the United States who so influenced my life."[20]

JUDGEMAKER

Judge Thompson's advice was critical to the appointment of federal judges in Oklahoma. His assessment of a candidate's potential to be a good jurist was invaluable in the process.

President David L. Boren

Judge Thompson's greatest legacy may be the incredible influence he had on the selection of federal judges who followed him.

Judge David Russell

Since Judge Thompson assumed the federal bench in 1975, the number of judges in Oklahoma's three federal districts has grown dramatically. In 2010, there were six active district judges, two senior judges, five full-time magistrate judges, and one part-time magistrate judge in the Western District. Because political leaders in both major parties trusted his judgment, he has frequently been called upon to suggest names or give his views on prospects for vacant judicial positions.

President George H.W. Bush appointed Robin Cauthron as a district judge in a new position in the Western District in 1991. Her story is "very close" to Judge Thompson's heart. She was an honor student at the University of Oklahoma College of Law before the judge hired her as a law clerk in 1977. Cauthron never had "given a thought" to being a judge until she worked for him. But once she observed the judge for several years, she wanted to be "just like him." Cauthron said:

> With his good common sense in inserting just the right words and phrases into his orders and opinions so as to make them both understandable and acceptable to the lay public; never losing his temper, or treating anyone with disrespect, or holding himself above others; and always maintaining a sense of humor and humility caused me to want to be a judge.[1]

Judge Thompson's common sense is what impressed Cauthron the most. She said:

> He has always brought a very practical, common sense approach to sometimes very difficult public policy questions. This common sense approach, with his very real empathy with the litigants themselves is legendary.[2]

Before taking the federal bench, and after leaving her post as law clerk, Cauthron served as Special District Judge in McCurtain County and United States Magistrate Judge. Cauthron was Chief Judge of the Western District from 2001 to 2008.[3]

Judge Thompson was instrumental in Cauthron being appointed federal judge. He highly recommended her nomination to United States Senator Don Nickles. Once Nickles recommended Cauthron to the White House, her Senate confirmation occurred without delay. Judge Cauthron's ascent from being his law clerk to later Chief Judge of the court is one of Judge Thompson's proudest stories.

Judges of the Western District in 1993. Front row, left to right, Luther Bohanon, Chief Judge Thompson, and Fred Daugherty. Back row, Robin Cauthron, David Russell, Lee West, Wayne Alley, and Tim Leonard.

Even during times when the President has been a Democrat, and Oklahoma had a Democratic senator, Judge Thompson's input was sought in regard to the selection of federal judges. Former Oklahoma Democratic Attorney General Michael C. Turpen said, "There is not a federal judge appointee in the past four decades that hasn't sought the advice and counsel of Judge Thompson to help them maneuver the maze of the federal judgeship appointment process."[4]

Turpen knows that to be true. During the years in which George H.W. Bush and George Bush were in the White House, Turpen often wrote letters of support for federal court candidates. Turpen knew the judge was involved in the process because Judge Thompson might say, "I saw your letter and am proud of your support of a Republican nominee. That's real statesmanship."[5]

Tim D. Leonard, an appointee of President George H.W. Bush, joined the Western District as federal district judge in August, 1992, replacing Layn Phillips. Leonard was a graduate of OU and the OU

The court of the Western District in 1996. Left to right, Judges Wayne Alley, Tim Leonard, Ralph Thompson, Robin Cauthron, Luther Bohanon, Vicki Miles-LaGrange, David Russell, Fred Daugherty, and Lee West.

When Judge Thompson completed his seven-year term as Chief Judge of the Western District in 1993, his portrait was officially hung in the United States Courthouse. Left to right, Elaine Thompson DeGiusti, Maria Thompson Abbott, Lisa Thompson Campbell, Barbara Thompson, and the judge.

College of Law, an assistant Oklahoma attorney general, member and minority leader of the Oklahoma State Senate, and United States Attorney for the Western District from 1989 to 1992. Leonard assumed senior status in August, 2006.[6]

In 1994, when Judge West took senior status, President Bill Clinton appointed Vicki Miles-LaGrange to the Western District. A graduate of Vassar College and the Howard University School of Law, she was a law clerk for Judge Woodrow Seals in the Southern District of Texas, graduate fellow in the Criminal Division of the United States Department of Justice, assistant district attorney in Oklahoma County, the first black woman to serve in the Oklahoma State Senate, and United States Attorney for the Western District. When she took the bench, she was the first black woman to serve as a federal district judge in the Tenth Circuit. Both Leonard and Miles-LaGrange had Judge Thompson's full support.[7]

Judge Thompson also promoted and supported the selection of Jerome Holmes as the first black judge of the Tenth Circuit Court of Appeals in 2006. In his investiture ceremony, Holmes said:

> I want to thank Judge Thompson who is a wonderful man, a wonderful judge, and a steadfast friend and supporter. If a man could have one person in his corner to fight the fight, they would be inclined to look in the direction of Judge Thompson.[8]

CHAPTER 20

DARKNESS
AND LIGHT

While other things happened in 1995,
the Murrah Building bombing put everything in
the rightful "what's really important" category.

Judge Ralph G. Thompson

Shortly after 9:00 a.m. on April 19, Judge Thompson was in his third-floor office in the United States Courthouse. At 9:02:55, he turned away from his oversized office window that faced the grounds of the Alfred P. Murrah Federal Building directly across the street. It was his daily routine to dictate at his desk until 9:00 a.m. before proceeding to the courtroom. He often enjoyed watching small children being walked to the daycare facility in the Murrah Building.[1]

He left the window, removed the dictation tape from his recorder, and turned to walk to the desk of his secretary, Sharon Henshall. At that moment, just five seconds after turning from the window, a monstrous explosion rocked not only the Murrah Building but the United States Courthouse as well. Windows buckled and blew out, the ceiling fell in, and shards of glass pierced the wood paneling in the office. No one could have survived standing in front of the window.[2]

Not knowing the extent of the tragedy, the judge joined his secretary and court room deputy as they clasped hands and made their way down the hallway toward the red "EXIT" sign that barely was visible through the dust in the air from collapsed ceilings.

The judge first thought the building had experienced a natural gas explosion. However, once he exited the building and saw the devastation and carnage of the Murrah Building, he concluded privately that surely a bomb from a terrorist cell had caused the damage. His work on the FISA Court gave him great insight into the capabilities of people who wanted to hurt the United States.[3]

"The Murrah Building was rubble," he remembered, "people were hanging out of windows and on the ledges of what remained. There was fire, smoke, and screams. Bloody people fleeing southward passed us." Standing at the intersection of Northwest Fourth Street and Robinson Avenue, he could not help but notice the confluence of those fleeing south from the building and the mothers of children racing north toward the daycare center in the Murrah Building.

The judge recognized federal Court Clerk Robert Dennis staggering down the street toward him, covered with concrete dust. In shock, somehow Dennis had miraculously survived, having dug his way out of the rubble after standing by the elevator shaft on the ground floor of the bombed building. His back was covered in blood that was not his own.

In the days and weeks ahead, the world discovered that two disgruntled former American soldiers, Timothy McVeigh and Terry Nichols, had created a fertilizer bomb and placed it in a rented Ryder truck that McVeigh parked

Barbara was honored as the National Mother of the Year at the Waldorf Astoria hotel in New York City in 1995 by American Mothers, Inc.

Oklahoma Governor Frank Keating presents Barbara a proclamation on her selection as Oklahoma's Mother of the Year in 1995.

at the Fifth Street entrance to the Murrah Building. Many were wounded and 168 federal workers, visitors, and children lost their lives. It was the most violent act of domestic terrorism in the nation's history.[4]

There were anxious moments for the Thompson family in the hours after the bombing. News accounts broadcast around the world identified the bombed building as the "federal courthouse building." Many listeners and viewers believed the United States Courthouse had been bombed. One radio station reported that Judges Thompson and Russell were missing. Judge Thompson had escaped his damaged office and Russell actually was in the Dallas-Fort Worth Airport. Friends and family rushed to the Thompson home to be with Barbara. Judge Thompson was without communication. There was no telephone service until he reached an automobile repair shop several blocks away and called home.[5]

Daughters Elaine and Maria were in law offices a few blocks away and he finally found them. Lisa, at FBI headquarters in Washington, D.C. was in a command post giving a secured briefing when the red telephone rang and the bombing was reported. Other agents knew the location of the judge's office and walked a stunned Lisa back to her office. Fortunately, a thoughtful Oklahoma City FBI agent called and told her it was the Murrah Building, not the courthouse.

For weeks, day after day, the judge watched from his window as rescue workers dug through the rubble to recover bodies of victims. He was touched by the solemnity of workers rolling the bodies on gurneys to a temporary morgue at the First Methodist Church, then removing their hard hats and briefly bowing their heads in respect before returning to their ghastly task.[6]

He reflected:

> It was a deliberate, horrible tragedy that destroyed and ruined many lives. But, out of the evil event came the goodness in people—stories of courage, professionalism, generosity, devotion to duty, caring , sacrifices, and patriotism that have helped define the people of Oklahoma at their best.[7]

The day after the Murrah Building bombing, the Thompsons flew to New York City to the annual convention of American Mother's Inc. Barbara had been chosen Oklahoma's Mother of the Year and the trip had been planned for months. The judge was asked to make remarks at a banquet of the 75-year-old organization dedicated to the promotion of motherhood and family. He told the wholesome audience at the

United States Senator Kay Bailey Hutchison of Texas presents Judge Thompson with the Oklahoma Hall of Fame medallion upon his induction in 1995, Oklahoma's highest honor. The judge's grandfather, Dr. William Bennett Bizzell, was inducted into the Hall of Fame in 1936.

Waldorf-Astoria Hotel, "We have just come from our hometown, having left the gore and abject evil there. Being with you is like coming from darkness into light." He meant it.[8]

The judge was preoccupied with the devastation back home, but was there to honor Barbara. It was a secret for her, but he had been given brief advance notice that Barbara had been chosen as the National Mother of the Year. Barbara made gracious acceptance remarks and was wonderfully received.

In November of the same year, Judge Thompson received the highest honor his native Oklahoma could bestow—induction into the Oklahoma Hall of Fame. At a black-tie event at Oklahoma City's Civic Center Music Hall, the same building where he had first seen Barbara 31 years before, he was presented for induction by United States Senator Kay Bailey Hutchison of Texas, his dear friend since the Nixon campaign of 1972. The judge was only two years old when his grandfather, Dr. Bizzell, was inducted into the Hall of Fame in 1936.

Among many other friends, he received a congratulatory note from Chief Justice William Rehnquist. The Chief Justice said, "Judge Thomp-

Judge Thompson as King of the Beaux Arts Ball in 1995. Courtesy John Douglas Photography.

son represents the best of Oklahoma. His judicial accomplishments coupled with his distinguished public service make him more than qualified for this recognition."[9]

In his acceptance speech, he thanked his family, colleagues, and supporters. He said he was grateful for the privilege of public service—the privilege of serving as a federal judge for more than 20 years. He said he was grateful for Oklahoma, "a state that has so generously given me opportunities and whose character and courage are now known to the world."[10]

He also paid tribute to the men and women who had so valiantly performed in the aftermath of the Oklahoma City bombing and citizen volunteers everywhere:

> I am particularly grateful for all those in our community who so richly deserve recognition and get so little; those for whom there are no medallions and magical moments; those who protect us, teach us, heal us; those who dream and build our communities and in so many ways enrich our lives. On this night of our beautiful tributes, may you know how much we honor you.[11]

The third notable event of 1995 was the judge's selection as King of the Beaux Arts Ball, a prominent civic/social event in Oklahoma City held annually in support of the Oklahoma City Museum of Art. The "King" is selected on the basis of distinguished achievements and contributions to the community and is considered to be a "significant community honor."[12]

Judge Thompson joined a prestigious group of Oklahoma City leaders as King of the annual Beaux Arts Ball. Front row, left to right, Ed Cook, Bill Cleary, Admiral John Kirkpatrick, Sidney Upsher, Tony Calvert, Stanton Young, and Tom Dulaney. Back row, Dan Hogan, G.T. Blankenship, John Mee, Richard Clements, John Kilpatrick, Doc Jordan, John Parsons, Judge Thompson, Judge Fred Daugherty, and Bill Swisher.

CHAPTER 21

A JUDGE'S JUDGE

Y.A.A.F.J.A.L.I.

*Letters Judge Thompson wrote on a piece of note paper taped
to his bench in the courtroom. The letters stand as a reminder for
YOU ARE A FEDERAL JUDGE—ACT LIKE IT.
Judge Thompson was the member of the Oklahoma federal
bench whom I would call for advice because of
his impeccable ethical standards.*

Judge Claire V. Eagan

*Judge Thompson is truly a judge's judge. It's as if he has
a big magic wand—he makes things happen.*

Judge Vicki Miles-LaGrange

To many federal judges across the land, Judge Thompson is known as a "judge's judge." Claire Eagan, Chief Judge of the Northern District of Oklahoma, called him "the consummate federal judge." When Eagan was appointed United States Magistrate Judge in 1998, she met Judge Thompson for the first time at the Tenth Circuit Judicial Conference.[1]

Eagan knew him only by reputation. Soon, if a matter of judicial conduct or etiquette came up, she called him for advice. "I found him," she said "intelligent, even-tempered, fair, collegial, and wise."[2]

Former American Bar Association President Bill Paul said:

> He is truly a judge's judge. A hallmark of his success is his great good humor. He can make you laugh, about even the most serious matter. Not only is he universally admired and respected at home (and that is probably the most severe test of all), he is admired and respected nationally.[3]

Leonidas Ralph Mecham, former Director of the Administrative Office of the U.S. Courts, observed the judge in service to the national federal judiciary over a long period of time. It was Mecham who recommended him to Chief Justice Rehnquist for several major assignments. Only a handful of federal judges in the nation serve on committees that oversee policy for the entire federal court system. "For Judge Thompson to receive not only one, but four such key responsibilities," Mecham said, "will enable you to understand more fully how highly regarded he is in the Judicial Branch and was to the two Chief Justices that he served so well."[4]

Mecham called Judge Thompson his "mentor," because of "his outstanding experience, keen intellect, and exemplary character." "He is a star and one of the great heroes of the Judicial Branch," Mecham said.[5]

The judge's good friend, former Oklahoma Governor Frank Keating, credits him with convincing him to enter public service by standing for election to public office. Keating said, "He always told me that I should run for office because that is what a public citizen should do." "He was my first professional mentor," Keating said, "and showed me a real appeal for politics with his intelligence and devotion to giving through public service."[6]

"Judge Thompson has been a mentor to scores of young lawyers," William J. Ross said. "He always knows what to say when a young lawyer is undecided about career choices. He is blessed with the most delightful sense of humor that serves him well. At moments of stress, he can call on this gift to lighten the situation."[7]

The judge also was a mentor for attorney Mack Martin, who said, "It is because of his wisdom and willingness to reach out to those who have served before him that we feel such a strong bond of allegiance." On many occasions, Martin sought the judge's "insightful judgment and counsel."[8] Martin said, "One would be hard pressed to find a man with a deeper sense of respect for the law or a truer commitment to fulfill his judicial duties fairly and honorably."[9]

Martin calls the judge a "consummate professional." He said, "This was true even during the heat of trial when emotions and tempers might flare. He ranks among one of the most, if not the most revered judges in front of whom I ever appeared."[10]

Attorney Don Holladay believes Judge Thompson's greatest contribution is enhancing the public image of federal judges. He said, "His way of going about his duties, and how he was seen as a judge by both the bar and the public, became a model for other judges." Holladay also said the judge mastered "keeping the right distance" between judges and lawyers. "He kept a certain distance from the camaraderie of the profession, particularly within that segment of the legal community that appeared before him," Holladay said. "That may be an unfair observation, but is intended as a compliment. Deep down, most of us like just the right amount of distance. Judge Thompson seemed to have mastered the yardstick."[11]

"Oklahomans have come to expect him as always acting like a judge," said Ed Kelley, editor of *The Oklahoman.* Kelley said, "A judge is never really off the job, for wherever he goes, so goes the persona that fellow citizens expect from one. With or without a robe, a judge is expected to display wisdom, integrity, and temperament, even if it's just in a casual conversation at the neighborhood post office."[12]

"Just by being himself," Kelley said, "Judge Thompson has created an image to many Oklahomans of what a federal judge is supposed to be. He's made it a high standard, a legacy that has contributed mightily to public life in our great state. He is grounded in ways that the Founding Fathers would have wanted from a prominent member of one of the three branches of government."[13]

Former District Attorney, Oklahoma City Mayor, and OU College of Law Dean Andy Coats said, "On the bench, he presided over difficult and complex cases with firmness and dignity, but also with grace and charm, kindness and patience."[14] Prominent Washington, D.C. lawyer and former presidential special counsel DeVier Pierson, whose family ties with Judge Thompson go back nearly a century, said he has never known a better man than the judge. "He is an exceptionally able man of great integrity who has been a leader in the judiciary for many years."[15]

"Absolute fairness is evident in Judge Thompson's courtroom," said Judge Robert Henry:

> He treats the ACLU the same way he treats the U.S. Attorney or the Department of Justice. Everyone comes in with a tablet eraser and a clean slate with him. He is just, fair, and thoughtful, really what the framers of the constitution had in mind when establishing an independent judiciary as one of the three branches of government.[16]

Judge Henry says one of the reasons other judges across the land respect Judge Thompson is their awareness of his unique ability to listen, whether it is during a trial or at a meeting of judges and lawyers. Henry said:

> As a judge, it is hard to give each party and each lawyer your full attention. It is a shortcoming of many judges. However, Judge Thompson has mastered the ability to listen. He gives each case its required dignity. That is why parties leave feeling like they have had their day in court. Win or lose, they've had a fair shake.[17]

Judge Thompson's reputation as a fair and impartial federal judge was evident to veteran attorney Page Dobson. "While treating counsel with great respect," Dobson said, "Judge Thompson insisted on diligent preparation and adherence to the guiding rules under which we practiced. Always prepared, he asked the probing questions, sometimes before they occurred to us." Dobson described the judge's spirit as "indomitable," and appreciated the fact that his candor in the courtroom created an atmosphere that proved he "considered sunlight as the best disinfectant."[18]

"Judge Thompson has served with grace, intellect, and honor," said longtime attorney and friend Burck Bailey.[19] Former Oklahoma Speaker of the House Rex Privett reflected on the judge's lifetime of public service, "His record in the legislature and as a federal judge was never tarnished. He was a dedicated public official intent on promoting only the best for Oklahoma."[20]

Others have commented and written about Judge Thompson's excellence as a "judge's judge." United States District Judge William G. Young of Massachusetts said:

> He is the exemplar of everything I hope to be as a trial judge. His warm, winning, and even-handed personality makes him unexcelled in his ability to communicate to juries, litigants, and the bar both the great and the lesser concepts of our constitution and laws. Firm, calm, and reflective, he has the capacity and ethic to make our adversary system function at its best...his service as Chief Judge for the Western District of Oklahoma is universally recognized as outstanding...He is the shining example of what we hope every federal judicial officer should be.[21]

One of Judge Thompson's most enjoyable tasks as a federal judge was to preside over naturalization proceedings, officially conferring United States citizenship upon applicants who meet requirements for citizenship. Unless he was out of town, he rarely missed the monthly ceremony in the federal courthouse.[22]

The court made a special effort to make the naturalization ceremonies special. The judge said:

> By their very nature they were immensely emotional and proud moments for the new citizens and movingly warm and patriotic moments for all of us. I particularly loved them because of my special interest in our country's immigrant history, and my appreciation of those who have made such an effort to become citizens of our country.[23]

Often the naturalization ceremonies were accompanied by an instrumental ensemble. In his welcoming remarks, the judge loved to tell the new citizens about a small boy from Siberia arriving on a ship in New York Harbor carrying everything he owned in a cardboard box. Irving Berlin saw the Statue of Liberty and was happy and thrilled with his new land, although he had no plans for the future. Judge Thompson said, "I wanted the new citizens to understand that Mr. Berlin had indeed made his way and had become one of our country's most beloved songwriters, writing 'God Bless America,' which had just been played for them." It was always a sentimental moment.[24]

Attorney Joseph Wells, also a veteran musician with the Oklahoma City Symphony, helped organize groups of musicians to play patriotic music before the naturalization ceremonies. Many times, the musicians asked to meet the judge. Wells said, "I would take them back to his office and, without hesitation, he would greet my friends and make them feel like he was the one that was honored to have them in his courtroom." [25]

In his 32 years of presiding over or participating in the court's naturalization proceedings, the judge conferred citizenship upon 10,800 new citizens. Ironically, that number was compiled by San Nguyen, Western District Deputy Court Clerk for Naturalization Affairs, himself a refugee from Vietnam. Nguyen, trained as a lawyer in Vietnam and a CIA employee, was a passenger on the last helicopter to lift off from the United States Embassy roof during the fall of Saigon.

Judge Thompson has always loved history and writing. In 1998, he combined the two interests. He teamed with author Bob Burke to co-author a biography of Oklahoma native Bryce Harlow. The book, *Bryce Harlow: Mr. Integrity,* published by the Oklahoma Heritage Association, was submitted by the association for consideration for a Pulitzer Prize in non-fiction, and was named the outstanding Oklahoma History Book of 2000 by the Oklahoma Historical Society. Harlow was an Oklahoma City native who became President Dwight Eisenhower's speech writer and trusted advisor and was one of the most respected men in Washington, D.C., while serving several presidents. Harlow was the first cabinet-level appointee of President Richard Nixon after the 1968 election.

The Harlow project was close to the judge's heart because Harlow's nephew, James Harlow, Jr., was his Beta fraternity roommate at OU and a close friend for decades. Former Secretary of State Henry Kissinger agreed to write the foreword to the Harlow biography. The judge was able to conduct a lengthy interview with former President Gerald Ford. Ford returned the judge's telephone call while he was in the middle of a hearing. An aide slipped a note to him and he promptly adjourned court to talk with Ford for an hour and twenty minutes.[26]

Judge Thompson also contributed to research for the Harlow book by interviewing former President George H.W. Bush, Chief Justice Rehnquist, George Shultz, James A. Baker, III, Donald Rumsfeld, Melvin Laird, Lamar Alexander, Howard Baker, Jr., Robert Dole, General John Eisenhower, Pat Buchanan, William Safire, General Andrew Goodpaster, and many other leaders of the Harlow era.[27]

After the Harlow book was published, Judge Thompson received a cordial letter from President Ford:

> You have done a superb job. I am sending it to my library with an accompanying note—"This is a very accurate book on the turbulent times in the Nation's Capital." Congratulations.
>
> I am asking my staff to purchase five more copies for my library and our four children.[28]

Judge Thompson and Burke traveled to Washington, D.C., for a book signing attended by two dozen present or former members of Congress. Former Tennessee Governor, presidential aide, and United States Senator Lamar Alexander said," You have done a real service for our country by telling his story, and for doing it so well."[29] Harlow's son, Larry, said, "You have captured the essence of the honest life and service that my father lived."[30] Political advisor and presidential assistant Lyn Nofziger wrote, "Bryce Harlow came back into my life today…Without a doubt, across the board, Bryce has to have been the most respected man of his time in political Washington."[31]

About Judge Thompson's writing, Jane Harlow said, "He is a Renaissance man. Everything I have read that he was written is superb. His writing is inspiring as well as beautifully crafted."[32]

Judge Thompson's well-documented caring-for-others attitude also carried over to his staff. Attorney Joe Reinke served as the judge's law clerk after graduation from law school. "Outside of my father, Judge Thompson had the single greatest influence on my life. I would have done anything to make certain he doesn't think less of me." Reinke believes the judge is unique in his "magnificent handling of power with grace, wielding incredible power without maligning those around him."[33]

Marilyn Edens worked as Judge Thompson's law clerk for 15 years, although she had first met him when she was a student at OU and worked with him on an OU alumni committee. Recognizing him as a mentor, Edens sought the judge's advice when she decided to attend law school. He had taken the bench as a federal judge and Edens was hesitant to contact him. She remembered, "But he not only remembered me, he generously offered his time and advice about the law school experience and the practice of law."[34]

Judge Thompson's compassion was demonstrated to Edens on many occasions. When her elderly mother's health declined, she had to be absent from work. She said, "There was never a time that Judge Thompson questioned my absence. In fact, he continually offered his assistance and advice. He simply believes that family is first and foremost." When Edens husband suffered a heart attack, "Judge Thompson magically appeared to help." When her husband died, the judge delivered the eulogy. When Edens had a lengthy recuperation from cancer treatment, he offered support and counsel and never worried about her absence from work.[35]

CHAPTER 22

FOLLOWING THE LAW

*Judge Thompson always followed the law
even when the result was controversial.*

Judge Richard L. Bohanon

Many of the federal court cases assigned to Judge Thompson evoked public debate. In June, 1997, based upon a complaint from one citizen, Oklahoma City police officers scoured the city looking for copies of a critically-acclaimed motion picture, *The Tin Drum,* after a state district judge gave an informal opinion, without a hearing, that the film contained child pornography. The movie, which won the Oscar for Best Foreign Language Film of 1979, was based upon a 1959 novel by Gunter Grass, winner of the Nobel Prize for Literature in 1994.[1]

As soon as word leaked out that the police were acting as censors by seizing and removing copies of the film from bookstores, video tape outlets, and a private residence, civil rights groups and free speech advocates objected. The police action sparked international commentary and debate.

Michael Camfield, a member of the American Civil Liberties Union, filed a federal lawsuit which was assigned to Judge Thompson. The complaint asked the federal court to stop police from arresting Oklahoma County residents who wanted to watch *The Tin Drum*. A nationwide group representing video tape stores and distributors filed a second action asking that the censorship activities cease. A third case, filed by Oklahoma County District Attorney Bob Macy, sought a ruling on the film's alleged obscenity and asked for a permanent ban on its distribution.[2]

The "R" rated movie had won both the Academy Award and the Cannes International Film Festival Prize. It had been widely distributed in the United States and throughout the world for nearly 20 years. An edited version had been shown on television and it was available for rental in video stores and libraries. Judge Thompson and his staff could not find, and no evidence suggested, one single instance where the movie had been withdrawn from public access or subjected to any police or judicial censorship, much less ever being adjudicated as "child pornography."[3]

The legal action and the judge's pending ruling in the case was big news. Local newspapers and radio and television newscasts gave headline attention to the matter. Media and anti-censorship organizations across the country monitored his handling of the case in which motions were filed to require the return of all confiscated copies. The basis of the litigation was that the police action was an unconstitutional restraint on First Amendment rights.

The first and primary legal question that had to be considered was— could the police remove the film from public access without a prior adversarial hearing? Police officials testified that Oklahoma County District

Judge Richard Freeman had "ruled" that the film was child pornography after a copy was shown to him by a representative of the Oklahomans for Children and Families. ACLU attorney Michael Salem knew that was not the case. Instead, Freeman had simply given what he called "an advisory opinion," without a hearing.[4]

For months, the legal wrangling continued. The Oklahoma County Metropolitan Library Commission intervened in the case and officially opposed District Attorney Macy's attempt to permanently ban the movie from Oklahoma County.[5]

A temporary injunction was granted by Judge Thompson on Christmas Eve that ordered Oklahoma City police to return videotape copies of *The Tin Drum* to their rightful owners. After the emotionally charged debate, his ruling went straight to the heart of the legal argument:

> The court concludes that constitutional law requires that, before public officials take such action, they must first provide the interested parties an opportunity to present their contentions, evidence, and legal arguments for consideration before a court. Such a requirement is, under the law, an essential procedural safeguard.[6]

The order had the effect of forcing police to return confiscated copies to Blockbuster and Hollywood video stores, a Bethany public library branch, and private homes, including the plaintiff's, Michael Camfield. However, the emotional argument in Oklahoma County had a chilling effect upon distribution of the *The Tin Drum*. In early January, 1998, *The Daily Oklahoman* reported that video stores remained "undecided" on whether or not to restock their shelves with copies of the film. Library officials announced they would wait on the court's ruling on whether or not the entire film was obscene.[7]

The newspaper, on its editorial page, said it understood the judge's ruling that copies of the movie should not have been confiscated without a prior adversarial hearing. The newspaper said:

> But the law, even in Bill Clinton's America, retains many protections not only for parental rights but also for common sense. Childhood still is regarded, even in the law, as a time of vulnerability. That allows contemporary communities to leave in place some, but not all, curbs on youth access to salacious and/or dubious material.[8]

Judge Thompson personally agreed with the editorial position. It was consistent with his ruling.

The judge ruled that, under the facts and law, the film did not violate child pornography laws. He wrote:

> While the state has every right and duty to prohibit and criminalize such a profound evil as child pornography…the court concludes that the film in issue is not one that violates the law as claimed.[9]

The ruling had credibility. The judge had a long established reputation for being extremely tough on defendants convicted in child pornography and child victim cases.

After the ruling, Lee Brawner, executive director of the Metropolitan Library System, said, "We are happy with the ruling. We will be making available a film to our patrons that they never should have been denied the right to access."[10]

In a December, 1998, ruling in the lawsuit brought by the Video Software Dealers Association, Judge Thompson specifically found that the Oklahoma City police officers who rounded up copies of *The Tin Drum* violated a federal privacy law when they, without a search warrant, obtained the names of customers of video stores who had rented the movie. Some video stories claimed the officers had intimidated them and threatened them with arrest if they did not hand over the video rental information.[11]

The judge's rulings were affirmed on appeal.

CHAPTER 23

SENIOR STATUS

*Judge Thompson's career has truly been
that of a shooting star.*

Judge Lee West

In 1999, Judge Thompson made the decision to assume senior status, a designation of semi-retirement for federal judges allowed by Congress since 1919. A federal judge must be 65 years old and have served a statutory length of time to assume senior status with full salary and a potential part-time work load.[1] However, he made the very unusual choice to continue with a full-time judge's allocation of cases.

To celebrate the transition from active judge to senior judge, an elaborate ceremony was held in the federal courthouse on December 22, 1999. His family, fellow judges, court staff, and many friends appeared to talk about his life.

Judge Lee West joked:

> When I was a small boy growing up in the depths of
> Little Dixie, my father told me, "If you live long enough and
> look hard enough, you may someday find a good, decent man
> who is a Republican." Well, it's taken me a little over 70 years,
> but I think I finally located one in Ralph.[2]

Judge Wayne Alley said of him, "He is very thoughtful and in his professional life gives the deepest of study in his difficult cases." Judge Robin Cauthron, who had served first as the judge's law clerk, said, "He leaves a legacy in this courthouse for collegiality and courtesy and compassion. He leaves a legacy to the administration of justice through his work that cannot be ignored."[3]

Judge Tim Leonard used original "poetry" to describe his friend and colleague:

> While a few who were unprepared
> Trembled in fear,
> Most lawyers were glad it was Judge Thompson's court
> In which they had to appear,
> Because his opinions were always
> Concise and clear,
> And not far from stare decisis
> Did he ever veer.[4]

Oklahoma's two United States senators were present for the senior status ceremony. The judge's close friend, United States Senator Don Nickles added humor to the proceedings when he said, "Judge Thompson has shown great wisdom. His decision to marry Barbara was perhaps the

Judge Thompson's good friend, United States Senator Jim Inhofe, speaks at the judge's senior status ceremony with other judges and staff looking on.

best decision of his career." Senator Jim Inhofe talked about meeting the judge on the first day they served in the House of Representatives, how both of their fathers had suggested they needed to meet each other. Inhofe jokingly wondered out loud why the ceremony was taking place. He quipped, "It's my understanding you get the same money and you work less. I don't know what we are celebrating today!"[5]

Tenth Circuit Judge Robert Henry talked about the collegiality of the court, which he described as the most collegial district in the circuit. He gave Judge Thompson primary credit for the warmness he saw among the judges. Henry, always a wordsmith, said:

> Ralph Thompson is, to borrow a scientific term, a constant for me. He would deny it, but all in the black robes here know that he is the dean of this district. He is the architect of many of the careers in his room, judicial and otherwise… I think we are very much in the shape that newly-arrived French ambassador Thomas Jefferson was when he was asked in Paris if he were Dr. Benjamin Franklin's replacement. He answered, "No, I'm Dr. Franklin's successor. Dr. Franklin cannot be replaced." And neither can Ralph.[6]

As part of the senior status ceremony, Judge Henry read a letter from former President Gerald Ford. In part, the letter read, "As president, I was proud to nominate you in 1975 as federal judge…and I am equally proud of your outstanding service on the bench for the past 24 years."[7]

Chief Justice Rehnquist added his congratulations, "Your many contributions to the judiciary are appreciated by your colleagues and I am particularly grateful for your service on the Judicial Conference of the United States."[8]

Louis J. Freeh, director of the FBI, thanked Judge Thompson for always being fair to the nation's top law enforcement agency. He wrote, "You are deserving of the admiration and respect you enjoy among the ranks of the FBI, and the nation owes you a debt of gratitude for your lifetime of public service."[9]

The judge was humbled by the words of adulation from his friends and colleagues. Many former staff members were present. He pointed out that among his former law clerks were two law professors, the federal public defender for Oklahoma, a magistrate judge, many distinguished lawyers, and his "adored colleague on the court," Judge Cauthron. He promised he would not slack on his duty to the court:

> I do not intend for things to come to a halt, or to take long naps during workdays[looking at Judge West]. I will be on the job. Still, knowing that I have this strange attraction to such things as polar bears in the Arctic, the backstreets of Hanoi, the markets of Singapore, the lions of Africa, the character in the craggy face of a Panhandle pioneer, or the street scenes of Paris, and occasionally flying an unusual airplane, I do reserve the right to pursue a few adventures from time to time.[10]

When a federal district judge takes senior status, a vacancy occurs on the court. Judge Thompson's position was filled in 2001 by Joe L. Heaton, appointed by President George W. Bush. Heaton was a graduate of Northwestern Oklahoma State University and the OU College of Law, a legislative assistant to United States Senator Dewey Bartlett, a member of the Oklahoma House of Representatives for four terms, United States Attorney for the Western District of Oklahoma in 1992 and 1993, and First Assistant United States Attorney for the five years prior to being appointed to the federal bench.[11]

Judge Wayne Alley also took senior status, resulting in President

The judges of the Western District in 2002. Front row, left to right, David Russell, Chief Judge Robin Cauthron, Tim Leonard, and Stephen Friot. Back row, Judge Thompson, Wayne Alley, Joe Heaton, Lee West, and Vicki Miles-LaGrange.

Bush's appointment of Judge Stephen P. Friot in 2001. Before he assumed the federal bench in the Western District, Friot, a graduate of OU and the OU College of Law, had been a premier private practitioner in Oklahoma City since 1972.[12]

As his caseload remained the same, Judge Thompson and fellow judges continued their daily lunches together at the Faculty House on the OU Health Sciences Center campus and other local restaurants. The lunches often turned to story time, with judges remembering historic, humorous moments involving judges of the Western District.

He enjoyed telling the story of Judge Alfred P. Murrah when he was being considered by President Franklin D. Roosevelt for appointment to the federal district court. His sponsor, Senator Josh Lee, was meeting with Roosevelt in the Oval Office. Roosevelt said, "Josh, this young Murrah looks fine, but I thought there was some medical problem we should talk about." Senator Lee was perplexed and said, "I don't know about any medical condition, but let me step outside and call Murrah." Lee reached Murrah by telephone and asked him if he had kept any medical problem from him and what he should say to the President about it. Murrah said,

"Senator, just tell President Roosevelt there is nothing wrong with Murrah that a lifetime appointment wouldn't cure!"[13]

Another favorite story was of a colleague sentencing a Nigerian defendant with a heavy British accent. The man repeatedly addressed the judge as "Your Excellency." Finally, the defendant's lawyer interrupted the man and said, "Your honor, may I have a private word with my client?" The judge agreed. However, the lawyer did not realize the sensitive microphone at the lectern would broadcast the following conversation all over the courtroom. The lawyer told his client, "Stop calling him 'Your Excellency,' you are to address the court as 'Your Honor.'" The defendant answered, "All right, but I rather think he likes it." Judge Thompson and his fellow judges at lunch voted and agreed that the judge in question probably had liked it.[14]

On another occasion, during one of his trials, a witness paused to collect his thoughts before answering the key question of the case. Parties and jurors were sitting on the edge of their seats when, breaking the silence, was the piercing, high-volume sound of a rooster crowing. Stunned, the judge wondered "what in the world was happening." One of the lawyers was digging through his briefcase and the rooster stopped crowing. The red-faced lawyer apologized profusely, explaining that his rooster alarm clock had malfunctioned. Judge Thompson remembered, "No one in the courtroom could keep a straight face. We all got a big laugh out of it and the drama of the testimony was lost." He liked the idea of a rooster alarm clock and purchased his own, which he awakened to each morning for years.[15]

Sometimes, lawyers misspoke. During a case involving several expert witnesses, one party's lawyer was snidely baiting the witness into claiming the other party's expert was "incompetent." But, in his haste, he didn't ask, "Are you claiming our expert is 'incompetent?'" Instead, he asked, "Are you claiming our expert is 'INCONTINENT?'" As muffled snorts and giggles were heard through the courtroom, the lawyer said, "Your honor, perhaps I should rephrase the question." The judge was quick to agree.[16]

One of the favorite courtroom tales involved a personal injury case being heard before Judge Alley. The plaintiff's lawyer called an expert witness to testify about the plaintiff's emotional distress. The expert was asked to leave the witness stand, approach a blackboard, and write on the blackboard the areas which he expected to discuss. When the expert wrote, "The Meaning of Life," Judge Alley quickly interrupted and said,

"Doctor, you may return to your seat because the meaning of life is not a proper subject for expert testimony. Expert testimony is allowed only when it will provide information and opinion not in the general knowledge of the jury." Alley said, in his opinion, each juror knew as much about the meaning of life as did the expert.

The plaintiff's lawyer objected to the dismissal of his witness. Judge Alley said, "Overruled!" Then, the defendant's counsel rose to his feet and said, "I, too, object!" Alley said, "You have no standing to object. I have just ruled in your favor." The defense lawyer said, "I know, your honor, but I have always wanted to know 'the meaning of life.'"[17]

An oft-told story at lunches or meetings of judges involved Judge Thompson "being taken in" by behind-the-scenes mischief planned by Judge West with his helper, Judge Russell. West was nationally known for raising and training bird dogs. Judge Thompson was having problems training a new English bulldog and asked if he could borrow an electric collar from West that was used to train bird dogs. The collar emitted shocks to the dog as part of its training.

West remembered, "It was a wonderful opportunity for Russell and me to test our friendship with Ralph." They conspired. When they approached him with the collar, it was pre-planned that Russell would hold the collar and West would pretend to turn on the current. It was off, so Russell said, "It just feels like a little tickle and doesn't hurt." Then the collar was handed to Judge Thompson who put his fingers on the prongs. When West turned the collar to full force, he was startled. West described the scene:

> When I hit it with the full charge, his lips went white and his hair literally stood straight out. He screamed and flung the dog collar to get rid of it. He actually said a few bad words. I thought to myself, maybe we've gone a little far this time.[18]

Judge Thompson was quick to say, "So much for judicial collegiality!" Fortunately, for the three dear friends, they made up and continued their "fast friendship."

Throughout his judicial career Judge Thompson received high marks from lawyers who frequented his courtroom. Each year, *The Almanac of the Federal Judiciary* contained a section of "Lawyers' Evaluation" of each federal judge in the nation. In 2001, the publisher summarized interviews with lawyers:

Thompson has an excellent demeanor and is always courteous to lawyers. "He's very bright." "He's a fine judge." "He's always well-prepared." He has an amazing ability to anticipate the legal issues before they come up and has them researched." "He is somebody, that, if you have a problem, you can go to and talk to." "He gives everyone a chance to have their say." "He doesn't let anything get out of control." "He's right down the middle." "He believes in defendants' rights and wants to err on the side of caution, so if there is a close call, he gives it to the defendant." "In sentencing, he's strict. He's a tough, law and order judge."[19]

Attorney Burton Johnson said, "Judge Thompson always showed wisdom beyond his years."[20] Lawyer Larry Ottaway said the judge had a "deep understanding" of the trial process and gave each lawyer the opportunity to adequately represent his or her client.[21] Attorney John A. Kenney applauded the judge for always taking "quick, decisive, and tough action" in difficult situations without affecting a case from the jury's standpoint.[22]

A testimonial of Judge Thompson's fairness and common sense came from attorney Harry A. Woods, Jr., who said, "I have seen him manage a trial with an even hand, sometimes in precarious positions when an errant word could result in a mistrial. His common sense was unmatched."[23] Attorney William H. Campbell attributed Judge Thompson's success and longevity to simply treating everyone who walked into his courtroom with "incredible respect and dignity."[24]

As Judge Thompson's public service exceeded three decades, awards were commonplace. Following his election to alumnus membership in Phi Beta Kappa in 1975, and, in 1983, to The Order of the Coif, the top academic honor that can be bestowed upon law students, additional honors followed. In 1991, he was named Phi Beta Kappa of the Year by the Oklahoma City Phi Beta Kappa Association, a group that both he and his father served as president. When the judge was presented the honor, he was brimming with pride when he noted that his daughters, Elaine and Maria, had just been elected, as students, to Phi Beta Kappa at OU.

The judge was awarded the OU Regents' Alumni Award in 1990 and its Distinguished Service Award, OU's highest honor in association with its Alumni Association, in 1993. He presided at the inauguration of

President David L. Boren in 1995.

In 2001, he won the *Journal Record* Award for distinguished service to the legal profession. In his 40th year since becoming a lawyer, the judge followed in the footsteps of previous award winners that included legends such as his father, Lee B. Thompson, Granville Tomerlin, Elliott Fenton, Fred Dunlevy, John Couch, James Fellers, Luther Bohanon, Fred Daugherty, and Howard K. Berry, Sr.[25] In 2003, Judge Thompson received the Oklahoma City Public Schools Foundation's Wall of Fame Humanitarian Award.

OU Law Professor R. Dale Vliet presents Judge Thompson his certificate of honorary membership in The Order of the Coif in 1983 for high distinction in scholarly achievements since graduating from law school.

When Judge Thompson was named Oklahoma City's "Phi Beta Kappa of the Year" in 1997, he was presented the award by longtime friend Hannah Atkins, his former colleague in the Oklahoma House of Representatives, former Oklahoma Secretary of State, and United States Delegate to the United Nations.

In 1993, Judge Thompson was awarded OU's Distinguished Service Award. Left to right, Elaine Thompson, the Judge, Barbara Thompson, Maria Thompson, Lisa Campbell, and Frank Campbell.

FLYING AND PHOTOGRAPHY

Becoming a pilot was the fulfillment of my boyhood dream.
It was part of my nature. I also learned to appreciate
the art of capturing the special things and
moments of life with a camera.

Judge Ralph G. Thompson

Ralph was nearing completion of civilian pilot training when he was appointed federal district judge in 1975. He was so determined to wrap up the training before the new responsibilities of the judgeship took over his life that he often logged night flying hours before daylight. He was sworn in as a judge on October 20, 1975, and received his pilot's license five days later. While he did not have much time for recreational flying after he assumed the bench, he was slated to have some of the adventures of his life in the air thanks to others.

Judge Thompson had good friends "in the right places" to earn him cockpit time in unique aircraft. He and friend, Colonel Bob Lammerts, retired Marine Corsair pilot, flew his open cockpit Stearman bi-plane. It brought back memories of the airplanes that flew over his grandparents' home in Norman during World War II. Later, the judge and his pilot pals, Jim Fentriss and Jim Inhofe, flew in Inhofe's Stearman, The Spirit of Tulsa. He enjoyed doing loops, rolls, and other aerobatic maneuvers in the "wonderful open cockpit plane."[1]

When General Richard Burpee was commander of the Oklahoma City Air Logistics Center at Tinker Air Force Base in 1983, Judge Thompson and Barbara were dining with the Burpees on base when he asked Burpee what was the favorite airplane he had ever flown. Burpee quickly cited the T-6, commonly called the "terrible Texan," because of its propensity to ground loop during landings. Burpee had trained in the T-6 many years before as an aviation cadet.[2]

The following day, Judge Thompson called Burpee and said he had arranged for both of them to fly T-6s at Wiley Post Airport in Oklahoma City. Bill Dahlgren flew with Burpee and the judge flew with Jim Fentriss. The general said, "It was a beautiful clear day and we flew for about an hour in formation all over the city. I was in seventh heaven and the judge flying on our wing was busy taking photographs and capturing the moment."[3]

After landing, Judge Thompson asked Burpee if he had ever flown a P-51 Mustang. When Burpee replied it had been his dream to do so, the judge pointed across the ramp where a P-51 was parked. The judge had prearranged the opportunity for the two of them to fly the Mustang.[4]

Thanks to the Air Force, Judge Thompson was given a flight in a F-16 jet fighter, joining an active duty pilot in the tandem seat, dual control, training version of the aircraft. Once the plane was in the air, the judge was given generous time at the controls with loops, rolls, Chandelles, and split-S maneuvers. He also was allowed to fly the Air Force's

A-7 Corsair II, a single-engine jet air-to-ground fighter.[5]

The Thompsons flew to London for the judge's next great flying adventure. Through a British historian and travel friend, the judge was invited to come to England to fly the British Spitfire, a hero of the Battle of Britain. The aircraft helped save England from Nazi invasion by defeating the German Luftwaffe and denying them air superiority on which the invasion depended. The particular Spitfire that he flew was the aircraft credited with shooting down the first enemy plane on D-Day during the Normandy invasion in World War II and was credited with other combat victories.[6]

The plane had been converted to a tandem seat, dual-control trainer. The judge sat in the back seat with a veteran pilot in the front seat as the Spitfire took off from a grass strip from the old Royal Air Force field at Duxford. With the smooth roar of the Rolls-Royce Merlin engine, the Spitfire was put through one hour and twenty seven minutes of aerobatics in the skies of the Battle of Britain. For the judge, with generous time at the controls, it was one of the most unforgettable experiences of his life. Later, the friendly guests at the tiny nearby Nutshell Pub, the smallest pub in England, welcomed him with "a pint" to celebrate his first flight in a Spitfire.[7]

His last flying adventure was at Vance Air Force Base in Enid, Oklahoma. He flew with an instructor pilot in the Air Force super-sonic

Old friends, United States Senator Jim Inhofe, left, and Judge Thompson prepare to fly Inhofe's Stearman bi-plane, *The Spirit of Tulsa.*

trainer, the T-38. "I couldn't get enough of it," he said, "performing aerobatics in such a spectacular airplane." After his disappointment of leaving the Air Force pilot training program decades before, he was just happy to be a pilot and to be treated to unique and memorable flying experiences.[8]

His other passion has been photography. His interest in photography began with the joy of taking photographs of Barbara and the children when they were young. It spread to photographing other friends' children and to nature and wildlife. "The transition from children to wildlife was pretty easy," he said. His and Barbara's love for travel complimented his entrance into photography as a serious hobby. He was fascinated with other people, places, and cultures, and photographing them became a life passion.

He is fascinated "capturing the images of nature and its creatures and of ordinary people doing ordinary things in interesting places and circumstances." He sees things that others do not. Photography has sharpened his eye to see forms, colors, details, relationships, textures, designs, and behavior. He said, "Being more observant has been life enhancing for me."[9]

Through the years, he has photographed people, places, and things on every continent. He prides himself in capturing the moment and the wild subjects and leaving them as he found them—alive, uninjured, and

Left to right, Jim Fentriss, General Dick Burpee, and Judge Thompson with big smiles after formation flying in venerable T-6s at Oklahoma City's Wiley Post Airport in 1983.

undisturbed. His photographic missions have led him to Polar bears in Canada, elephants, hippos, giraffes, lions, and cheetahs in Africa, penguins in Antarctica, mountain goats and Bald Eagles in Alaska, and mountain lions, wolves and bears in Montana and Wyoming.

Some of his photographs have been published. A daybreak scene at Red Square in Moscow in 1964 appeared in *Friends,* a General Motors publication. Several photos have been included in *Photographer's Forum-Best of Photography.*[10]

The Daily Oklahoman has featured Judge Thompson's travel and wildlife photographs on two occasions. In September, 1999, the entire "Destinations" section of the Sunday newspaper added six photographs to the text to help describe his trip to Africa. In April, 2001, ten photographs accompanied his story about his trip to Antarctica. The feature article was titled, "Unspoiled Continent—Antarctica piques interest of explorers."[11]

On purpose, the judge has never sold a photograph, but has given many to others which adorn their homes. He also enjoys donating them to fundraising events for charitable causes such as United Appeal and Habitat for Humanity and to benefit schools and churches. It gives him great pleasure to present photographs of a child or grandchild to a friend. "I've never lost a friend doing that," he said.

Judge Thompson was privileged to fly the famed British Spitfire at the Royal Air Force Base at Duxford, England, in 1997.

He published a book of his photographs titled *Essences I, People, Places and Things.* In the preface, he wrote:

The title: "Essences" is not a word. I made it up. I mean it to be the plural of essence, which is the one word that best describes why I took these photographs. They seemed to be the essence of wherever I was at the time. Because there are so many, I exercised a little literary license and added an "s."

Some of the photographic adventures have been challenging. Special photographs of mountain lions, wolves, bears, and Bald Eagles have come after waiting long hours in the snow and cold. A close encounter with a cobra, tense times with lions in Africa, and crawling through Viet Cong tunnels near the Cambodian border in Vietnam have been part of the adventure.[12]

The judge's photography has been made better by his association with prize-winning wildlife and nature photographer Tom Murphy, whose images have been featured on public television and in *National Geographic* and other publications. Judge Thompson said, "As a mentor, Tom has taught me 'how to see' and how to more expertly and creatively capture what is seen." The two have shared challenging moments in different places of the world photographing many creatures of the wild. Tom and his wife, Bonnie, have become good friends of the Thompsons.[13]

The judge flew the T-38 supersonic trainer with instructor pilot, Major Ryan Link, left, at Vance Air Force Base at Enid, Oklahoma.

One of Judge Thompson's published and award-winning nature and wildlife photographs, "Mother's Day," was taken in Montana in the winter of 1993.

"Symmetry," taken by Judge Thompson in Kenya, East Africa, in 1999.

On a trip to Australia, Judge Thompson took this photograph of an Aboriginal man.

"Reading in Saigon," taken by the judge in Saigon, Ho Chi Minh City, Vietnam in 1996.

Judge Thompson took this photograph of a napping polar bear near Churchill, Manitoba, Canada, in the winter of 1994. He called the photograph, "Senior Status," and presented it to his judicial colleagues when they have taken senior status.

CHAPTER 25

A LOVING AND ACCOMPLISHED FAMILY

*A good family, good friends, and good health
are the most important blessings of life. To be sure,
I have had all three in abundance.*

Judge Ralph G. Thompson

Judge Thompson saw in his parents a blueprint for making his own family successful. He never knew two people more totally devoted to each other than his parents. "Their total integrity, good character, generosity, and well-earned regard as a perfect lady and a true gentleman gave us the ideal example," he said.[1]

Many families have been torn by friction through the decades—but not the Thompsons. The judge has enjoyed lifelong closeness with his brother, Lee, and sister, Carolyn. "We have laughed our way through life," he said. Lee, his late wife, Ann, and Carolyn and her husband, Don Zachritz, long ago formed "The Humility Committee," to keep brother Ralph from getting a swelled head because of his many accomplishments. Lee said, "We were not afraid to get all over his case if we had the slightest inkling of this happening. Ann was chairman of the board and was not shy."[2]

In a more serious tone, Lee said, "His accomplishments have brought a great sense of pride to me. His awards are many and meaningful and it warms my heart. I am very proud to call him my brother."[3] The judge is a proud and devoted brother as well.

He is also proud of his sister, a highly-regarded church and civic volunteer, and brother-in-law, Don, a successful Oklahoma City businessman and civic leader. They have enjoyed more than 50 years of happy marriage. Lee is a successful Certified Life Underwriter and civic leader in Enid. In 2008, Judge Thompson and Barbara, Lee, and Don and Carolyn teamed up on a Mediterranean cruise with stops in Barcelona, Monte Carlo, Corsica, Sorrento, and Rome. Lee's children, Kathi, Lee B. Thompson, III, "Trippy," and Suzy, and Carolyn's children, Anne, Jeff, and David, and their families have added to the fun and pleasure of the growing family.[4]

Of her brother, Carolyn said, "Ralph's most consistent lifelong trait is his ability to be super enthusiastic about whatever he is doing at the time."[5] The judge has enjoyed an enduring kinship with his cousins, Bill and the late Barbara Bizzell Barry, Mary Ann Thompson Denman, and the late Dr. Wayman Thompson, Jr., and their families. Wayman and the judge were only one month apart in age and were like brothers. After his untimely death in 1969, Judge Thompson maintained a close friendship with his wife, Ann Rivers, and their daughter, Susan. The judge and Barbara have also been close to Barbara's younger sister, Patricia, and her husband John Schoen and their children, Johnny and Laura.[6]

To honor their parents, Judge Thompson, Lee, and Carolyn established the Lee B. Thompson Scholarship at the OU College of Law and funded the Elaine Bizzell Thompson Garden at the site of her father, Dr. Bizzell's statue, on the OU campus in Norman.

Not long after the judge and Barbara were married, they began planning a family. They lived in a comfortable rented bungalow at 1102 Park Manor on the edge of Nichols Hills when their first baby, Lisa, was born. The family, that included an English bulldog, enjoyed the house and their neighbors.

The Thompsons moved to larger quarters, at 1109 Huntington, a house that became their home for the next 27 years. "It was good that we moved," the judge said, "because when our twins, Elaine and Maria, were born we became a family of three little girls under 27 months old and an English bulldog. In our neighborhood, 31 children lived in one block. Life was good."[7]

Barbara said, "Life with Ralph as my loving partner is rich with positive experiences—the true gentleman, the thoughtfulness, the military bearing and precision, the love of the law of his father, and the kindness, caring, and consideration of others, a trait of both his parents." When Ralph was recommended for a federal judgeship, Barbara's immediate reaction was that he would make a good judge. She said, "His nature is to be fair. He has an innate sense of fairness. He's a good decision maker."[8]

As Oklahoma's and the National Mother of the Year in 1995,

The Elaine Bizzell Thompson Garden was dedicated in front of the William B. Bizzell Library on the OU campus in Norman on Mother's Day, 1988. Left to right, Carolyn Thompson Zachritz, Judge Thompson, Elaine Bizzell Thompson, Lee B. Thompson, Jr., and Lee B. Thompson.

Barbara traveled throughout the nation speaking in support of American Mothers, Inc., and the organization's efforts to promote worthy causes benefiting families and childcare.

Barbara's French teaching career began on educational television with the Oklahoma City public schools. She later taught in the Putnam City schools and at Heritage Hall Middle School.

She was appointed Honorary Consul of France for Oklahoma by the French government in 2000. During her ten-year term, she assisted hundreds of Oklahoma and French citizens in important and sometimes compelling and critical situations. In 2006, she received France's Legion of Honor, the Chevalier de la Legion d'Honneur, that country's highest honor for civilian service which has existed since the days of Napoleon. The honor was conferred by French President Jacques Chirac and announced by Jean-David Levitte, the French ambassador to the United States.[9]

Among other honors, Barbara was recipient of The University of Oklahoma Regents Award and the OU College of Arts and Sciences 2002 Distinguished OU Alumnus Award. She received the 2007 Jeannine Rainbolt College of Education Meritorious Service Award. She was president of the OU Bizzell Library Society and president of the OU

On a Mediterranean cruise in 2006, left to right, Lee B. Thompson, Jr., Carolyn Thompson Zachritz, Don Zachritz, Barbara Thompson, and the Judge.

Barbara, appointed Honorary Consul of France for Oklahoma, receives the French
Legion of Honor, that country's highest honor for civilian service, from Patrick Berron,
Consul General of France, right, in 2006.

Mom's Association. In 2007, Barbara was named a Friend of Foreign
Languages by the Oklahoma Foreign Language Teachers' Association.
She received the Outstanding Alumna Award from the OU Panhellenic
Association and the Chi Omega Alumnae Achievement Award from the
Chi Omega Alumnae of Oklahoma. She has served for many years as a
member of the board of directors of the Oklahoma Historical Society,
both appointed and elected. She was originally appointed to the board by
Governor Henry Bellmon.[10]

In 2011, Barbara received the Oklahoma City Junior League's highest honor, the Mary Baker Rumsey Lifetime Commitment Award, for
her lifetime of volunteer achievement and commitment to community
service. Judge Thompson said, "Barbara has done all this, and more, qui-
etly and modestly, never calling attention to herself and always putting
the other person first, while making real contributions for the betterment
of our state and our people, especially our children."[11]

To longtime friends and new acquaintances alike, it is obvious that
Barbara has the same endearing feelings about her husband. She said, "I

say with great affection that Ralph is the best, always a loving, caring, engaged husband, father, and in recent years, grandfather, without peer!" With accolades that most husbands strive for, Barbara calls her husband "my best friend," "my confidant," "my partner," and "a most attentive husband." [12]

The Thompsons are enthralled with their children and grandchildren. The judge said, "Lisa, Elaine, and Maria are the most wonderful people any parent could ever hope for and, to us, they are, too, Mothers of the Year, every year. And our adored eleven grandchildren? Well, how much time do you have?"

All three daughters began their schooling at St. John's Episcopal School in Oklahoma City where they received an excellent grounding in a happy and nurturing atmosphere with fine teachers.

Lisa went on to Casady School and graduated Magna Cum Laude with the Trustees' Award given by the Headmaster and faculty. A beautiful ballet dancer, she performed in many performances of *The Nutcracker* as an apprentice to the Oklahoma City Ballet Company and attended the New York Summer School of Arts.

"Being a Thompson was all about character," Lisa said. "Daddy instilled traditions by telling us about his childhood. He shared the pranks and silly stories, times of uncertainty, hopes, dreams, and his childhood friends who meant the world to him." [13]

Their father prepared Lisa, Elaine, and Maria for the real world by relating stories of "how he fell in love" with their mother and what it meant to him "when he lost a special friend to sickness or an accident."

As a gangly teenager with braces, trying to navigate her social life at Casady, Lisa received special attention from her father. She said, "My Daddy helped me feel beautiful even when I was convinced I wasn't. He sympathized with me when my English compositions and math challenges seemed impossible. He helped me keep a sense of humor and... always found a way to celebrate my skills." [14]

Next, it was on to the University of Oklahoma. At OU, Lisa was president of her pledge class of Kappa Kappa Gamma and graduated with a degree in English. She was a member of the President's Leadership Class and served the university as a campus tour guide. In 1988, she was Oklahoma's Cherry Blossom Princess for the Cherry Blossom Festival in Washington, D.C. That same year she graduated from OU and moved to the nation's capital to join the FBI.

Assigned to the FBI's National Security Division, she wrote briefing books for the FBI director. As an Intelligence Operations Specialist, she began a top secret, critical, and interesting career in the nation's foreign counterintelligence activities.

Lisa married Frank Andrew Scott Campbell, a Washington, D.C. lawyer, on May 25, 1991, at All Souls Episcopal Church in Oklahoma City. Frank left private practice to become assistant general counsel of the FBI and later became Deputy Assistant Attorney General of the United States in the Justice Department's Office of Legal Policy. After 14 years of government service, he founded his own consulting firm. Lisa interrupted her 15-year career at the FBI to raise her three children in their 100-year-old home in northwest Washington, D.C.

Lisa is an active volunteer leader in her childrens' schools. Christianne and Chloe attend the National Cathedral School and Colin the Norwood School in nearby Maryland. All are excellent students.[15]

Lisa has fond memories of her childhood. "Daddy's hard work, discipline, accountability, honesty, and having parents who really love me are examples I am trying to pass on to my own children," she said. She also remembers waiting for her father to come home from Air Force duty. She said, "He could come home, dressed in his handsome blue uniform with lightning bolts on his cap and I was so proud of him."[16]

Left to right, Frank Campbell, Judge Thompson, Lisa Thompson Campbell, baby Christie Campbell, and FBI Director Louis J. Freeh at FBI headquarters in Washington, D.C.

Lisa was an accomplished ballet dancer.

Lisa Thompson Campbell and husband, Frank, crossing the finish line at the Marine Corp Marathon in Washington, D.C.

Lisa described what she calls her "Daddy's Walk:"

He walks with purpose and enthusiasm everywhere he goes. He walks in every door with a smile, a determined presence, and a hearty greeting. His secretary could always recognize him coming down the hallway of the courthouse. Even on my wedding day, as we were walking down the aisle, he was walking me with his usual determined gait of pride and gusto. I had to say, "Daddy, let's go a little bit slower. I want to treasure the moment."[17]

Elaine and Maria chose Bishop McGuinness Catholic High School after graduating from St. John's Episcopal School. Both devoted twins had closely parallel careers. Both were award-winning gymnasts and performing ballet dancers. They had shared the honor of "outstanding graduate" and "outstanding musician" at St. John's. At McGuinness, both were varsity cheerleaders and members of the National Honor Society.

The federal courthouse housed some very unlikely visitors during the Thompson daughters' ballet seasons. Judge Thompson spent many fall Sunday afternoons entertaining his daughters and their ballet dancer friends between the matinee and evening performances of *The Nutcracker*

Lisa and her family enjoying Canada. In front, Colin Campbell. Back row, left to right, Chloe, Frank, Lisa, and Christie Campbell.

Elaine, Lisa, and Maria provided great joy to the Thompson family.

by Ballet Oklahoma. Rather than return to their homes, the little ballerinas went to the judge's chambers in the federal courthouse. Barbara said, "There were little girls everywhere. There was a room for snacking, a room for resting, a room for homework, and a room for dancing." Court security officers enjoyed the very unusual break from their routine.[18]

The judge was "team doctor" for his daughters and their friends at every family outing. He had a shoebox of medications. Barbara remembered, "He had medicine for almost any minor affliction. Splinter removal was his specialty."[19]

Following in the footsteps of their older sister, as well as their family tradition, both Elaine and Maria chose OU as their college destination and both pledged Kappa Kappa Gamma.

All three Thompson daughters enjoyed happiness and success for all of their years at OU. They were proud of their family's long standing ties to the university. They loved the presence of their great grandfather Bizzell's imposing statue facing the library bearing his name on the beautiful South Oval of the campus and were proudly aware of the scholarly distinction and deep affection that it symbolized. That is an awareness shared by all of the Thompson family.

Elaine performs on the bars as an award-winning gymnast at Gymnastics Oklahoma.

Maria, also an award-winning gymnast, concludes her floor exercise.

The Thompson family hiking in the Rocky Mountains of Utah in 1982. Left to right, Elaine, Maria, Lisa, Barbara, and the Judge.

Elaine was a member of the President's Leadership Class, Mortar Board, Crimson Club, was selected for the Women's Letzeiser Honor List, and was elected to Phi Beta Kappa. In 1989, she studied French language, culture, and literature at La Sorbonne in Paris and received a Bachelor of Arts in Letters from OU in 1991.[20]

Both Elaine and Maria followed the tradition set by their father and grandfather in attending law school at OU, becoming their family's third generation of OU Law graduates, receiving their Juris Doctor degrees in 1994.

Elaine became associated with a leading Oklahoma City law firm and later became assistant general counsel of Hobby Lobby, Inc. While at the firm, she met and fell in love with Tim DeGiusti, an honor graduate of OU in Ethics and Religion and from OU Law, and later a federal judge. They were married February 21, 1998, at All Souls Episcopal Church. As a "bonus," the Thompson family was blessed with Tony and Joey DeGiusti, Tim's young sons from a prior marriage.

Maria, Lisa, and Elaine as students at the University of Oklahoma.

Tony, an OU graduate, is now a deputy United States Marshal and Joey is an undergraduate at OU. Elaine and Tim added to the family two more children, Ellen and Jack, both excelling at Westminster School in Oklahoma City.

Elaine is named for her grandmother, Elaine Bizzell Thompson. The DeGiustis live in the Thompson family home where Judge Thompson spent his teenage years. Elaine is thankful for her father exposing her sisters and her to a "healthy balance of many things that helped us to be well rounded."[21]

Happy family activities took many different forms. Her father's piano playing, entirely "by ear," was special for Elaine:

Sometimes I would sit on his lap while he played, and I would put my hands on his hands to learn. He indulged our games and was our piano player for pretend singing concerts with our friends. He would play the tunes to songs we made up without commenting on the silly titles and lyrics.[22]

For Elaine, her father's parenting style was positive, effortless, and natural. She said:

He is a proud and loving father. With our mother, he has attended every school event, gymnastics meet, piano recital, ballet performance, track meet, band concert, cheerleading event,

Three generations of OU Law graduates. Left to right, Elaine Thompson DeGiusti, class of '94, Judge Thompson, class of '61, Lee B. Thompson, class of '27, and Maria Thompson Abbott, class of '94. Courtesy University of Oklahoma.

With Lisa, the family celebrates Elaine and Maria's graduation from OU in 1991 at the foot of the statue of Judge Thompson's grandfather, Dr. William Bennett Bizzell, OU's fifth president.

and graduation, with enthusiasm.[23] Even in their 40s, Elaine and her sisters all call their father "Daddy." Elaine said, "It reflects our affection for him and the lifetime of love he's given us."[24]

Elaine, as a busy mother, wife of a federal judge, and member of the Oklahoma Bar Association, also uses her legal training and leadership skills as a leader in school and charitable causes and as a volunteer in the community.

Maria also graduated from OU with a Bachelor of Arts in Letters with Distinction in 1991. She, too, was a member of the President's Leadership Class, Mortar Board, Crimson Club, was selected for the Women's Letzeiser Honor List, and elected to Phi Beta Kappa. After graduating from the OU College of Law in 1994, she practiced with a distinguished Oklahoma City law firm until she "retired" to raise her children.

How Maria met her husband, Craig, is an appealing story. While in law school, she made an appointment with a Norman dermatologist to examine a problem on her foot. The physician she was scheduled to see was not there, so Maria had to see a "moon-lighting, handsome young

Elaine and her family. Left to right, Jack, Tony, Elaine, Tim, Beau, Ellen, and Joey.

Thompson grandchildren at play. Front row, left to right, Colin Campbell, Christie Campbell, Claire Abbott, and Eric Abbott. Second row, Chloe Campbell, Ellen DeGiusti, and
Rachel Abbott. On top is Jack DeGiusti.

dermatology resident," Dr. Craig Abbott. The doctor-patient relationship
later blossomed into a romance.[25]

Maria and Craig were married on June 1, 1996, also at All Souls
Episcopal Church. Craig had a son, Kyle, by a previous marriage, another
blessed "bonus" for the Thompson family. He is a gifted student at the
University of California at San Diego. Maria and Craig have three
other children, Claire, Eric, and Rachel, all accomplished students at
Westminster School.

Maria points to her childhood of learning basic values from her
parents. She learned effort, fairness, honesty, generosity of spirit toward
others, and the importance of close family and friends. She said:

> Our childhood reflects Daddy's attitude toward life and oth-
> ers—down to earth, genuine, and devoted. Despite the authority and
> prestige of his positions, his sense of humor, strong sense of fairness,
> and genuine interest in others, has kept us all very well grounded.[26]

Maria and her husband, Dr. Craig Abbott, enjoy a Santa Fe sunset.

"To me," Maria said, "all of this adds up to a dad who has always involved me in his life—one who has always been there for me to be happy and secure and to help me fulfill my potential and my dreams."[27]

Maria continues her membership in the Oklahoma Bar Association and uses her legal training and leadership skills as an active volunteer in school, civic, and charitable causes. She enjoys her support in husband Craig's busy dermatology/pathology practice. Craig also pursues his interest in zoology as a life director of the Oklahoma Zoological Society and as chairman of the board of visitors at OU's Sam Noble Museum of Natural History, one of the world's largest university-based natural history museums.[28]

All three daughters describe an impish side to the judge. They said:

As a grandfather, after the serious business of holding court all day, he would play peek-a-boo with us at the front door when we would come to visit. He would make silly faces for his grandchildren by arranging bananas and apples and squash on the dining room table, to the delight of all, and

Maria and family on a trip to Yosemite National Park in California. Left to right, Eric, Claire, Kyle, Rachel, Craig, and Maria.

would play our favorite camp songs on the piano while his grandchildren danced to do their best to raise the roof.[29] Reflecting on his family life, the judge said:

Watching our daughters develop so beautifully and happily through the years, becoming talented, wholesome, popular, capable, and contributing young women, wives, and mothers makes one thing very clear—no adventures, positions, or honors combined could ever come close to the importance of the pure joy and pleasure that all of our daughters have given us and that includes their great husbands and adorable children.[30]

In his remarks on the ceremonial occasion when he took senior status as a federal judge, he expressed his sentiments:

To Barbara, my loving and lovely wife, you are, to me, the wife, mother, and grandmother of the year, every day of every year. To our daughters, Lisa, Elaine, and Maria (their names always have sounded like a song to me) my greatest gift is your love. My greatest pride is in you. My greatest success would

The Thompsons on a trip to Versailles, France, in 1987. Left to right, the Judge, Maria, Lisa, Elaine, and Barbara.

be to make you proud of me. You can sure pick husbands. Frank Campbell, Craig Abbott, and Tim DeGiusti are three of the finest young men I have ever known. Your children, our grandchildren, are, well, works of art. And to my parents, I thank them for giving me the priceless gift of their examples of good character, high standards, the value of striving, generosity, fairness, concern for others, and, I hope, their patented family indomitable spirit.[31]

The judge considers his family the pride and joy of his life. That is evident to friends such as Jane Harlow, whose late husband, Jim, was the judge's college roommate. She said, "Ralph is the ultimate family person. He was devoted to his parents as well as his siblings, wife, children, and grandchildren."[32]

The Thompson family in 2008. Front row, left to right, Chloe Campbell, Jack DeGiusti, Ellen DeGiusti, Rachel Abbott, Claire Abbott, and Eric Abbott. Back row, Frank Campbell,

Colin Campbell, Lisa Campbell, Joey DeGiusti, Christie Campbell, Tony DeGiusti, Elaine DeGiusti, Tim DeGiusti, Kyle Abbott, Craig Abbott, Maria Abbott, Barbara Thompson, and Judge Thompson.

CHAPTER 26

FRIENDS
AND TRAVEL

*Ralph is an accomplished adventurer, explorer, and photographer,
but it is his rare sense of kindness and appreciation he shows
for others that sets him so far apart.*

Judge Layn R. Phillips

In 1995, with all three girls gone from home, Judge Thompson and Barbara left their home of 27 years and moved to a new home on Northwest 39th Street. With plenty of bedrooms and a nice pool, it has been a perfect place for family gatherings. It also gave the Thompsons the pleasure of living across the street from dear friends, the late Dr. Henry and Josie Freede, a noted philanthropist, distinguished civic leader, and another fellow inductee of the Oklahoma Hall of Fame.

"Ralph is the kindest, most thoughtful neighbor anyone could have," Josie Freede said. He picks up her papers every morning and puts them outside her door. If he goes out of town, he leaves a note with the papers telling Josie where he will be and leaves a phone number. In time of scary weather, the judge keeps in touch with Josie and comes and gets her to sip cocoa and wait out the storm in the Thompson basement.[1]

When Josie's mother died, she ran across the street barefoot and asked the judge to come quickly to see what was wrong. Josie said, "He calmly took care of everything. He arranged for a doctor to come and for the funeral home to pick up mother. Months later, I was going to thank the doctor, but Ralph had already taken care of that too."[2]

Judge Thompson's friends have been special in his life. In 1968, at the conclusion of his first term in the Oklahoma House of Representatives, he received several prestigious honors, provoking immediate action by some of his best friends. The Challenged Awards Review Board (CARB) was formed by Jerry Tubb, Jim Chandler, Scott Nickson, Bob Amis, Jack Cain, Tom Lynn, Bob Bowles, and Dr. Paul Houk. The board convened at the Beacon Club and promptly roasted the judge with strong rebuttals of the nice and complimentary things the newspapers had said about him. CARB reconvened on other occasions.[3]

"Throughout my life," the judge said, "friends have meant everything to me. There has not been a single time, circumstance, success, or failure that has not been made better by my having my close friends." He has tried to live by Ralph Waldo Emerson's words, "The only way to have a friend is to be one."[4]

Daughter, Maria, has a theory why her father has so many friends:

He has an extraordinary ability to make and keep friends and make people feel comfortable. His old friends are cherished and new friends are engaged. He seems to have the attitude that everyone has an interesting life and stories to tell. He gives people the benefit of the doubt. For as long as I can remember, I have been sought out by people who said, "I love your Dad."[5]

Judges Phillips, Thompson, and Russell explore Antarctica in 2001.

"Ralph is most considerate of his friends." said close friend, retired Air Force Major General William P. Bowden, "When he is gathered with one or more, he has total focus on that person who is speaking. It is his way of showing respect."[6]

One of the judge's closest personal friends for decades is United States Senator James Inhofe, who said:

Ralph Thompson is one of kind. He is an encourager. He has the gift of encouraging those around him to expect greater things for themselves through hard work and dedication to their craft. But he doesn't stop there—he rejoices with them in their successes.[7]

Many of the judge's close friendships are as a result of traveling the world. He fell in love with travel while in the Air Force. An international moment was being in Tokyo, Japan, and seeing a performance of the Russian Moiseyev Dancers. He said, "My appetite for seeing other people, places, and things was being richly fed. Happily, it has been ever since."[8]

The judge often took Barbara and their daughters to the Judicial Conferences of the Tenth Circuit, an annual meeting of the federal judges in the states covered by the circuit. The conferences took the family to the Colorado Rockies, Jackson Hole, Wyoming, Snowbird, Utah, and other beautiful, historical, and wondrous locations. In the early years, they loaded their Oldsmobile station wagon and made adventures at every stop along the way.

In 1987, the family took a "joyful" European tour, celebrating Lisa's 21st birthday in Paris. The Thompsons returned to England and France in 1992 to deliver Elaine and Maria to Oxford for the OU Oxford Law program that summer. While in London, they enjoyed a visit with Sir Peter Imbert, head of Scotland Yard, and, after a round of sherry, were his guests at his weekly executive luncheon. Later, one of Sir Peter's officers escorted the Thompsons on a rare visit behind the face of Big Ben, London's famous clock tower.[9]

Judge Thompson's colleagues and close friends, Judge David Russell and former Judge Layn Phillips, have literally traveled the world together the last two decades. They have visited every continent. In 1996, the three flew to Singapore, took the Eastern and Oriental Express to Kuala Lumpur, Indonesia, then flew to Saigon, now Ho Chi Minh City, Vietnam.

Good friends and intrepid travelers, Judges Layn Phillips, Ralph Thompson, and David Russell, on the veranda of the legendary Raffles Hotel in Singapore in 1996

They stayed in the historic Continental Hotel, visited the old presidential palace, the boarded-up former American Embassy, and the "Hanoi Hilton," where American flyers were imprisoned.[10]

The threesome traveled extensively in the former South Vietnam, through the Mekong Delta, and to an area near the Cambodian border where they crawled through Viet Cong-dug tunnels at Cu Chi and saw the Cao Dai temples at Tai Ninh City. Many of the younger Vietnamese had never seen people from the West and were fascinated with fair, blue-eyed Americans and touched their bare arms in wonderment.[11]

San Diego, California, lawyer and decorated Vietnam combat veteran Bob Brewer joined Judges Thompson, Russell, and Phillips in the Vietnam experience. They flew from Saigon to Hanoi and visited Ha Long Bay north of Hai Phong. While in Saigon, they met Hoang Van Cuong, the internationally-famous Vietnam War photographer. Judge Thompson received a signed photograph from Van Cuong before the visitors left Vietnam for a few days in Hong Kong, including a meeting with a justice of the Hong Kong Supreme Court.[12]

Judge Thompson, right, meets famous Vietnam war photographer Hoang Van Cuong at his studio in Ho Chi Minh City in 1996 after the photographer's release from seven years in a Communist "re-education" camp.

Although he had been there several times before, Judge Thompson never tired of the fascinating blend of British and Chinese cultures in Hong Kong. He said, "Its sights and sounds, its scents, its sampans and skyscrapers, its endless crowds of people from everywhere were always thrilling to me." Walking down the streets of Hong Kong, he saw complete diversity, from East Indians in their saris and turbans, to gentlemen in their Bond Street pin stripes, and others in cone hats.[13]

In 1999, the Thompsons joined a group of other federal judges and friends on an unforgettable safari to Africa. Joining the Thompsons on the trip were Judge David and Dana Russell, former Judge Layn and Kathryn Phillips, United States District Judge Tom and Mary Brett, Pat Ryan and daughter, Megan, and Bob Brewer and his wife, United States District Judge Irma Gonzalez, of California.

He concluded his description of the African adventure in a feature article in *The Oklahoman*:

Africa is far behind us now. Our overnight in Zurich

reminded us of what a total contrast in cultures we have experienced—Switzerland, the ultimate in pristine civilization, and the villages of Africa, such a stark view of a primitive culture.[14]

Barbara has been a good traveling companion for her husband. She was enthralled with Africa. The group of 17 stayed in tents in a remote compound in the Amboseli National Game Reserve. She was surprised that their tent was equipped with a private bath. There was an uninterrupted view of the savannah from their compound and "a magnificent" view of Mt. Kilimanjaro, the highest point on the African continent.[15]

Barbara was intrigued with a visit to a Masai village. "It was a series of rounded, cow dung huts surrounded by a three-foot wall of sticker bushes," she said. She was startled at how clean the inside of one of the huts was. Life was simple, yet dangerous for humans and livestock. The cows slept within the walls at night to avoid the ravages of wild animals. The "clean, tall, lean, and handsome" people in the Masai village performed their traditional dances for the American travelers. Barbara was "unsettled," not that she had to pay, but that she had to pay the chief of the village for jewelry she had bought from women who had made and displayed their wares spread out on blankets in front of their huts.[16]

Three days before the group left Africa, Judge Thompson nearly stepped on a seven-foot Egyptian cobra that crossed the lava path in front of him. A skeptical native suggested that he had probably seen a rabbit. However, a few minutes later, Judge Phillips and his family entered their open air lodging and were confronted with the deadly snake. Several of the Masai who worked at the lodge killed the viper. The Phillips family, traveling with small children, decided it was time to leave Africa.[17]

In 2000, the Thompsons returned to London as guests of dear friends, Bill and Barbara Paul. Bill was president of the American Bar Association and was being warmly hosted by the British legal community. "Riding on Bill's coattails," the Thompsons had the pleasure of sharing time with high British officials. They were also reunited with friends, Supreme Court Justices Anthony Kennedy and Sandra Day O'Conner, and Attorney General Janet Reno. They were proud when Bill Paul joined British dignitaries in rededicating the Magna Carta at Runnymede with a monument bearing a beautiful inscription that Paul had authored.

The Oklahoma group also attended the Queen's Garden Party. Since the Queen's party, every time the judge sees old friend and fellow guest

The judge and Barbara enjoy a sunset in Kenya, East Africa, with Mount Kilimonjoro as the background in 1999.

The Thompsons leave the Queen's Garden Party at Buckingham Palace in London in 2000.

General Bill Bowden, he asks him within earshot of others, "When was the last time you were with the Queen? [18]

In 2001, Judges Thompson, Russell, and Phillips flew to Argentina and set out for Antarctica aboard a converted Russian ice breaker. They were hit by a hurricane, an 11 out of the worst of 12 on the Beaufort Scale, during the 760-mile trip across the Drake Passage. It was the worst storm the veteran Dutch sea captain had ever experienced. Winds of 60 knots with 30-40 foot waves buffeted the ship. They had to hold on to railings to keep from rolling out of their bunks.[19]

Once through the storm, the travelers entered a place that seemed to be "not of this world." They saw vast stretches of uninhabited, pristine ice with beautiful icebergs, glaciers, mountains, and hundreds of thousands of penguins and seals. After several days of shore landings near the southernmost point of earth, they sailed to the Falkland Islands, strangely beautiful, but barren and windswept.

When Judge Thompson returned to Oklahoma City, he wrote of his adventure for *The Sunday Oklahoman:*

Antarctica: It's been called the highest, the driest, coldest, windiest, emptiest, and loneliest continent on Earth—the bottom of the world.

So, why on earth would anyone want to go there?...
Perhaps it is because it is all of those things—so remote, so isolated and foreboding that it piqued our curiosity and sense of adventure. Plus, for me, it was another opportunity to experience and photograph some of the unusual nature and wildlife of the world.[20]

There was more adventure for the Thompsons in 2001. They selected an area along the Dordogne River in France to immerse themselves in just one area of that European country. They headquartered in the village of Sarlat and explored other charming villages along the river for two weeks. They returned to Paris for their flight home on September 11. Suddenly, the day became known as "9/11," and all airline flights were cancelled. Security in Paris, especially around the American Embassy, was high. They will never forget the extraordinary outpouring of sympathy, friendship, and support from the French people. The judge remembered:

Little American flags suddenly appeared out of thousands of windows. Parisians stopped us on the street to express their

A solemn moment in France. On the day after "9/11," Judge Thompson and Barbara were honored when they were invited to lower and fold the two American flags at the cemetery at Omaha Beach in northern France.

sympathy. Flowers were knee deep at the corner of the park across the street from the American Embassy. The newspaper *Le Monde* carried the headline, "We are all Americans."[21]

The Thompsons were held over in France for 11 days. On one of the days, they revisited the American cemetery at Omaha Beach where thousands of Americans lost their lives on D-Day. Each of the Thompsons was honored by being invited to lower the two American flags at the retreat ceremony at the close of the day and carry them to their nightly resting places. For them, "it was a touching moment."[22]

From 2002 to 2004, they visited three of the Hawaiian Islands and Victoria, British Columbia. In 2005, Judge Thompson and Layn Phillips traveled to Munich, Germany, Salzburg, Austria, and Brussels, Belgium. They visited the sites of the Battle of Waterloo and the Battle of the Bulge. In 2006, the Thompsons visited the Canadian island cabin of his colleague, Judge Stephen Friot and Nancy, and traveled to Ottawa, Canada, returning through the Adirondacks. They also returned to France so the judge could photograph the lavender fields of Provence.[23]

Judges Thompson, Russell, and Phillips visited Australia and Tasmania in 2008. The main purpose of the trip was to see the Australian Open. Later in the year, the Thompsons joined friends, Eva and Kent Bogart, in their home, Villa Frangipani, on St. Maarten in the Netherlands Antilles.

There was a return trip to Australia for the three world travelers and their spouses in 2009, including a "marvelous" side trip to New Zealand. In September, 2009, the Thompsons saw five countries in Europe, mostly by train. It began in Paris with French diplomatic friends, then to Lyon, Zermatt, and St. Mortiz, Switzerland, via the famous Glacier Express. The trip continued through the Swiss Alps, Austria, Germany, and to the Cotswolds of England.[24]

Of traveling throughout the world, he said, "My love for travel began in Taiwan years ago. I hope it continues for a long, long time."[25]

CHAPTER 27

RETIREMENT AND BEYOND

Even though he is retired from the bench, Judge Thompson
has remained a solid public servant and champion of
a fair and independent federal judiciary.

Governor Brad Henry

In 2007, Judge Thompson prepared to welcome his son-in-law, Tim DeGiusti, as a fellow judge of the United States District Court. DeGiusti, an Oklahoma City native and an honor graduate of OU and the OU College of Law, shared a military background with the judge, having served in the United States Army and Army Reserve as a Judge Advocate General (JAG). The honor graduate of his class of the Army JAG, he also was eventually the youngest Staff Judge Advocate in the history of Oklahoma's 45th Division/Brigade. During the time DeGiusti and his future wife, Elaine, were dating, the commonality of military and law experience made "meeting my girlfriend's father" much easier. When DeGiusti and Elaine met, they both worked at the same Oklahoma City law firm.[1]

In February, 2007, President George W. Bush, with the sponsorship of Oklahoma Senators Jim Inhofe and Tom Coburn, nominated DeGiusti to fill the vacancy that occurred when Judge Tim Leonard assumed senior status. Judge Thompson was excited about DeGiusti joining him on the court. He knew him not only as a good son-in-law, but was aware of the respect DeGiusti commanded as a lawyer in private practice.[2]

The plan for DeGiusti to join the court seemed flawless. He had the proper background, his screening by the FBI went smoothly, and his bi-partisan political support was solid. However, while he was reading information about the Senate confirmation process, DeGiusti saw a reference to a little known federal statute that prohibited two members of an immediate family from serving in the same federal judicial court. "I read it several times," DeGiusti said, "and wondered, 'Does this apply to me?'" Concluding that it did, he called his father-in-law and said, "I need to talk to you about something."[3] The judge wondered what possibly could necessitate a special meeting.

With a copy of the obscure statute in hand, DeGiusti went to the Thompson home fully ready to ask that his nomination be withdrawn. When the judge read the statute, he also recognized that the law, approved by Congress without fanfare a few years before, "most certainly" applied to his situation. His first response was, "I'll retire." DeGiusti protested, saying, "Oh no! I'll withdraw my nomination so you can stay on the court!"[4]

But the judge's mind was made up. "There was not a hint of hesitation in his voice," DeGiusti remembered. The judge told DeGiusti, "I have had a long career as a federal judge. Your time is just beginning. There is no way I will let you pass up this opportunity."[5]

Elaine Thompson DeGiusti proudly "robes" her husband, Tim, at the new federal judge's swearing-in ceremony on October 9, 2007.

The next day, Judge Thompson and DeGiusti informed the appropriate officials of the dilemma. It called for the judge's retirement to happen as soon as DeGiusti's nomination was confirmed by the United States Senate. President Bush's nominations for others had moved painfully slowly through the Democratic-controlled Senate. However, thanks to his bi-partisan support, the work of Senators Inhofe and Coburn, and the backing of Democrat Senator Patrick Leahy, chairman of the Senate Judiciary Committee, the DeGiusti nomination was confirmed by unanimous vote of the Senate on an accelerated schedule.[6]

Judge Thompson composed his retirement letter to President Bush that said, in part:

> Since my appointment by President Ford, it has been the greatest honor of my life to have served as a U.S. District Judge for nearly 32 years. I now proudly step down to make way for this splendid new federal judge who is sure to become one of your proud legacies.[7]

His office staff prepared to fax his retirement letter at the required time. On the day of DeGiusti's Senate confirmation, the President was poised to finalize his appointment to the federal bench. It was then that Judge Thompson's letter was sent. Within a few hours, the careful plan to facilitate DeGiusti's appointment and to avoid violating the federal statute was carried out perfectly.[8]

It was a bittersweet moment for Judge Thompson who had reached the age of 72. He said:

> While I had not planned to retire, loved my work on the court and my colleagues, and felt that I had a few good years left in me, it was nonetheless a very proud moment, indeed. I was gratified that the tradition of the appointment of highest quality judges continued.[9]

Upon the transition from father-in-law to son-in-law, *The Oklahoman,* in an editorial titled, "Family Affair," said:

> To us, Thompson's years on the federal bench epitomize that of the ideal jurist: Smart, with a command for and respect of the law, but always instinctively fair. His long tenure has created and inspired an outstanding crop of younger judges whom he has counseled and promoted. Oklahoma—indeed the nation—will miss the judicial work of this outstanding public servant.[10]

Former Oklahoma Governor Frank Keating said of the judge's retirement, "It was an act of extraordinary selflessness—that he would give up his dearly loved position as a federal judge, a job that he has done with such honor, so his son-in-law could take the reins."[11]

Judge Thompson left the court in good hands. Vicki Miles-La-Grange was Chief Judge, with active judges David Russell, Robin Cauthron, Stephen Friot, and Joe Heaton; senior judges Lee West and Tim Leonard; and Magistrate judges Doyle Argo, Bana Roberts, Gary Purcell, Valerie Couch, Robert Bacharach, and Shon Erwin.[12]

In leaving what had been his life for 32 years, he was thankful for his staff. Larry Marks, his court reporter, had worked with the judge for 30 years. Each of his law clerks, Marcia Rupert and Marilyn Edens, he considered to be "absolutely top flight lawyers and wonderful people." Together with Sharon Henshall, the judge's devoted

Judge Thompson and his staff upon his retirement in 2007. Left to right, courtroom deputy court clerk Mike Bailey, law clerk Marcia Rupert, administrative assistant Sharon Henshall, law clerk Marilyn Edens, and court reporter Larry Marks.

administrative assistant for 27 years, and courtroom deputy Mike Bailey, the entire staff assumed the same positions with Judge DeGiusti. Of his staff, the judge said, "Quoting Winston Churchill, 'I am easily satisfied with the best.'"[13]

The judge's unexpected retirement required him to decline the appointment of Chief Justice John Roberts to serve on the Foreign Terrorist Alien Removal Court, a panel created by the "Patriot Act" to secretly assess the government's designation of suspected terrorists and approve their removal from the country. He would have been one of five federal judges from different circuits to sit on the court.[14]

By 2007, Judge Thompson had been on the federal bench for 32 years, a single year shy of a third of a century. His reputation was stellar. Judge Joe Heaton, who has known him since attending Young Republican meetings in his hometown of Alva, said, "By personal example, he has set a very high standard for all of us who served with him on the bench. He has the legacy of integrity, and nothing is more important than that."[15]

Judge Tim Leonard, who looks at Judge Thompson as a mentor and friend, said:

> Even as a lawyer appearing before him, I never saw him lose his temper. He always had a very cool demeanor. If you were going to type-cast the way a judge should run a courtroom, Ralph would be the example. In addition to his judicial temperament, his unquestioned integrity is another example of why he is respected across the nation.[16]

Judge Stephen Friot cited his colleague's ability to separate politics from judging:

> For his entire adult life, Ralph has been a man of deep and sincerely held political convictions. However…I can safely say that his performance of his duties as a United States District Judge was never tainted by politics or political considerations… I am not aware of a single instance in Ralph's long judicial career in which his political beliefs had any impact on his ability or inclination to render justice without respect to persons.[17]

Judge Vicki Miles-LaGrange believes Judge Thompson's greatest legacy may be his graciousness. She said:

> He never forgot, not for a single day, why he was on the bench. His graciousness put everybody at ease so that parties felt more free to relate their side of the controversy. He listened to each argument and piece of testimony as if that person was the only person in the courtroom. It did not matter who the parties or the lawyers were, he gave them his full attention, and with great grace, gave them their day in court.[18]

United States Senator Kay Bailey Hutchison said:

> Judge Thompson is one of the most remarkable people I have ever met. He is regarded by all who know him as intelligent, eminently reasonable, and principled. Public service has been the hallmark of his distinguished career. He has truly led the kind of upstanding and accomplished life that sets a grand example for the rest of us.[19]

After his retirement, Judge Thompson was "profoundly" honored by all judges of the Western District, the Northern District of Oklahoma,

Reunited with Justice Anthony Kennedy, center, celebrating the centennial of the OU College of Law in 2009, with OU President David Boren, right.

and the Chief Judge and all living former Chief Judges of the Tenth Circuit Court of Appeals, by becoming their nominee for the Devitt Distinguished Service to Justice Award, the highest honor a federal judge can receive. He was especially proud of the nomination because he had twice served on the Devitt Award selection committee.

The Devitt Award is named for the late Edward J. Devitt, longtime Chief Judge of the United States District Court for the District of Minnesota, and honors a judge who, among other criteria, performs "activities that have helped to improve the administration of justice, advance the rule of law, reinforce collegial ties within the judicial branch, or strengthen civic ties with local, national, and international communities."

Devitt Award recommendation letters came from lofty circles, including some of the preeminent federal judges in the nation. Tenth Circuit Chief Judge Robert Henry said, "The touchstone of Judge Thompson's life has been a dedication to the service of his fellow citizens—community, state, and nation...He has devoted his life to public service, and the scrupulous advancement of the rule of law."[20] Chief

Chief Justice John Roberts, left, with Barbara and Judge Thompson in 2009.

Judge Vicki Miles-LaGrange, joining the other Western District judges, wrote, "His considerable wisdom and legendary even-handed judicial demeanor, his gentlemanly personality and supreme collegiality set the tone for a Court regarded as one of the most collegial in the nation."[21]

Northern District Chief Judge Claire Eagan, joining the other judges of her court, said, "There is no doubt that, during his tenure, he was considered the judge to whom anyone could entrust a complex case of national importance."[22] United States District Judge Wm. Terrell Hodges of Florida said, "He was a friend and supporter of anyone interested in justice."[23] United States District Judge Lloyd D. George of Nevada, said, "I have developed a respect for Judge Thompson's intellect, high moral fiber, leadership skills, and intense work ethic. But it is the balance in his life that I observed which truly speaks to his exceptional nature."[24]

Oklahoma Governor Brad Henry wrote, "He has been the model jurist and public servant, setting the highest possible standard for others to emulate."[25] "It is difficult to imagine a more accomplished judicial career," said OU President David L. Boren. "Clearly, the State of Oklahoma—and our nation—have benefitted immensely from the service of Ralph Thompson. His example of dedication, competence, character, and integrity continue to inspire lawyers, judges, and all our citizens to excellence in public service."[26]

There was no slowing down. Judge Thompson was chosen for a position on the Council of Federal Arbitration, Inc., a group of highly-select former federal judges who arbitrate significant commercial disputes. The International Institute for Conflict Prevention and Resolution honored him by naming him to its Panel of Distinguished Neutrals. He continues to teach trial advocacy at Harvard Law School and is a highly sought-after speaker. Oklahoma Governor Henry appointed him to the Uniform Law Commission.

Travel, photography, family, public service, and serving on selected cases as an arbitration judge still all share the forefront of Judge Thompson's life. Even though he is no longer an active federal judge, he said:

> By every measure, instinct, education, training, and experience, I am—and always will be a federal trial judge. However well I have performed in that role will define my professional life, as evaluated by others. I think of my grandfather Bizzell's words that guided his life, "I hope to have the courage to do right, the will to be just, and the Christian virtue of being kindly, sympathetic, and open minded."

> I do hope that I have been a faithful servant, as I have tried to be, to those lofty standards and to the court's role of doing justice. To me there is not a higher calling.[27]

EPILOGUE

Finally, a love affair—Oklahoma, its history
and its uniqueness, as seen by Judge Thompson.

For years, he has been intrigued with how far Oklahoma
has come in such a short time, both as a state and as individuals.
He enjoys telling the story of Oklahoma with affection through
stories of achievement. It is a fitting closing to this story of his life.

He calls his remarks—

FROM MODEST BEGINNINGS

The story of Oklahoma is a story told through the lives of people—remarkably, because our state is so young, people many of us have known.

In speaking to a group in Boston a few years ago, some of whom proudly traced their families to the *Mayflower,* I enjoyed drawing the comparison of the youthfulness of our state with the age of theirs. It was easy to do. Some of Benjamin Franklin's relatives are buried in the backyard of their meeting hall; yet our state, I explained, was actually younger than my father who was still practicing law at the time, (I think they thought I was a cowboy with very shallow roots.)

"Modest Beginnings" because our state and most of the people who pioneered it began, literally, with nothing—nothing but opportunity, optimism, determination, faith, self reliance, and the willingness to work hard.

Achievement from modest beginnings is the fulfillment of our Founding Fathers. One of them, reportedly Thomas Jefferson, said:, "Let us dream of an aristocracy of achievement arising out of a democracy of opportunity."

Isn't that beautiful? Not an aristocracy as such, of course, but an aristocracy of achievement arising out of a democracy of opportunity.

Thomas Jefferson would have loved Oklahoma.

In this vein, historians have described our state's beginning by recognizing that it was, indeed, determination, not "pedigree" or ancestry, that counted. There certainly wasn't much of that either. One said:

> Opportunity, self-help and rugged determination have been as traditional to Oklahoma as oil wells, red earth, wheat and cattle, big skies, friendly, open people and a bright golden haze on the meadow.

Another wrote more solemnly, and with nice alliteration, "Bred on extremes and adventure, seasoned in crisis, Oklahoma's past reflects resiliency, resourcefulness, and resolve."

And, it is so true. Because those who built Oklahoma built literally from a prairie. And, as they built, they saw the virtual decimation of that prairie in the dust bowl days, endured two world wars and a devastating economic depression. The winds blew, the wars raged, the banks failed and so did the crops. Many people lost everything—everything but their will. But they persevered, survived, and succeeded, giving an early example of what Nelson Mandela later said, "Courage is not the absence of fear, but the triumph over it."

The story of our young state is rich with examples of those from modest beginnings who made successes of themselves, however that term is defined, so many that their "story book—only in America" successes seem to be the rule rather than the exception.

One of my favorites is the story of Dr. David Ross Boyd, a distinguished Harvard scholar who came to Norman as OU's first president, to start the university. When he stepped off the train he saw an absolutely treeless plain—not one university building—and not a tree to be seen. As he began to build the university, he also planted trees. Many of the beautiful trees on the OU campus today are the ones he planted.

Boyd, as a teacher and a planter, was portrayed beautifully a few years ago, in a play at the University of Oklahoma, written by one of my most admired scholars, OU's Dr. J.R. Morris. One scene showed him planting the trees, watering them himself, and nursing them through a harsh winter, while many were telling him that neither the trees nor the university could survive. In a following scene he returns from a trip one early spring evening, finds the leaves budding, and knows that they made it through the winter. And then Boyd says these words, which were written both as a credo for the educator, and as an enduring metaphor, the teacher/the educator as a planter. And to me, considering Oklahoma's modest beginnings, they are also eloquently symbolic of the optimism and faith and vision of all the early day Oklahomans profiled here. As he sees the budding leaves unfolding, he says:

At last, the leaves they said would never be.
My fellow man loses faith so easily
When he lacks the final say.
You can't make a seedling become a tree;
That's left to nature's mystery.
But the faithful planter always believes
That he will see unfolding leaves,
As sure as there's a spring.

Here are a few examples of Oklahoma's "unfolding leaves":

Alfred P. Murrah. A young orphaned boy literally rode the rails on a freight train from Alabama to Oklahoma City where he was kicked off, as he described it, "lonely, hopeless, friendless and miserable." He had nothing, nothing but his dreams, was taken in by a caring couple in Tuttle, worked his way through high school, as valedictorian and president of his class, worked his way through college, and worked his way through law school. Later on, the orphan boy who rode the rails was selected by President Franklin D. Roosevelt as the youngest federal judge ever appointed and became one of our country's most distinguished judicial leaders.

C.R. Anthony. The son of a tenant farmer, several years short of legal age and with only six years of schooling, left his Missouri home on horseback and rode to Tennessee determined he would never spend a day in a county poor farm like the one he had grown up beside. He worked for his keep as a farm laborer and at a saw mill. He later caught a train to Holdenville to join his brother, wearing the first new "store bought" pants of his life. Fortunately, and fortuitously, he got a job in a dry goods store. Little did he dream (or did he?) that he would one day own a chain of dry goods stores across 21 states in more than 300 towns and cities bearing his name.

The Five Ballerinas. During the 1920s, hundreds, maybe thousands, of little Indian girls were born in rural Oklahoma, but none quite like these. Growing up in Fairfax, a little Osage girl went on to become prima ballerina of the Ballet Russe de Monte Carlo and America's most famous ballerina as the star of the New York City Ballet. She was Maria Tallchief. Her sister, Marjorie Tallchief. was the first American to become prima ballerina of the Paris Opera Ballet—all the way from Fairfax, Oklahoma.. A little French and Shawnee-Cherokee girl from Vinita, who began dancing at pow wows, also joined the Ballet Russe de Monte Carlo, at the age of fourteen, later becoming its principal ballerina. She returned home to establish both the Oklahoma City Ballet, now Ballet Oklahoma, and the School of Dance at the University of Oklahoma. A little girl's dream come true. Her name is Yvonne Chouteau.

Moscelyne Larkin was from Miami, the daughter of an Indian father and a Russian mother. From her rural Oklahoma beginnings she, too, became an international star of classic Russian ballet with Ballet Russe. A little Choctaw girl who remembered swimming in creeks and almost never wearing shoes growing up on her Oklahoma farm became the toast of Europe as yet another prima ballerina of Ballet Russe de Monte Carlo: Rosella Hightower.

And one thing more. From such modest beginnings all five of these brilliant and internationally acclaimed stars were inspired for life, as children, by seeing Ballet Russe on tour in Oklahoma City. Can anyone doubt the importance of our local support of the arts?

Wiley Post. Obstacles came in different forms. A young twelve-year-old dropout from Maysville went on to become known as one of the world's great aviation pioneers, setting an around-the-world record of eight days, inventing the pressurized helmet and suit which were the forerunners of today's space suits, and discovered the jet stream, the high altitude wind current that changed flying. He is perhaps best remembered by his death with Will Rogers. What is not widely known is that before learning to fly, he was a convicted armed robber who, while serving a ten-year sentence, was pardoned by the governor of Oklahoma. He turned his life around, overcame the loss of one eye, and went on to make enormous contributions to aviation, becoming one of the world's greatest aviators, and one of Oklahoma's greatest historic figures.

Lee R. West. One of my colleagues, as a high school graduate, with everything he owned in a cardboard box tied with a rope, hitchhiked from Antlers to Norman to attend OU. He worked all sorts of jobs, somehow made his way, graduating as an honor student, with a law degree, and later with a masters of law degree from Harvard. The son of an illiterate father, he used his first pay check as a young Marine officer to buy indoor plumbing for his parents back in Antlers, the first of their lives. After being Chairman of the Civil Aeronautics Board, he is a very distinguished federal judge today. He came from the absolute depths of poverty.

William G. Paul. By the way, guess who picked up Judge West hitchhiking to OU? It was another young incoming freshman from a dairy farm in Pauls Valley, a Garvin County farm boy whose brilliant career led to his becoming president of the American Bar Association, the leader of 404,000 American lawyers, the largest voluntary professional organization in the world, and thus becoming one of the leading legal figures of the world.

One measure of Bill Paul's distinction happened while presiding at the rededication of the Magna Carta, at Runneymede, as president of the ABA. He unveiled a monument bearing an eloquent inscription that he authored which will endure for all time— a lasting tribute not only to the rule of law, but to this distinguished leader who has dedicated his life to the rule of law. I was proud to be with him as he was honored by Queen Elizabeth, II, Prime Minister Tony Blair, and the top officials of the United Kingdom. The theme was "Common Law, Common Bonds." What better example of one who achieved Jefferson's dream? But oh, there are so many others:

Judge Robert A. Hefner. He never attended a grade school or a high school. His self study was reading at night, even by campfire, while herding sheep by himself in the wild open range of West Texas. Even in those barren and lonely circumstances his ambition was to become a lawyer, but it certainly seemed like an impossible dream. Then things got worse. His family lost their farm and his father died. Still he studied on his own by kerosene lamp, eventually qualifying for admission to North Texas Baptist College and later graduating with distinction from the University of Texas Law School.

Hearing of the colossal oil discovery called Spindletop, near Beaumont, Judge Hefner decided to become part of the oil pioneers, later moving to Ardmore where he became a leading citizen and lawyer and prosperous oil man, as well as mayor. This one-time little shepherd boy realized his dream not only by becoming a brilliant lawyer, but by becoming a Justice of the Oklahoma Supreme Court, and then Mayor of Oklahoma City. The little shepherd boy kept his shepherd's bell beside him throughout the years to remind him of his modest roots. By the way, while at Ardmore, Judge Hefner lived next door to another Oklahoma giant in the making—a little boy named John W. Nichols—co-founder of Devon Energy, the largest American-based independent oil and gas producer.

Carl Albert. The story of Oklahoma is not complete without recalling the poor little boy in bare feet and bib overalls from Bugtussle who became a Rhodes scholar and, eventually rose to become Speaker of the United States House of Representative.

Alice Robertson. She was the daughter of impoverished missionaries to the Creek Nation, who sacrificed virtually everything to send her to a fine school, Elmira College, in New York. The refinement there was a long way from the life of cooking beef bones and hominy in an iron vessel over an open fire among the Indians. But she persevered. Through her connections she became known to President and Mrs. Ulysses S. Grant, former President Rutherford B. Hayes, and future President James Garfield, who appointed her to a position in the Office of Indian Affairs.

Later Robertson met President Benjamin Harrison and became friends with President Theodore Roosevelt. At 66 years of age, she was not only the first woman elected by Oklahoma to Congress, she was the only woman in Congress at the time, a conservative Republican elected in a strong Democratic district. She came from virtually nothing, but epitomized the rugged independent, indomitable Oklahoma woman, making history both in her election and in her tireless efforts to ease the plight of the Indian people with whom she had been raised.

Lyle H. Boren. The little boy whose destitute West Texas farmer family rode in a covered wagon into southern Oklahoma in search of water; a boy who on graduation night did not own a white shirt or a suit; who had to stuff cardboard in the soles of his only pair of shoes; who sold a cow to help with his college tuition, and ultimately became a distinguished member of Congress from Oklahoma.

Ralph Ellison. A son of Oklahoma City's Deep Deuce, a high school dropout, a child of segregation, who authored the masterpiece, *Invisible Man,* and became one of the literary elites among America's writers and thinkers. He had more than poverty and the Dust Bowl to overcome. But he, too, made his impossible dreams come true and contributed hugely to the cultural life of his country.

Robert S. Kerr. His grandfather had been murdered by Quantrill's Raiders in the family front yard when his father was only nine months old. Born in a windowless log cabin south of what became Ada, he picked cotton, struggled to earn his education and just as he began his law practice he lost his wife and baby son in childbirth. Alone, grieving and deeply in debt he started over. He told his father he wanted three things in life, "a family, a million dollars, and the governorship of Oklahoma"—seemingly impossible dreams. In one of the most remarkable of all "From Modest Beginnings" life stories, he succeeded, and exceeded, in every one. Oil industry giant, governor, and "uncrowned king" of the United States Senate.

I could go on and on. These are examples of the many other lives richly deserving to be honored--and all have formed the very character of our state. All of these children, without any material resources and, it would seem, without hope or promise, were children of Jefferson's dream. They planted their hopes in his "democracy of opportunity" and, through their achievements, saw the promise of their lives unfurl like "unfolding leaves,"

... as sure as there's a spring.

Ralph G. Thompson

ENDNOTES

CHAPTER 1:
A STRONG FAMILY HERITAGE
1 Recollections of Ralph Gordon Thompson recorded during the winter and spring of 2010, Archives, Oklahoma Heritage Association, hereafter referred to as Ralph Thompson interview.
2 Ibid.
3 www.independencetx.com, the official website of Independence, Texas.
4 Ibid.
5 *Encyclopedia of Oklahoma History and Culture* (Oklahoma City: Oklahoma Historical Society, 2009), "William Bennett Bizzell," by Kitty Pittman, hereafter referred to as *Oklahoma Encyclopedia.*
6 Ralph Thompson interview.
7 *Daily Eagle* (Bryan, Texas), June 3, 1925.
8 *The Daily Oklahoman* (Oklahoma City, Oklahoma), June 23, 2010.
9 Program of dedication of William Bennett Bizzell Memorial Library, December 14, 1949, Heritage Archives.
10 Ibid.
11 Interview with Denzil Garrison, December 3, 2009, Heritage Archives.
12 Interview with United States Marshal Mike Roach, November 18, 2010, Heritage Archives.
13 *The Daily Chieftain* (Vinita, Oklahoma), July 8, 1901.
14 Ralph Thompson interview.
15 Clayton Keith, *History of the Jackson Family in America* (Pike County, Missouri: News Power Print, 1916).
16 Ralph Thompson interview.
17 Ibid.
18 Ibid.
19 Ibid.
20 Ibid.
21 Ibid.
22 Ibid.
23 Ibid.

CHAPTER 2:
WARTIME BOYHOOD
1 Ralph Thompson interview.
2 Ibid.
3 Ibid.
4 Letter from Suzanne Riley Lawson to Bob Burke, March 7, 2010, Heritage Archvies.
5 The Daily Oklahoman, March 8, 1941.

6 Ralph Thompson interview.
7 Ibid.
8 Ibid.
9 Ibid.
10 Ibid.
11 Letter from Lee Thompson, Jr., to Bob Burke, April 15, 2010, Heritage Archives, hereafter referred to as Lee Thompson, Jr. letter.
12 Ralph Thompson interview.
13 Ibid.
14 Ibid.
15 Ibid.
16 Ibid.
17 Ibid.
18 Ibid.
19 Lee Thompson, Jr. letter.
20 Ralph Thompson interview.
13 Ibid.
14 Ibid.
15 Dallas Morning News (Dallas, Texas), May 15, 1944
16 Sooner Magazine (Norman, Oklahoma), June, 1944.
17 Ralph Thompson interview.

CHAPTER 3:
THE EDGEMERE EXPERIENCE
1 Ralph Thompson interview.
2 Ibid.
3 Ibid.
4 Ibid.
5 Ibid.
6 Letter from James Fentriss to Bob Burke, April 4, 2010, Heritage Archives, hereafter referred to as James Fentriss letter.
7 Suzanne Riley Lawson letter.
8 Ralph Thompson interview.
9 Ibid.
10 James Fentriss letter.
11 Ralph Thompson interview.
12 Ibid.
13 Ibid.
14 Ibid.
15 Letter from Charles Osgood to Ralph Thompson, March 16, 2007, Heritage Archives.
16 James Fentriss letter.
17 Ralph Thompson interview.
18 Ibid.
19 Ibid.

20 Ralph Thompson interview.
21 Ibid.
22 *New Classen Life,* No. XVII, No. 68.
23 Ralph Thompson interview.
24 Ibid.
25 Bob Burke, Royse Parr, and Kenny Franks, *Glory Days of Summer* (Oklahoma City: Oklahoma Heritage Association, 1999) p. 9.
26 Ralph Thompson interview.
27 Ibid.

CHAPTER 4:
A QUALITY EDUCATION
1   Ralph Thompson interview.
2   Ibid.
3   Ibid.
4   Ibid.
5   Ibid.
6   Ibid.
7   Ibid.
8   Ibid.
9   Ibid.
10 Ibid.
11 Ibid.
12 Ibid.
13 Ibid.
14 Ibid.
15 Ibid.
16 *The Daily Oklahoman,* October 19, 1955.
17 Ralph Thompson interview.
18 Ibid.

CHAPTER 5:
SPECIAL AGENT
1   Ralph Thompson memoir.
2   Ibid.
3   Ibid.
4   www.osi.andrews.af.mil, the official website of the Air Force Office of Special Investigations.
5   Ibid.
6   Letter from Colonel Albert Naum to Colonel Benjamin Forrest, February 15, 1959, Heritage Archives.
7   A history of Ardmore Army Air Field and Ardmore Air Force Base can be found at www.brightok.net.
8   Ralph Thompson memoir.
9   Ibid.
10 Ibid.
11 www.gio.gov.tw, the official website of the

Republic of China.
12 Ralph Thompson memoir.
13 Ibid.
14 Ibid.
15 Ibid.
16 Ibid.
17 Ibid.
18 Ibid.
19 Ibid.
20 Ibid.
21 Ibid.
22 Ibid.
23 Ibid.
24 Ibid.
25 Ibid.
26 Ibid.
27 Ibid.
28 Ibid.
29 Air Force Evaluation by Lt. General Winfield W. Scott, Jr., March 8, 1984, Heritage Archives.
30 Ralph Thompson interview.
31 Letter from Richard Burpee to Bob Burke, March 25, 2010, Heritage Archives.

CHAPTER 6:
THE LAW AND ROMANCE
1   Ralph Thompson interview.
2   Ibid.
3   Ralph Thompson interview.
4   Ibid.
5   Ibid.
6   Ibid.
7   Ibid.
8   Ibid.
9   Ibid.
10 Interview with Barbara Thompson, June 2, 2010, Heritage Archives, hereafter referred to as Barbara Thompson interview.
11 Affidavit to Origin of Disability of Captain Geo. Billow, Co. I, 107th Reg., Ohio Infantry, The National Archives.
12 Ibid.
13 Ralph Thompson interview and Barbara Thompson interview.
14 Ralph Thompson interview.
15 Ibid.
16 Ibid.
17 Ibid.
18 Ibid, *New York Times,* November 26, 1991.
19 Ralph Thompson interview.

20 Ibid.
21 Ibid.
22 Barbara Thompson interview.
23 *The Journal Record* (Oklahoma City, Oklahoma), May 17, 2007; *Time* Magazine, April 16, 1965.
24 *The Journal Record,* May 17, 2007.
25 *Time* Magazine, April 16, 1965.
26 Ralph Thompson interview.
27 Ibid.
28 Ibid.

CHAPTER 7:
TWO TERMS AND THREE BABIES
1 Ralph Thompson interview.
2 Ibid.
3 Ibid.
4 Ibid.
5 Ibid.
6 *The Daily Oklahoman,* April 26, 1966.
7 Ibid., May 12, 1966.
8 Ralph Thompson interview.
9 Barbara Thompson interview.
10 *The Daily Oklahoman,* November 8, 1966.
11 Letter from James Inhofe to Bob Burke, December 2, 2010, Heritage Archives, hereafter referred to as James Inhofe letter.
12 Ralph Thompson interview.
13 Ibid.
14 Ibid.
15 Letter from Rex Privett to Bob Burke, April 12, 2010, Heritage Archives.
16 Ralph Thompson interview.
17 Ibid.
18 *The Daily Oklahoman,* July 9, 1967.
19 Ibid., April 19, 1967.
20 Ibid.
21 *The Daily Oklahoman,* January 12, 1968.
22 Ibid., February 8, 1968.
23 Ibid., February 25, 1968.
24 Ibid., June 23, 1968.
25 Ralph Thompson interview.
26 Ibid., November 9, 1968.
27 Ralph Thompson interview.

CHAPTER 8:
THE RACE FOR LIEUTENANT GOVERNOR
1 Ralph Thompson interview.
2 Ibid.
3 Ibid.

4 Ibid.
5 Ibid.
6 *The Daily Oklahoman,* August 26, 1969.
7 Bob Burke, *Good Guys Wear White Hats: The Life of George Nigh* (Oklahoma City: Oklahoma Heritage Association, 2000), p. 154.
8 *The Daily Oklahoman,* December 21, 1969.
9 Ralph Thompson interview.
10 *The Daily Oklahoman,* December 28, 1969.
11 Ibid.
12 Ibid.
13 Ibid.
14 Ralph Thompson interview.
15 Ibid.
16 *Tulsa World* (Tulsa, Oklahoma) October 25, 1970.
17 *Tulsa Tribune* (Tulsa, Oklahoma), October 27, 1970.
18 *The Daily Oklahoman,* November 3, 1970.
19 *Good Guys Wear White Hats,* p. 157.
20 Ibid., November 9, 1970.
21 Ralph Thompson interview.
22 Interview with George Nigh, August 5, 2010, Heritage Archives.

CHAPTER 9:
APPROACHING THE FEDERAL BENCH
1 Ralph Thompson interview.
2 Ibid.
3 Ibid.
4 Ibid.
5 *The Daily Oklahoman,* December 9, 1971.
6 Ibid.
7 *The Daily Oklahoman,* December 17, 1971.
8 Ralph Thompson interview.
9 Ralph Thompson interview.
10 Ibid.
11 Ibid., Barbara Thompson interview.
12 Ralph Thompson interview.
13 Ibid.
14 Ibid.
15 Don V. Cogman, *My Journey: A Memoir and Musings on Life* (Bloomington, Indiana: iUniverse, Inc., 2009), p. 187.
16 Ralph Thompson interview.
17 Ibid.
18 Ibid.
19 Ibid.
20 *Congressional Record,* October 6, 1975.
21 Ibid., October 9, 1975.

22 *The Daily Oklahoman,* October 21, 1975.

23 Text of speech of Ralph Thompson, October 20, 1975, Heritage Archives.

CHAPTER 10:
FEDERAL JURIST

1 Alexander Hamilton, *The Federalist No. 78,* published in the *Independent Journal,* June 14, 1788.

2 www.fjc.gov, the official website of the Federal Judicial Center.

3 Bob Burke and David Russell, *Law and Laughter: The Life of Lee West* (Oklahoma City: Oklahoma Heritage Association, 2005), p. 8.

4 www.fjc.gov, the official website of the Federal Judicial Center.

5 Ralph Thompson interviews.

6 Ibid.

7 Ibid.

8 Ibid.

9 Ibid.

CHAPTER 11:
COLORFUL AND INTRIGUING CASES

1 The State of Oklahoma, et al v. Federal Energy Regulatory Commission and USA, 494 F. Supp 636 (WD Okla. 1980), affirmed 661 F.2nd 832 (10th Cir. 1981).

2

3 Ralph Thompson interview.

4 *The Daily Oklahoman,* June 6, 1980.

5 Indian Territory Operating Company v. Bridger Petroleum Corporation, 500 F. Supp. 449 (WD Okla. 1980).

6 Letter from Eugene Kuntz to Ralph Thompson, July 27, 1981, Heritage Archives.

7 Eaves v. Penn, 426 F. Supp. 830 (W.D. Okla. 1976), affirmed 587 F.2nd 453 (10th Cir. 1978).

8 Jones, et al vs. Oklahoma Secondary School Activities Association, et al and Benson, et al, Intervenors, 453 F. Supp 150 (WD Okla. 1977).

9 Ibid.

10 Ralph Thompson interview.

11 *The Daily Oklahoman.,* April 27, 1978.

12 Ibid., December 1, 1978.

13 Ibid., Ralph Thompson interview.

14 Ralph Thompson interview.

15 Ibid.

16 Interview with Lee Roy West, March 7, 2010, Heritage Archives, hereafter referred to as Lee West interview.

17 Ralph Thompson interview.

18 Ibid.

19 Ibid., December 22, 1981.

20 Ibid., December 23, 1981.

21 *USA v. Sowers* (10th Cir. 80-1974, 1982) unpublished.

22 *USA v. David D. Brunson,* 54 F.3rd 673 (10th Cir. 1995).

23 Ibid.

24 *USA v. Graham Kendall,* 76 F.2nd 1426 (10th Cir. 1985).

25 Ibid.

26 Ibid.

27 *The Daily Oklahoman,* June 20, 1985, USA v. Conner, 752 F.2nd 504 (10th Cir. 1985), USA v. Doughterty, 106 F.2d 1514 (10th Cir. 1987)

28 Ibid.

29 Ibid.

CHAPTER 12:
GIVING EACH CASE ITS REQUIRED DIGNITY

1 Ralph Thompson interview.

2 Letter from Debra James Marshall to Bob Burke, May 25, 2010, Heritage Archives.

3 Letter from William G. Paul to Bob Burke, June 29, 1020, Heritage Archives.

4 Letter from Reid Robison to Bob Burke, June 22, 2010, Heritage Archives.

5 Letter from Drew Neville to Bob Burke, March 18, 2010, Heritage Archives.

6 Ibid.

7 Ibid.

8 Letter from Mack Martin to Bob Burke, March 22, 2010

9 Ralph Thompson interview.

10 Ibid.

CHAPTER 13:
IMPACT ON SOCIETY

1 *Bell and McCord v. The Little Axe Independent School District No. 70,* et al, affirmed by the United States Court of Appeals, Tenth Circuit, June 26, 1985, 766 F.2d 1391, hereafter referred to as *Bell and McCord.*

2 *National Catholic Reporter,* March 16, 1984.

3 *Bell and McCord.*

4 *National Catholic Reporter,* March 16, 1984.

5 *Bell and McCord.*
6 Michal Salem letter.
7 Ralph Thompson interview.
8 Ibid.
9 *McCord and Bell.*
10 Ralph Thompson interview.
11 *The Daily Oklahoman,* November 5, 1981.
12 Ibid.
13 Ralph Thompson interview.
14 Ibid.
15 Ibid.
16 Ibid.
17 Ibid.
18 Ibid.
19 Interview with William Price, August 14, 2010.
20 Ralph Thompson interview.
21 *The Daily Oklahoman,* September 23, 1983.
22 Ibid.
23 In the matter of the Reinstatement of William C. Page to membership, 94 P.3rd 80, June 22, 2004.
24 Ibid., September 20, 1989; Interview with Robert Henry, August 12, 2010, Heritage Archives, hereafter referred to as Robert Henry interview.
25 Letter from William Price to Bob Burke, September 15, 2010, Heritage Archives.
26 Robert Henry interview.
27 Ralph Thompson interview.
28 *The Daily Oklahoman,* September 24, 1989.
29 Ibid.
30 *Tulsa World,* September 21, 1989.
31 Ralph Thompson interview.
32 *The Daily Oklahoman,* March 30, 2001.
33 *People* Magazine, May 28, 2001.
34 Ibid.
35 Ibid.
36 *The Washington Post,* November 28, 2001.
37 www.edmondgeary.wordpress.com.

CHAPTER 14:
HARVARD AND JUDICIAL PHILOSOPHY
1 www.law.harvard.edu, the official website of Harvard Law School.
2 Ralph Thompson interview.
3 Ralph Thompson interview.
4 Ibid.
5 Letter from Peter L. Murray to Judge David Russell, December 6, 1999.
6 Ralph Thompson interview.

7 Ibid.
8 Ibid.
9 Ibid.
10 Text of speech by Ralph Thompson, December 1, 1976, Heritage Archives.
11 Ibid.
12 Speech by Ralph Thompson to OU College of Law convocation ceremony, May, 1978l, Heritage Archives.
13 Speech by Ralph Thompson to the American Civil Liberties Union, April 5, 1979, Heritage Archives.
14 Address of Ralph Thompson to Oklahoma City University School of Law commencement, May 9, 2004, Heritage Archives.
15 Ralph Thompson interview.
16 Ibid.
17 Ibid.

CHAPTER 15:
REFORMING THE JUVENILE JUSTICE SYSTEM
1 *Terry D. v. L.E. Rader,* 93 F.R.D. 526 (W.D. Okla. 1982).
2 *The Daily Oklahoman,* January 12, 1982.
3 Ibid., February 21, 1982.
4 Ibid., March 2, 1982.
5 *Terry D. v. L.E. Rader,* 93 F.R.D. 526 (W.D. Okla. 1982).
6 *The Daily Oklahoman,* March 2, 1982.
7 Ibid., June 18, 1982.
8 Ibid., May 27, 1984.
9 Ibid., April 6, 1996.

CHAPTER 16:
CHIEF JUDGE
1 *The Daily Oklahoman,* February 12, 1986.
2 Letter from Patrick Leahy to Ralph Thompson, March 27, 1991, Heritage Archives.
3 Management Statistics for US Courts, Director, Administrative Office of the US Courts; Interview with Robert Dennis, August 16, 2010, Heritage Archives, hereafter referred to as Robert Dennis interview.
4 Ibid.
5 Ibid.
6 Ibid.
7 Ibid.
8 Ibid.
9 Letter from Robin Cauthron to Bob Burke,

April 14, 2010, Heritage Archives, hereafter referred to as Robin Cauthron letter.

10 Robert Dennis interview.

11 Official biography, Federal Judicial Center.

12 Ibid.

13 Letter from Steven Taylor to Bob Burke, February 19, 2010, Heritage Archives.

CHAPTER 17:
DIRECTOR OF THE FBI

1 Ralph Thompson interview.

2 Ibid.

3 Ibid.

4 Ibid.

5 Drew Neville letter.

6 Ibid.

7 Ralph Thompson interview.

8 Ibid.

9 Ralph Thompson interview.

10 DeVier Pierson letter.

11 Ralph Thompson interview.

12 *The Daily Oklahoman,* July 25, 1987.

13 Letter from OU Presidential Search Committee, August ____, 1988, Heritage Archives.

14 Ralph Thompson interview.

15 Ibid.

16 Ibid.

CHAPTER 18:
NATIONAL SERVICE

1 Ibid., August 9, 1981.

2 Letter from Wm. Terrell Hodges to American Judicature Society, February 26, 2010, Heritage Archives.

3 Ralph Thompson interview.

4 Letter from Lloyd D. George to the American Judicature Society, March 31, 2009, Heritage Archives.

5 Letter from Fern Smith to Bob Burke, June 28, 2010, Heritage Archives.

6 Ralph Thompson interview.

7 Ibid.

8 Ibid.

9 Letter from Louis J. Freeh to Bob Burke, November 26, 2010, Heritage Archives.

10 Ibid.

11 Ibid.

12 Ibid.

13 Letter from David Boren and Don Nickles to President George H.W. Bush, June 27,

1991, Heritage Archives.

14 *The Journal Record,* June 29, 1991.

15 Letter from Don Nickles to President Ronald Reagan, June 25, 1981, Heritage Archives; Ralph Thompson interview.

16 Ralph Thompson interview.

17 Ibid.

18 Ibid.

19 Ibid.

20 Ibid.

CHAPTER 19:
JUDGEMAKER

1 Robin Cauthron letter.

2 Ibid.

3 Official biography, Federal Judicial Center.

4 Letter from Mike Turpen to Bob Burke, July 3, 2010, Heritage Archives.

5 Ibid.

6 Official biography, Federal Judicial Center.

7 Ibid.

8 Transcript of investiture proceedings of Circuit Judge Jerome Holmes, November 29, 2006, Heritage Archives.

CHAPTER 20:
DARKNESS AND LIGHT

1 Ralph Thompson interview.

2 Ibid.

3 Ibid.

4 Ibid.

5 Ibid.

6 Ibid.

7 Ibid.

8 Ibid.

9 Tribute to Ralph Thompson, by Chief Justice William Rehnquist, November, 1995, Heritage Archives.

10 Acceptance speech of Ralph Thompson, Oklahoma Hall of Fame, November, 1995, Heritage Archives.

11 Ibid.

12 Helen Ford Wallace in *The Oklahoman,* September 15, 2010.

CHAPTER 21:
A JUDGE'S JUDGE

1 Letter from Claire Eagan to Bob Burke, August 20, 2010, Heritage Archives.

2 Ibid.

3 Bill Paul letter.

4   Letter from Leonidas Ralph Mecham to Bob Burke, March 4, 2010.
5   Ibid.
6   Interview with Frank Keating, April 13, 2010, Heritage Archives.
7   Letter from William J. Ross to Bob Burke, March 1, 2010, Heritage Archives.
8   Letter from Mack Martin to Bob Burke, March 22, 2010, Heritage Archives.
9   Ibid.
10 Ibid.
11 Letter from Don Holladay, July 8, 2010, Heritage Archives.
12 Letter from Ed Kelley to Bob Burke, August 24, 2010, Heritage Archives.
13 Ibid.
14 Letter from Andrew Coats to Bob Burke, October 27, 2010, Heritage Archives.
15 Letter from DeVier Pierson to Bob Burke, November 12, 2010, Heritage Archives, hereafter referred to as DeVier Pierson letter.
16 Robert Henry interview.
17 Ibid.
18 Letter from Page Dobson to Bob Burke, May 25, 2010, Heritage Archives.
19 Letter from Burck Bailey to Bob Burke, February 22, 2010, Heritage Archives.
20 Rex Privett letter.
21 Letter from William G. Young to Devitt Award Selection Committee, May 6, 2009, Heritage Archives.
22 Ralph Thompson interview.
23 Ibid.
24 Ibid.
25 Joseph Wells letter.
26 Ralph Thompson interview.
27 Ibid.
28 Letter from Gerald Ford to Ralph Thompson, March 23, 2000, Heritage Archives.
29 Letter from Lamar Alexander to Ralph Thompson, undated, Heritage Archives.
30 Letter from Larry Harlow to Ralph Thompson, May 24, 2000, Heritage Archives.
31 Letter from Lyn Nofziger to Ralph Thompson, March 25, 2000, Heritage Archives.
32 Letter from Jane Harlow to Bob Burke, April 5, 2010, Heritage Archives, hereafter referred to as Jane Harlow letter.
33 Interview with Joe Reinke, July 23, 2010, Heritage Archives.
34 Letter from Marilyn Edens to Bob Burke,

April 24, 2010, Heritage Archives, hereafter referred to as Marilyn Edens letter.
35 Ibid.

CHAPTER 22:
FOLLOWING THE LAW

1   www.tindrum.net.
2   *The Daily Oklahoman*, August 9, 1997.
3   Ralph Thompson interview.
4   Michael Salem letter.
5   *The Daily Oklahoman*, August 12, 1997.
6   *Video Software Dealers Association v. City of Oklahoma City* 6 F. Supp.2nd (W.D. Okla. 1997), affirmed in part, dismissed in part; *Camfield v. City of Oklahoma City*, 248 F. 3rd 1214 (10th Cir. 2001).
7   *The Daily Oklahoman*, January 2, 1998.
8   Ibid., January 4, 1998.
9   Ibid., October 21, 1998.
10 Ibid.
11 Ibid., December 19, 1998.

CHAPTER 23:
SENIOR STATUS

1   28 U.S.C, section 371.
2   Transcript of Senior Status Ceremony, December 22, 1999, Heritage Archives.
3   Ibid.
4   Ibid.
5   Ibid.
6   Ibid.
7   Letter from Gerald Ford to Ralph Thompson, November 10, 1999, Heritage Archives.
8   Letter from William Rehnquist to Ralph Thompson, November 1, 1999, Heritage Archives.
9   Letter from Louis J. Freeh to Ralph Thompson, November 7, 1999, Heritage Archives.
10 Transcript of Senior Status Ceremony, December 22, 1999, Heritage Archives.
11 Official biography, Federal Judicial Center.
12 Ibid.
13 Ralph Thompson interview.
14 Ibid.
15 Ibid.
16 Ibid.
17 Ibid.
18 Interview with Judge Lee West, June 30, 2010, Heritage Archives, hereafter referred to as Lee West interview.
19 *Almanac of the Federal Judiciary*, Aspen Law

& Business, Volume 1, 2001, p. 200-201.

20 Letter from Burton Johnson to Bob Burke, February 15, 2010, Heritage Archives.

21 Letter from Larry Ottaway to Bob Burke, February 27, 2010, Heritage Archives.

22 Letter from John A. Kenney to Bob Burke, June 19, 2010, Heritage Archives.

23 Letter from Harry A. Woods, Jr., to Bob Burke, June 24, 2010, Heritage Archives.

24 Letter from William H. Campbell to Bob Burke, July 8, 2010, Heritage Archives.

25 *The Journal Record,* May 2, 2001.

CHAPTER 24:
FLYING AND PHOTOGRAPHY

1 Ibid.

2 Letter from General Richard Burpee to Bob Burke, March 25, 2010, Heritage Archives, hereafter referred to as Richard Burpee letter.

3 Ibid.

4 Ibid.

5 Ralph Thompson interview.

6 Ibid.

7 Ibid.

8 Ibid.

9 Ibid.

10 Ibid.

11 Ibid.

12 Ibid.

13 Ibid.

CHAPTER 25:
A LOVING AND ACCOMPLISHED FAMILY

1 Ralph Thompson interview.

2 Lee Thompson letter.

3 Ibid.

4 Ralph Thompson interview.

5 Interview with Carolyn Zachritz, October 1, 2010, Heritage Archives.

6 Ralph Thompson interview.

7 Ibid.

8 Barbara Thompson interview.

9 *The Oklahoman,* September 3, 2006.

10 Ralph Thompson interview.

11 Ibid.

12 Barbara Thompson interview.

13 Letter from Lisa Thompson Campbell to Bob Burke, June 1, 2010, Heritage Archives, hereafter referred to as Lisa Campbell letter.

14 Ibid.

15 Ibid.

16 Ibid.

17 Ibid.

18 Barbara Thompson interview.

19 Ibid.

20 Letter from Elaine Thompson DeGiusti to Bob Burke, April 28, 2010, Heritage Archives, hereafter referred to as Elaine DeGiusti letter.

21 Ibid.

22 Ibid.

23 Ibid.

24 Ibid.

25 Letter from Maria Thompson Abbott to Bob Burke, May 14, 2010, Heritage Archives, hereafter referred to as Maria Abbott letter.

26 Ibid.

27 Ibid.

28 Ibid.

29 Ibid., Elaine DeGuisti letter, Lisa Campbell letter.

30 Ralph Thompson interviews.

31 Ibid.

32 Jane Harlow letter.

CHAPTER 26:
FRIENDS AND TRAVEL

1 Letter from Josephine Freede to Bob Burke, July 8, 2010, Heritage Archives.

2 Ibid.

3 Ralph Thompson interview.

4 Ibid.

5 Maria Thompson Abbott letter.

6 Letter from William P. Bowden to Bob Burke, April 3, 2010.

7 James Inhofe letter.

8 Ralph Thompson interview.

9 Ibid.

10 Ralph Thompson interview.

11 Ibid.

12 Ibid.

13 Ibid.

14 *The Daily Oklahoman,* July 31, 1999.

15 Barbara Thompson interview.

16 Ibid.

17 Ibid.

18 Ralph Thompson interview, William P. Bowden letter.

19 Ralph Thompson interview.

20 *The Sunday Oklahoman,* April 22, 2001.
21 Ralph Thompson interview.
22 Ibid.
23 Ibid.
24 Ibid.
25 Ibid.

lection committee, March 31, 2009, Heritage Archives.
26 Letter from David L. Boren to Devitt Award selection committee, March 27, 2009, Heritage Archives.
27 Ralph Thompson interview.

CHAPTER 27:
RETIREMENT AND BEYOND

1 Interview with Timothy D. DeGiusti, July 14, 2010, Heritage Archives, hereafter referred to as Tim DeGiusti interview.
2 Ralph Thompson interview.
3 Tim DeGiusti interview.
4 Ibid.
5 Ibid.
6 Ibid.
7 Letter from Ralph Thompson to George W. Bush, August 6, 2007, Heritage Archives.
8 Ibid.
9 Ralph Thompson interview.
10 *The Daily Oklahoman,* August 11, 2007.
11 Frank Keating letter.
12 www.okwd.uscourts.gov, official website of the United States District Court for the Western District of Oklahoma.
13 Ralph Thompson interview.
14 *The Federal Lawyer,* August, 2009, p. 31.
15 Interview with Joe Heaton, August 18, 2010, Heritage Archives.
16 Interview with Tim Leonard, August 23, 2010, Heritage Archives.
17 Letter from Stephen Friot to Bob Burke, March 8, 2010, Heritage Archives.
18 Interview with Vicki Miles La-Grange, August 20, 2010, Heritage Archives.
19 Letter from Kay Bailey Hutchison to Bob Burke, September 22, 2010, Heritage Archives.
20 Letter from Robert Henry and judges of the Tenth Circuit Court of Appeals to Devitt Award selection committee, February, 2009, Heritage Archives.
21 Letter from Vicki Miles-LaGrange to Devitt Award selection committee, March 31, 2009, Heritage Archives.
22 Letter from Claire Eagan to Devitt Award selection committee, March 25, 2009, Heritage Archives.
23 Wm. Terrell Hodges letter.
24 Lloyd D. George letter.
25 Letter from Brad Henry to Devitt Award se-

INDEX